PURPLE HEART CORNER

As we approached the formation, I heard a report over the intercom.

"Somebody is shooting at us!"

"Every station check for damage and report," ordered the copilot over his static-choked intercom. All stations reported no apparent damage, and we breathed more easily. Then came the frightening report that made my heart skip a beat.

"I smell smoke!" cried the tail gunner.

"Where is it?"

"I don't know, I just smell it!"

One of the gunners looked out the right window and reported heavy smoke pouring from the No. 3 engine and wheel recess under the right wing. We were on fire!

A B-24 on fire!

We had ten seconds or less!

TARGET PLOESTI

BY LEROY W. NEWBY

ZEBRA BOOKS
KENSINGTON PUBLISHING CORP.

ZEBRA BOOKS

are published by

Kensington Publishing Corp.
475 Park Avenue South
New York, NY 10016

First printing: Zebra Books September 1986

Printed in the United States of America

The use to which the government would put (the airship) would be in scouting and signal work.
      —*New York Times,* December 26, 1903

The reward is the ecstasy of combat.
      Baron Manfred von Richtofen

CONTENTS

PART FIVE: PLOESTI KAPUT

FOREWORD

Leroy Newby's *Target Ploesti* is a very satisfying book, and a valuable one on two levels. He has recorded his own story, the "little picture," and interwoven it with the official records of his combat group and Air Force—the "big picture." Newby meticulously describes the largely overshadowed efforts of the Fifteenth Air Force's B-24 Liberators flying from their Italian bases, and every ingredient is there: the Rumanian oilfields at Ploesti, deadly priority target and the nemesis of every Mediterranean Theater bomber crewman; Vienna, Munich, and the other "flak holes" are vividly described. The low-key treatment underlines the immense strain upon the men as they moved toward their goal: the completion of fifty combat missions. Newby explains exactly how a bombardier went about his work, and his description of why his group may have been spared by fighters is just one of many fascinating sidelights. His personal observations highlight the irony and the whims of Lady Luck. Reading the book, I sensed that the author perhaps looks back with a little disbelief at the young Lieutenant Newby who rode in the cramped nose of a Liberator named "Hangar Queen." *Target Ploesti* is the diary of a survivor of an aerial conflict, the like of which will never be seen again.

—Steve Birdsall

PREFACE

The basic elements of *Target Ploesti* and the report of the actions of the crew and group came from my mission diary, my recollections, years of accumulated notes, and the historical records of the 460th Bomb Group.

All persons mentioned were real. I witnessed all depicted events regarding our crew or group, unless otherwise indicated. Some events were reported to me and some were general knowledge among crews.

I make no claim to infallibility in regard to the chronology of some details. It is possible some incidents actually happened in a different sequence than reported. Any such errors in memory recall are unintentional, and in no way materially alter the point being made in their reporting.

For the purpose of increased clarity and interest, most conversations were invented, under an author's license, and were intended to show the general nature of such conversations under conditions portrayed.

Overview information about targets and Fifteenth Air Force activities were unknown to me when the events of the story took place, but was researched and added in order to show where the efforts of crew #71 of the 460th Bomb Group fit into the overall plan of POINTBLANK, the joint Fifteenth and Eighth Air Forces' combined offensive to destroy the German war-making capability. I also had never heard of POINTBLANK at that time.

The impetus to organize hundreds of dormant index cards into a meaningful outline began in the mid-sixties with my reading of *Ploesti*, by James Dugan and Carroll Stewart.* And there it rested.

Years later, I read *Log of the Liberators*, by Steve Birdsall,** which depicts the role of the B-24 Liberator in World War II, and includes a chapter entitled "Air War: Italian Style." I was then able to relate my experiences to what had been happening all around me in the Mediterranean Theater, and bring my manuscript to fruition.

The microfilm records of the 460th Bomb Group supported and, in fact, added to my recall of specific events long since forgotten.

I was amazed, after reviewing the records and reading Birdsall's book, to learn how little I knew about what was going on when I was there.

—Leroy W. Newby

*James Dugan and Carroll Stewart. *Ploesti* (New York: Random House, Inc., 1962).

**Steve Birdsall, *Log of the Liberators: An Illustrated History of the B-24* (New York: Doubleday, 1973).

ACKNOWLEDGMENTS

Special thanks to a number of people who have helped me in preparing and writing the manuscript of this book.

Danny Smith was a good sounding board for some details and use of certain incidents. He also supplied many of the photos that he took in action.

Ed Devney of The Devney Organization, Inc., New York, New York, was kind enough to send me several photographs of the 460th planes and men in action, and gave me permission to use material and photos from his excellent book, *The 460th Bomb Group.* Ed was the group's PR officer.

Karen Hendriks and Frances Steig drafted some of my early material.

Bob Wachowiak copyedited my first draft. Frances Steig and my brother Jack copyedited the second draft.

Chris encouraged me to write the book, and typed most of the manuscript that was sent to the publisher.

Patti and Dan put up with their Dad who was all the time upstairs "working on his book."

13

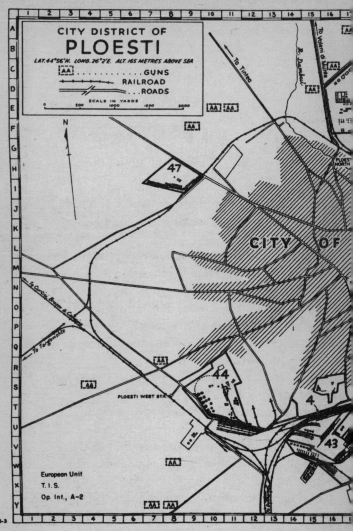

CITY DISTRICT OF
PLOESTI

LAT. 44°56'N. LONG. 26°2'E. ALT. 165 METRES ABOVE SEA

▭▭ . . . . GUNS
↔—↔ ─────── RAILROAD
═══════ . . . ROADS

SCALE IN YARDS
0   500   1000   1500   2000

N

European Unit
T. I. S.
Op. Int., A-2

M-3

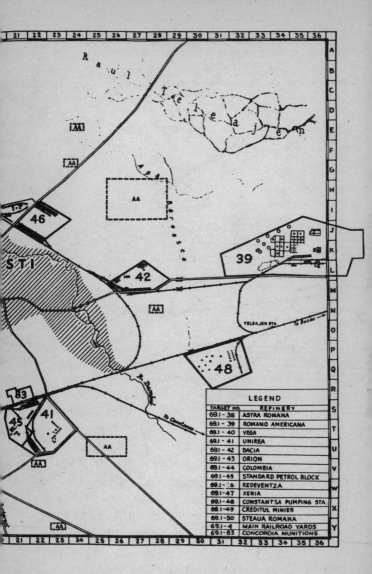

| 21 | 22 | 23 | 24 | 25 | 26 | 27 | 28 | 29 | 30 | 31 | 32 | 33 | 34 | 35 | 36 |

R a u l

T e l e a j e n

[AA]

[AA]

46

S T I

42

AA

[AA]

TELEAJEN STA.   To Buzău

48

83

41

45

AA

[AA]

LEGEND		
TARGET NO.	REFINERY	
69.1 - 38	ASTRA ROMANA	
69.1 - 39	ROMANO AMERICANA	
69.1 - 40	VEGA	
69.1 - 41	UNIREA	
69.1 - 42	DACIA	
69.1 - 43	ORION	
69.1 - 44	COLOMBIA	
69.1 - 45	STANDARD PETROL BLOCK	
69.1 - 46	REDEVENTZA	
69.1 - 47	XENIA	
69.1 - 48	CONSTANTSA PUMPING STA.	
69.1 - 49	CREDITUL MINIER	
69.1 - 50	STEAUA ROMANA	
69.1 - 4	MAIN RAILROAD YARDS	
69.1 - 83	CONCORDIA MUNITIONS	

Prologue: 12 August 1944

APPOINTMENT IN SAMARRA

The last of the four 1,200 h.p. Pratt & Whitney engines sputtered out, and the plane began her death dive from several thousand feet above the Italian plateau. *Hangar Queen,* a proud, majestic aircraft, glistening silver in the early afternoon sun, a smiling, voluptuous young lady adorning her side, had been faithful to her crew these past four months when her sisters were going down in flames all around her. Now she was faltering for the first time.

The Liberator crewmen and their bomber were returning from deep in enemy territory. All were on their fiftieth combat mission; a completed tour of duty and a ticket home were awaiting them.

The three-and-one-half-hour flight back from the flak clouds over the target seemed an eternity. *Nothing can go wrong. Can it? After all, we survived the terrible flak of Ploesti, Vienna, Wiener-Neustadt, Munich, and others. We even lived through Goering's Yellow Nose fighters' flying right through our formation, cannons and machine guns blazing.*

A simple downwind leg of a routine landing, but within the space of a few seconds all four engines, suddenly stopped, one after the other. Either a vapor lock in the gas lines, or belated battle damage. It didn't matter why or how. It happened. And a twenty-ton hunk of metal shaped like a B-24 was about to fall to earth, no differently than a giant boulder rolling off a cliff. Each man was filled with the most powerful emotion of his young life: anger! *They are snatching it all away from me when it was right in my grasp.* Then came frustration. *It's beyond my control to stop what is happening.*

The pilot had time only to react instinctively, putting the aircraft into a steep dive just a split second before actual air speed would have dropped below minimum flying speed. His fast action enabled him to maintain control and foil gravity, which was about to take control and pull the nearly stalled plane into the flat spin that meant certain death to all aboard.

"Feather all props," the pilot ordered calmly. The copilot responded at once by adjusting the blade angle to keep the props from spinning. Four windmilling propellers would have created tremendous drag and greatly reduced the likelihood of the aircraft gaining life-support air speed during its low altitude emergency dive.

"Air speed!"

"135 . . . 140 . . . 145 . . . 150."

"Roger!"

The air speed indicator was inching its lifesaving swing to higher readings. Gravity, at first the aircraft's foe, was now its friend, the only source of power for giving lift back to the speed-demanding Davis-designed wing of the falling B-24.

Two crew members, so angry at the imminent loss of all they had worked and hoped for, chose the course of the Baghdad servant in Somerset Maugham's "Appointment in Samarra"* who, upon being jostled in the market by Death's messenger, mounted his master's horse and fled to Samarra where Death could not find him. At the first sign of distress, the bombardier, a substitute for the regular one, snapped on his chest chute, opened the bomb bay doors, and dived out to escape what he believed would be his certain death. The nose gunner clambered up to the nose section, grabbed his chest chute, and started back to the open bomb bay for his escape just as the stricken aircraft began picking up lifesaving speed.

Several thousand feet is not high enough for a dead-engined B-24 to dive and expect to pick up air speed, regain control, and level out for a dead-stick landing. However, the pilot had no choice but to try, and well he did. Miraculously, the ground seemed to open and the falling coffin went zooming past ground zero into a valley, a deep ravine just west of the runway. The diving bomber hugged the contour of the slope just a few feet off the ground at about a forty-five-degree angle.

*"Appointment in Samarra" is an episode in a play written by Somerset Maugham, published in 1933, called *Sheppy*. It is included at present in *Part of the Works of Somerset Maugham*, c 1977, Arno Press, 3 Park Ave., New York.

The pilot's dilemma was frightening. He needed to maintain the steepest possible angle for the only source of power, yet he had to slowly reduce the angle in keeping with the changing contour of the slope, in order not to "land" the plane on the slope. It finally took the combined efforts of both pilots to pull back the controls as they neared the valley floor so that they soared up the other side and onto the lower plateau for a skillful wheels down, dead-stick landing in a farm field. Every factor required for their survival worked in their favor. The impossible became reality.

It was a fitting climax to the combat career of a man considered by his peers to be one of the best bomber pilots in the group.

Hangar Queen would have survived the landing and flown again with a new crew but for a low mound of earth in its path. This time the combined efforts of both pilots were not enough. Four strong feet on the brakes and muscles spiked with adrenalin were not sufficient to stop the plane short of the onrushing mound.

The ensuing crash, while fatal to the airplane, was not that severe for those braced in crash landing position. They all walked away except for the nose gunner, who was still under the flight deck when the crash occurred. Immobilized by the "G" forces of the bomber's dive in and out of the valley, he was pinned by the collapsed understructure. Even that would not have been fatal, but the gas tank above the bomb bay split open, pouring 100-octane gasoline into his prison.

The other men, despite victory in hand, tried desperately to free him, fighting the deadly fumes in relays with total disregard for the single spark that would blow them all to bits. Later it took a crane to extract his body, and their efforts were shown to be futile; but the crew members were quietly proud to have risked their lives for the man who was denied what each of them now had in his grasp. This was the indomitable spirit of the men of *Hangar Queen*.

The bombardier's body was found just a few feet from the edge of the first plateau where the bomber had escaped into the valley, his partially opened chute fluttering in the wind.

The master in Maugham's story went down to the Baghdad market and asked Death why she made a threatening gesture to his servant. "That was no threatening gesture," she said. "It was only a start of surprise. I was astonished to see him in Baghdad, for I had an appointment with him in Samarra."

PART ONE:
OCTOBER BIRTH

Chapter 1

ASSIGNMENT: FIFTEENTH
AIR FORCE

54 U.S. BOMBERS LOST IN DARING
LOW-LEVEL BOMBING
RAID ON PLOESTI OIL REFINERIES
1 August 1943

A new name had burst upon America—Ploesti!*
"Where *is* Ploesti?" Few, save a few high-ranking
U.S. military strategists, had ever heard of it. They
knew about Ploesti because a battle had been in the
planning stage for over a year, with 178 Libyan-based
B-24's to fly below smokestack level and into the
point-blank guns of Ploesti, Rumania. The defense
planners had the same time period to arrange their
reception for the raid they knew was coming.

*Ploesti, nestled in the southern foothills of the Transylvanian Alps, was
the first oil boom town in the world. It came into being two years before
they sank the first American oil well in Titusville, Pennsylvania.

This historic battle between air and ground forces is considered to have been one of the most thoroughly planned battles in the annals of warfare. It lasted less than an hour and was the second move in the grand chess match between the U.S. Air Force's offense and the Ploesti defense—a match that would take twenty-six months to complete.

The American public was aware of their country's commitment to daylight high-level bombing attacks on German targets, even though the RAF continued to do its bombing at night. They were even accustomed to relatively heavy losses, but 54 out of 178 lost attacking bombers was a shocker. It was an eye-opener, too, for over ten thousand young American flyers still in the Training Command. They heard that new hard-to-pronounce name, not knowing that in less than a year they would be experiencing the cause of so many bombers falling out of Ploesti skies.

The crew of *Hangar Queen* did not yet exist as an entity, but each of its eventual ten members heard the stupefying news at their training centers where they were learning their respective military specialties: pilot, navigator, bombardier, engineer, radioman and gunner. In October they would meld into a combat air crew, a fighting team, as part of a new offensive weapon being prepared for the final assault on Germany. This new weapon was not yet in existence on the day Ploesti became something of a household word, but by October military planners would be forming a new powerhouse, the Fifteenth Air Force, to be based in Italy under the command of Gen. James H. Doolittle. Six heavy bomb groups from the Twelfth Air Force in North Africa would form the nucleus and would be augmented by fifteen heavy bomb groups being groomed for the Eighth Air Force in England, to be diverted to the Fifteenth under the new plan.

The Fifteenth Air Force would have four main objectives, with priorities as follows:

1. To destroy the German air force in the air (by making it come up and fight) and on the ground, wherever it was within its operational range.
2. To participate in POINTBLANK (the joint Eighth Air Force and Fifteenth Air Force bomber offensive), which called for the destruction of Germany's war-making capabilities. Factories, oil refineries, oil transportation, and naval bases would be key targets.
3. To support the battle of the Italian mainland (mainly attacking communication targets in Italy, along the Brenner Pass route, and also in neighboring Austria).
4. To weaken the German position in the Balkans.

Later, targets in France would be added in preparation for ANVIL—the invasion of southern France.

On 1 November the Fifteenth Air Force flew its maiden mission. Four of the initial six groups took off from their Tunisian bases to bomb the naval base at La Spezia, Italy. Fifteen newly formed bomb groups patiently trained back home. One such group was the 460th, formed by Lt. Col. Robert T. Crowder of Lawrence, Kansas. Although started earlier at Clovis, it acquired most of its crews in October at Chatham Field, Savannah. Coloner Crowder believed that discipline breeds morale. His favorite quotation, from General Pershing, was "Send me men who can shoot and salute." He was determined that the 460th would become the best bomb group in the air forces. A month earlier, the "Black Panther" insignia and the "Black Panther Fife and Drum Corps" had been born, as part of his striving for high morale and the resulting excellence of performance. The 460th was the only U.S. bomb group to have such a musical organization.

End of the line for the *Hangar Queen*

The Saturday morning review was an opportunity for the Fife and Drum Corps to remind everyone of the growing spirit of the Black Panthers. As the Corps marched by, flags held high and martial music pouring forth, row upon row of smartly dressed U.S. airmen stood stiffly at attention . . . clean shaven, fresh haircuts, shoes brightly polished, and a prophylactic device in each hand. A "pro" in one cupped palm and a "con" in the other. (Savannah mothers would have been thrilled to have known about such thoughtfulness.) This was a new one to most of the men, but they took it in stride. Not the group chaplain, though. He fumed and seethed at each inspection. Others thought his plight funny.

One of the crews to join the 460th was crew #71, fresh from a month's first-phase training at Davis-Monthan Air Base in Tucson. There were ten single young men, most in their early twenties:

Charlie Hammett from Taylors, South Carolina, was the pilot and youngest man on the crew. His ambition was to have his own combat plane and name it "Blues in the Night," after a then-popular song. He would make his mark as a combat pilot, not as a namer of airplanes.
Ed ("Dusty") Rhodes from Lilly, Louisiana, was the co-pilot.
The navigator, Sherman Wood from Coldwater, Michigan, was the old man of the crew at twenty-six.
Dominic Minitti, the engineer and top turret gunner, hailed from Pittsburgh, Pennsylvania.
Danny Smith, assistant engineer and waist gunner, was a photographer from Gary, Indiana, and owned a horse that the crew would learn to love.
Bob Kaiser, the nose gunner, was from Brooklyn, New York. He loved to make up songs, which he would croon to his captive audience. We nicknamed him "Tyrone," after Tyrone Power.

Sid Woods, the tail gunner, came from Manchester, New Hampshire.

Howard Thornton was the radio man from Durham, North Carolina.

John Woodland, the other waist gunner, came from Jordan, New York.

I, Leroy (Ted) Newby from Crafton (near Pittsburgh, Pennsylvania) was the bombardier.

The highlight of our training program was a full formation mission to "bomb" the city of Richmond. Deputy Commander Lt. Col. Bertram C. Harrison decided to fly our plane, bumping Charlie Hammett to the copilot's seat and bumping Dusty off the plane.

On the way to the target we passed near the Marine air base at Cherry Point and were subjected to a fighter attack by a squadron of fighters who no doubt were enjoying the highlight of their training program. The sight of those fighters swarming in at us in groups of three, wave after wave, scared the daylights out of me. That was my life's greatest thrill up to that time. I knew they were only kidding, but I could see swastikas on their wings and began to realize what was in store for us.

We survived the attack and managed to lose the rest of the formation in some bad weather. Sherm had a difficult time getting oriented and couldn't find Richmond as quickly as Colonel Harrison thought he should have. The colonel was a West Point man and our group's answer to General Patton. Tough and demanding. Sharp-tongued too, as Sherm found out.

I fared little better. I couldn't find my target, a certain distinctive building, and we were over the city before I could get my bearings. During the colonel's on-the-spot commentary, the words "buck private" came up several times.

As the time grew near for the 460th's departure for the New York staging area, the sixty-eight crews began speculating on their chances of being one of the six who would not get one of the sixty-two brand new flyaway bombers. (These were new B-24-H's, which had not yet been in combat, the first model with a nose turret.) The lucky sixty-two crews would get to name their airplanes.

The news one day was bad. One of our crew members had seen the listings on a bulletin board, and crew #71 was one of the six to be denied its own flyaway plane. We would ride to war as passengers. We "have nots" were quite upset over this slight and did not appreciate the snide remarks and humorous comments by some of the "haves." One wag pointed to a carcass of a B-24 in a nearby hanger and said, "There's your plane." It was a "hangar queen," so named because it was a disabled aircraft kept around and cannibalized for its parts. It was a wreck; only one remaining propeller, all the engine cowlings gone, and parts of some engines missing. The name stuck. We were the "Hangar Queen Crew" from then on.

The group was scheduled to depart early New Year's day for Mitchell Field, so the New Year's eve activities would not exactly be an ordinary celebration. This might possibly be our last such occasion; to make certain it would be properly noted, someone had flown down to Havana (on official business, of course) and brought back a planeload of rum. It *was* properly noted.

The star-filled sky on the 8th of January was the most beautiful sky I had ever seen. It was dark in the area, with no city lights to wash out the distant stars. It was a clear Florida sky. It could well have been my final look at an American sky.

Not a soul was asleep. It was 0330 hours, one hour out of the POE and two miles above the Caribbean. Pilot Paul Grinnell held an official looking envelope in this hand, with the word "SECRET" stamped on it. With a flourish, as the second hand reached the numeral 12 on his watch, Paul opened the secret document and said . . . nothing.

Was it England? South Pacific? North Africa? The reason he did not announce our destination was because he couldn't pronounce *Djeseida*, Algeria. Actually it was spelled incorrectly on the secret orders and was also shown to be in the wrong country. We didn't know it at the time but *Djedeida, Tunisia* was the correct spelling and address. None of us had ever heard of the place, which obviously made us no different from the person who wrote up the orders. None of us had ever heard of the Fifteenth Air Force either, but that was to be our new home according to the rest of the orders.

Arriving in Tunis we learned that our staging base would be Oudna, instead of Djedeida, Tunis. This was the most unforgettable town I ever visited. It had one outstanding characteristic: a smell like stale urine extending about a mile or so beyond the city limits; two miles if you were downwind. One reason for the smell was that it was a common practice for the Arabs to urinate right on the street or sidewalk.

I have seen some fine balancing and tumbling acts in my day, but none to compare with the virtuosity of one man's stellar performance right in the middle of a Tunis side street. Broad daylight. This barefooted artist in his tattletale gray robe decided to enjoy a bowel movement right there on the spot. This *was* a little different, so several flyboys stopped to admire his act. Upon completion, while still in the stooped position, he very adroitly shifted his balance onto his right foot, with a "Look, Ma, no hands" expression on his face, "cleansed" himself with the heel of his left foot, rubbed the heel in the dirt, rose to his feet, and started away. Spontaneous applause—probably the first standing ovation for a bowel movement in history. His toothless grin of appreciation was priceless.

At the nearby Djedeida staging base, a plane with its regular crew aboard, except for a replacement copilot, went racing down the runway at the hands of a pilot who had frequently made "hot" takeoffs. Instead of lifting off at a normal 120 mph or so, it was his practice to stay on the ground until about 140 mph and make a steep climbing takeoff. Safe enough when the copilot knows his plans.

The replacement copilot, unaware of his pilot's unorthodox takeoff habits, proceeded as he normally did, and when the air speed indicator read 140 mph, he presumed the plane was airborne and applied the brakes. This was standard procedure used to stop the wheels from rotating before retracting the landing gear up into the recessed area in the wing. Spinning wheels could cause damage in the retracted position. Unfortunately, the aircraft was still on the ground when the brakes were applied, and the giant Liberator, pride of its highly trained crew and ready for battle, nosed over and burst into flames. Nine young men died at once. The copilot was blown out through a split in the side of the plane and was found some distance from the plane, still strapped in his seat. He survived.

On to target

On 13 February our ground crews, who came by sea, arrived at the site of a newly laid metal landing strip near Spinazzola, Italy. As the ground crews were unpacking in Spinazzola, the flight crews were packing in Oudna for the last leg of the journey to the lair of the Black Panther.

Valentine's Day came early and stayed late. At 0630 hours a big sleek Liberator roared down the Oudna runway. The navigator was anxious to be aloft, to find "Dolly" field at Spinazzola, Italy. This small town was in the lower boot area, about where the ankle bone would be. "Dolly" was the code name of the 460th's airfield.

The other sixty-one Libs followed at short intervals, each to find its new home some 450 miles away. There would be no formation flying that day as the weather in Italy was bad—a condition that would continue for another forty-five days.

The navigation had to be by "dead reckoning" and radio as most of the trip was over water, and when land was reached heavy overcasts obscured most of the ground. Once over Italy, each plane lowered itself gently through the cloud barrier and went to "visual" or "pilotage" navigation, where the navigator could identify ground points from his map and compass and plot his course accordingly.

Our plane eventually found the airstrip at Spinazzola, which was located parallel and quite close to a mountain ridge, with a deep valley on the other side of the strip. The airstrip was on a plateau between the valley and the ridge. This configuration forced a very rigid landing pattern that placed the downwind leg partially over the valley, regardless of wind direction. The wind that day was from the north, so the landing pattern was counterclockwise—no problem for the sixty-one pilots that found Spinazzola.

The wind at Spinazzola was of no concern to the sixty-second crew. After descending beneath the heavy overcast many miles from Spinazzola, they were evidently uncertain of their whereabouts in this foreign land. The pilot and navigator apparently resorted to the age-old navigational procedure of following railroad tracks at a very low altitude, eventually finding a town whose name would generally appear on a station house.

Normally this is a very effective way to locate oneself when temporarily lost in an airplane, but they realized too late that the railroad tracks they were following went into a tunnel. The pilot made a gallant effort to pull up at the last moment, but the mountain was too steep. The demolished plane was found the next day near the top of the mountain, just 500 feet short of victory.

One man, who seemingly survived the crash, dragged a buddy out of the burning airplane and attempted to minister to him throughout the night. The surviving member was found the next morning with his dead companion nestled in his arms. The heroic flier* was taken to the Air Force Hospital in Bari, where he died the following day. Our first fatality put a damper on the elation of finally arriving at our destination.

Few of us had ever seen a single landing strip before, especially for use by four-engine aircraft. Most airports have two or more landing strips at different compass headings to accommodate variable wind conditions. Even an aircraft carrier can change its course to meet the wind direction. We would be stuck with whatever wind direction was available on a given day.

A heavily loaded bomber could weigh up to 60,000 pounds, and would need all the wind assistance it could muster to lift off the ground on the relatively short 6,000-foot runway provided. A direct north or south wind was fine, as we had a choice of runway directions.

*Lt. Homer H. Koch, who was later awarded the Soldier's Medal posthumously.

But as the wind moved toward the east or west, our help from wind lift diminished accordingly. This would be an important factor in our futures.

In the present, however, it was pouring down rain, and from the looks of the ground where the truck dropped us off it must have been raining for a week, or snowing. We stood ankle-deep in mud at a spot someone designated as our homestead. Another truck showed up a little later and they threw out some canvas, wooden poles, and rope. That was our home, the man said. None of the six of us assigned to this housing unit had ever assembled a pyramidal tent before, but we managed somehow to assemble all the parts into a dwelling. The situation was so unbelievably bad it was funny. Our folding army cots sank down so far, the canvas bed section nearly touched the mud. We found some wooden crates and stashed our bags on them until the tent floor dried out a few days later.

We not only did not have an airplane of our own, but our crew was split up in its living quarters. Dusty and I bunked in with four officers from another crew. Bob Holland was the pilot, Bob Zorns the copilot, Vince McCoy the navigator, and Morris Wollan the bombardier.

That night it turned bitter cold. In the morning our shoes were frozen to the ground and the inside of the tent covering was frosted over. It was snowing, and would continue for the next few days.

Our first official welcome came from "Berlin Sally" on the radio. "Welcome, Colonel Crowder and the Black Panthers of the 460th Bomb Group," she said. "We almost got your ground crew on the way over, and we will be looking for you in the air. While you are being

37

shot out of the skies over here, your girl friends and wives will be having a good time with their civilian boyfriends back home. Wouldn't you rather be there?" She was on the air quite a bit during the day, and while she didn't exactly replace *Amos and Andy* as a daily listening habit, we did tune her in a lot in order to hear our favorite music between commercials.

Inclement weather continued throughout February. And while we knew nothing about the conduct of the war except what we read in the *Stars and Stripes*, the Fifteenth was in fact flying very few missions until late in the month, when it struck some telling blows at several aircraft factories in southern Germany.

Early March had a continuation of bad flying weather, with snow, rain, and overcast skies almost every day. Our group was still preparing itself for entry into the war. We were amassing bombs, ammunition, and fuel, and were reasonably comfortable in our tents even though it was a mess outside. Most tents had a make-shift gasoline-burning furnace that would get so cherry red and hot you just knew it was going to blow up any minute. None did, but there were some tent fires.

Then it happened. Some enterprising enlisted men, cement masons in civilian life, rounded up some cement and made a beautiful concrete floor in their tent. Our C.O. heard about it and decided every tent should have the same. Orders went out to have a hard-surfaced floor in every tent by a certain date. We moved fast. We got hold of a truck and went to a nearby town that boasted a tile factory and purchased a load of roofing tile. In another town we bought some cement and sand. The pile of good intentions sat in front of our tent for about a week as we procrastinated, hating the messy job of emptying the tent and laying the tile. Our most plentiful commodity, time, finally ran out. Nothing more had been said, so we thought, or hoped, they had forgotten about it. Hardly any of the officers' tents were in compliance when the inspection team arrived, headed by Col. Bertram C. Harrison himself. Some had not even procured the materials. No one on the inspection team smiled. They just wrote on clipboards.

It was lesson time that night. Each offending tent unit was summoned to headquarters at 2200 hours. At the appointed time there was a score or so of tent units standing outside the old farmhouse that was the living quarters for the top officers. We waited in pouring down rain. No shelter. Finally they called out the names of one tent unit and invited them in out of the rain. When it came time for our invitation it was about 2315 hours. In a very few minutes we learned it was better out there in the rain.

Colonel Harrison conducted the unilateral discussion in his own unique style. He remembered Richmond. At least he *knew* me. We all stood in the exaggerated brace we learned so well in cadet days. Shoulders wide, chest out, chin tucked into the neck, and red-faced. We held that pose for about five minutes while he sat on his bed, reading a newspaper between comments. The old phrase, "buck private," and a new one, "Ship you to Anzio," kept coming up. I was totally embarrassed and deserved it.

His final words were to have the job completed by 0500 hours, at which time there would be a special reveille and tent inspection. As sorry as I felt for myself, I had room to empathize with those still outside in the rain who had not yet obtained any materials. They were certainly in for the shock of their lives.

We knew we could make it with our materials on hand, providing they were still there when we returned, but the ones who had done nothing were in a state of panic. With trucks provided, they flew into town where the tile factory was located, only to find it, of course, closed. Unable to locate the owners, they engaged in what was known as midnight requisitioning. They simply broke into the building and helped themselves. The cement factory in another town got the same treatment. I like to think they all went back next day and paid up.

What a mess! We moved all the cots and bags to one side of the tent and started in on the other side. Dusty and I mixed cement in the rain. Zorns and Wollen hauled cement in small buckets into the tent. Holland and McCoy laid the tile on a bed of fresh cement. I'm sure a real tile setter would have cringed to see us move all the cots and bags back onto the freshly laid tile so as to work on the other half. We finished about thirty minutes before inspection and were cleaned up and standing at attention when the Colonel and his staff came by. I thought I detected a twinkle in the colonel's eye. Not sure, though.

Later that morning Chaplain Dodds came by with a big grin on his face and asked if we needed his services. We told him we could have used him a few hours earlier.

Few kind words were said about Colonel Harrison that night, but the day would come when many of us would thank our lucky stars we had such a man at the helm. We would owe our lives, in part, to the man from Leesburg, Virginia.

Formation practice continued in March on the few days allowed us by the weather. I managed to get out to the bombing range fairly often to sharpen my skills at the Sperry bombsight. All my training had been on a Norden and I still wasn't quite used to the Sperry.

Saturday evening, 18 March, our four tent mates were unusually quiet. They were busy writing letters home by candlelight. Few words were spoken, each man thinking it might well be the last letter he would ever write. They were scheduled the next morning on the group's maiden mission. Dusty and I played chess by the light of the cherry-red furnace, trying to act nonchalant. With an 0330 hours wake-up call facing the warriors, it was a short evening. We all sacked out by 1930 hours.

PART TWO: BALKAN BAPTISM

Chapter 2

MOSTAR MILK RUN

"Lieutenant Holland, it's wake-up time," announced the corporal as he shone the flashlight in Bob's face.

"OK."

"Lieutenant Wollen. Lieutenant Zorns!"

"I'm awake," they chorused.

"Lieutenant McCoy."

"Go away."

No one called me, but I was awake too, pretending to be asleep, not wanting to intrude on their moment.

Soon water was being heated on the stove; a candle was lighted. A cigarette glowed in the semidarkness. Bob Holland was bravely whistling as he shaved. When they silently filed out of the tent I choked out, "Good luck." "I thought you were asleep." "I am."

At precisely 0610 hours the still of a quiet Italian spring morning was ripped by a 43,200 horsepower thunder as thirty-six bomber pilots started their No. 2 engines when the second hands of the chronometers pointed straight up.

At the briefing a half hour earlier all the pilots went through the ceremony of the "Hack!" The briefing officer solemnly counted down, "Five . . . four . . . three . . . two . . . one . . . HACK!" and a roomful of airmen pushed in the stems of their G.I.-issue watches simultaneously.

The No. 2 engine was started first because that was the engine that generated the electrical power for the rest of the airplane. Precision bombing starts with precision engine starting. A few seconds later, 43,200 more horses shouted at us in our more or less comfortable beds as the No. 3 engines were started. This was the engine that operated the pump for the plane's hydraulic system. Two more thunderous reports, and the gross of Pratt & Whitney engines that were to take the Black Panthers to Metkovic, Yugoslavia were roaring at full fortissimo, all two-thousand-plus cylinders hard at work. Sleep was out of the question.

It was an exciting moment for those of us left behind. Everyone was up and out of his tent to watch the takeoff. Several times in the past few weeks we had heard the steady drone of a bomb group in beautiful formation crossing the sky above our base on the way to some target. We saw ourselves in those planes, wondering why we sat on the ground while the war went on without us. *We can't be too important.* Our impatience had been bugging us, but now we could transfer our vicarious adventures to our own group as they began their takeoff. Soon it would be our turn. Butterflies in the stomach.

Dolly Tower had dispatched its first bomber into combat. One by one the thirty-ton monsters lifted off the ground at about thirty-second intervals, just a

46

couple of hundred yards from our tent area. Slowly they banked to the right and headed for the rendez-vous point over Altamura, about twenty miles away. There the mission lead plane began flying in a giant circle, and soon this nucleus of one was to grow into a full formation of bombers. When thus assembled, the group would head for Metkovic to bomb the "mar-shalling yards." (This was a new term for me. I had always called them "freight yards.") Unknown to us in the cheering section, the group did a very poor job of assembly, and when it joined the other groups for the trip to Yugoslavia, there was little resemblance to the neat formation of six tight "boxes" of six planes that was supposed to identify an airborne bomber group.

Metkovic was a milk run. A milk run was air-war jargon for a noncontested mission. Virgin groups were sent on milk runs for their first mission. No flak, no fighters, not much of a target; but it was good practice for beginners.

We who waited back home didn't know much about milk runs. We thought they were all tough. Everyone stood around at mid-morning with faces to the east, like rubbernecked rubes on their first trip to New York, waiting for the group to appear over the crest of the mountain that ran alongside our air base.

"There they are!" someone shouted as several Libs came into view. Soon more of our planes came strug-gling over the mountaintop. While we were pleased to see our planes returning, it wasn't the neat, clean formation we expected. The last two stragglers were about a minute behind the plane in front of them.

No matter, we cheered as we counted them. All had made it home. Dusty and I raced out to the squadron

47

area to welcome our tent mates back. After the "How was it?" routine and backslapping came the realization that we were due to be up next. The excitement of our tent-mates' icebreaker was replaced by a sick feeling in our stomachs. Dusty managed a weak grin as he said, "We're next."

The following day at our regular outdoor breakfast, prior to another practice mission, we all complained of grittiness in our oatmeal. Eating oatmeal with straight canned milk on it out in the snow was bad enough, but having grit mixed in was too much. My mouth felt as if a dentist had just cleaned my teeth. I never could rinse away all the grit. Our necks began to feel gritty as we walked in the snow through the olive orchard to the briefing room. The mystery of the grit was quickly explained at the briefing. Mt. Vesuvius had erupted the day before for the first time since 1906, and during the night the fine volcanic ash had traveled the hundred miles to Spinazzola and had come down with the snow.

After the briefing the trucks dumped us off at our respective hardstands and we stood by to await word to start engines. Hammett & Co. were standing around talking when we heard the sharp command, "Fire!"

Ten snowballs greeted us as we turned toward the command voice. "Rattlesnake Hank" was on the attack against the Hangar Queen Crew, who still had no airplane of its own to adorn with appropriate pictures like the big rattlesnake on the plane of its attackers.

The fight was on, but it ended abruptly when the Red-Red flare was fired from Dolly Tower. STAND-DOWN! That meant no flying that day. Volcanic ash in the air could damage engines.

Hammett & Co. flew over to Naples the next day in a borrowed plane, and we buzzed the top of Vesuvius, looking down into its depths from about two hundred feet as smoke wafted up at us. The hole at the top must have been a quarter mile or more in diameter, so we could see quite far down into the abyss, but not all the way. Fresh lava covered the side of the mountain and spilled on into part of a city near Pompeii. Beautiful, but sad. I had seen the aqueducts at Carthage and had visited the famed Casbah on the trip over, and now here I was, one of the few people ever to fly over a freshly erupted volcano. I was beginning to enjoy my new status as world traveler.

A few days after Mt. Vesuvius erupted, our group was declared "inoperative"—a polite word for "You-aren't-ready-so-don't-be-cluttering-up-the-skies-for-the-others!" Our slow group formation assembly and poor formation in general at Metkovic was the reason for our being "kicked out of the sky." That did it. The reaction of Colonel Harrison to the Richmond snafu and to the tent floor episode was tame compared to his reaction to this affront to his and Colonel Crowder's pride and joy, the Black Panthers—the group that was going to make aerial combat history.

For one solid week we practiced flying as it had never been practiced before. In the morning after the other groups had gone to do battle, half of our pilots took off in their planes with skeleton crews aboard, assembled into full group formation, and flew all over southern Italy. Colonel Harrison sat in the rear turret of the lead plane and communicated by radio with each pilot in the formation. "Communicated" is perhaps too mild a word for the one-way verbal thrashing taking place in that Italian sky. Any pilot who dared to stray more than ten feet from where he should be was called by name and *ordered* back into position. Formation flying was never intended to be flown as close as these men were now flying. The wing tips of the planes on either side of the lead planes were nearly poking into their windows. Some pilots, entering into the spirit of the occasion, would actually tap wings with each other—and that is tight formation.

The group would drill in this way for two or three hours, with the colonel cracking his electronic whip like a giant mule drive in the sky. As tough as he was, it was the best thing for these pilots, as they would soon learn.

The remaining crews were marching in close order drill on the ground, and in the afternoon the fliers and walkers exchanged places. Flying close formation was not easy, and any fun there was in piloting an airplane was lost in this kind of flying, as the pilot was doing physical work every second he was at the controls. The autopilot was not used in formation flying, the only exception being the one in the lead plane. When piloting a four-engine aircraft with one or more similar aircraft within a few yards of the plane, and with all planes flying at about two hundred miles an hour, a pilot has no margin for error. It was both a physical and mental strain. Pilots would return to their tent with blisters on their hands and aching arms, even though the flying was shared with the copilot.

After seven days of this regimen, the pilots of the 460th were routinely flying a tighter, more compact formation than was ever dreamed possible. "Hell Week" was worth it, after all! Colonel Harrison was perhaps the most hated man alive after a day or two of this punishment, but by the time the week was over the pilots to a man realized they had achieved something never before thought possible: sustained ultratight formation flying, without casualties.

Tight formation had two important advantages. First, it saved lives. As a formation of bombers became more closely knit, its fire power increased geometrically. Several fighters attacking a close formation of B-24's could face over one hundred .50-caliber machine guns firing thirteen rounds a second, converging their 1,300 bullets per second on them. A five-second burst would pour 6,500 bullets into the attacking planes. Not a very pleasant thought, for a German fighter pilot.

The more sloppy the formation, the less formation firepower can be directed to any one spot in the sky. The German pilots all knew this, and they liked to live, too. Given a choice, they would always opt for the groups flying the sloppiest formation and, conversely, shy away from the ones flying good tight formation. We had just bought into the best insurance policy in the Fifteenth Air Force.

Tight formation means better bombing results. If lead bombardiers performed accurate sighting and the "togglers"* did their jobs right, a tight formation

---

*"Togglers" was a term used for bombardiers farther back in the formation who did not use the bombsight. They flicked a toggle switch when the bombs came out of the lead planes.

would assure a high score for the mission. Each mission was rated on the basis of percentage of bombs within a thousand feet of the group aiming point. Each group had several planes equipped with aerial cameras that took sequential photos of bomb impacts. Post-mission appraisers identified and counted each bomb impact inside a 2,000-foot circle superimposed on the impact photos. Fifty percent was considered a very good score. A score of 70 percent was outstanding, considering the physical size and shape of a group formation.

With the good must come some bad. When a plane in a very tight formation was hit by flak, there was a strong possibility of it taking another plane down with it. A loose formation reduced that likelihood, so the tendency was to relax the formation over the target. Usually when a plane sustained a direct hit and burst into flames, the other planes would scatter at once. (If this should occur before the bombs were dropped, it would have a disastrous effect on bombing efficiency.) Beautiful formation temporarily would be gone, but once away from the target area the group would quickly reform to maximize its protective firepower for the trip home.

Formation integrity was the result of a battle of personal values—good bombing pattern potential versus survival. One look at a given formation tells you where the pilots' values lie at that moment.

Finally Hammett & Co. got its marching orders on the evening of 29 March 1944. We and our group would take our new flying skills to an easy target.

Where would it be?

That night Dusty and I were sweating as we wrote letters home. About seven I went outside and washed my face in the wash-up area near our tent, drawing some water from the fresh water supply to brush my teeth. I found myself again looking up at the star show and thinking of my last night in the United States. I somehow felt close to my Creator and couldn't help thinking that this night might be my last look. This was a pre-mission ritual I would follow from that night on. I finally hit the sack and slept surprisingly well.

The flashlight was in my face at 0330 hours. Dusty was up even before the beam reached him. I tried whistling while I shaved, but my mouth was too dry. I tried singing, but was told to shut up by one of the combat veterans. Breakfast was somewhat better than I thought it would be for such an early hour.

We met Sherm and Charlie for the walk through the olive orchard to the briefing room. While I had seen the olive orchard many times, the significance of the olive branches and our walk past them on the way to war struck me for the first time.

Our electrically heated flying suits weren't heated while walking on this windy, chilly morning, and we noticed it. We plodded along with our parachute harnesses in place (except for the leg sections which were unhooked and dangling at our sides), each of us carrying his flak helmet by the chin strap, a green box inside. In the green box was a life-supporting oxygen mask. On our heads were our leather flying helmets with built-in earphones and a dangling plug-in cord.

Thirty-six crews made that maiden trek, wondering

where they would be heading in an hour or so.

After everyone was seated on the two-by-sixes laid across some building blocks in the church/movie/briefing room, Colonel Crowder stepped up on the stage and gave us a little pep talk. Behind the colonel, covering the entire back wall of the stage, was a map of Europe. Six inches above the protective curtain was Berlin, one target we knew was out of our territory, so naturally they needn't cover it for the daily surprise.

With a flourish, the Intelligence officer marched up and opened our curtain on the war. All that was missing was the Fife and Drum Corps. Our virginal milk run was Mostar, Yugoslavia, not far from Metkovic. The officer said a few things about the importance of knocking out the airfield, and that there would be very little enemy opposition. He gave us our morning time hack so we could all go on our way with each of our watches showing the identical time.

After getting off the truck at our assigned hardstand, each man on the crew had some regular preflight duties to perform. The pilot, copilot, and flight engineer went through a long sequence of instrument and control checks as each step was read off a check sheet. The navigator checked over his maps and log sheet. The gunners checked their guns and ammo belts. Howie Thornton checked his radio and his intercom system.

I looked inside the bomb bay at the ten graffiti-covered 500-pound general purpose bombs, gulped a little, and whistled. This thing was getting serious, despite the chalked greetings to Hitler and the pointed suggestions to him for his personal behavior. Then I checked to see that the cotter pins were in each bomb's arming mechanism, as well as the safety wire that runs from the arming device and is fastened to the bomb rack.

Several men went down to the squadron supply tent and drew ten parachute packs, "Mae West" life jackets, flak suits, and escape kits. The copilot had to sign for the kits and would be responsible for their return if they were not used.

John Woodland tightened up his parachute harness leg strap and asked, "How's that look?" Sid Woods spoke up and asked, "Is it comfortable when you straighten up?"

"Yes."

"Then it's too loose."

The idea of the harness is to support your buttocks as you sit in it when the canopy opens and you come to a screeching halt—momentarily. It's like a chair in the sky. Loose leg harnesses do not form a seat; they slip down under your crotch and are reported to cause a very unpleasant sensation when the chute opens.

Mae Wests, which are inflatable life jackets, were checked for live CO_2 cartridges and then strapped in place. We had heard that some people were using the CO_2 cartridges to cool their beer and then placing the spent cartridges back in the Mae Wests, which were kept in the squadron pool. Unbelievable.

The flak suits were stowed for later use.

As I put my escape kit in my flying suit leg pocket, I thought about what all was in it and if I would ever have to use it. The kit was about five inches by five inches by one inch and was contained in a rubberized bag, or pouch. "Escape kit" was a misnomer. We were told, in several lectures since arriving, that we were to *evade* capture if shot down in enemy territory, and to *escape* from custody if possible. The kit contained items designed to help us *evade* capture. The big silken map of Southern Europe and the Balkans was a simulated handkerchief, or scarf. The brass button was actually a compass. A piece of thread was furnished, which you tied to the button, and when the button was suspended, a small dot on one edge pointed north. The small four-inch saw blade didn't seem big enough to saw through prison bars. A plain wallet contained forty-eight U.S. one-dollar bills, for bartering and bribery. People understood U.S. dollars.

I went back outside to put on the rest of my equipment and to take a final look at my new home-away-from-home for the next few hours. A pretty girl adorned its side. I was envious. I wished it were our own plane rather than a borrowed one. The proud owners hoped we would bring it back, but not as much as we did.

The B-24 had many nicknames, but "Flying Box Car" and "Pregnant Cow" were perhaps the two most descriptive. Airborne, the big box hanging below the single narrow wing did make the plane look a little pregnant. Actually, it was a beautiful and majestic sight, but on the ground it had the proverbial face that only a mother could love. It was built so low to the ground that the crew members had difficulty stooping down under the open bomb bays to climb into it.

In full regalia, we didn't look so pretty either. With our flying suits, flying boots, parachute harnesses, and Mae Wests all in place, we felt as if we were in corsets. The most apt description of us was that we looked like a bunch of penguins waddling around. So if you can picture ten penguins trying to climb under a low fence, you have an idea what we looked like as we struggled into our pregnant cow.

At start-engine time we heard the 172,800 horse-power chorus from close up. A jeep scurried from plane to plane, and when the assembly officer in the back seat waved his flag the appropriate four-engine battlewagon moved off its hardstand to join the others in a single-file clockwise path around the perimeter taxi strip. Soon there were thirty-six olive drab B-24 bombers in line, each with a big bold Black Panther on the left nose section, its green eyes and red mouth ready for action. Beside the emblem was the "name" of the particular aircraft. Names like "Rattlesnake Hank," "Our Hobby II," "T. S. Express," "Dinah Might," "Annabelle," "Bottoms Up," "Roseanna from Indiana," "Cuddles," "Boomerang" (my favorite), "Angel of the Sky," "Seldom Available," "Yakimo Kid," and countless others. Most included scantily clad young ladies.

As we lined up on the runway, awaiting our "go" signal from the starter, Sherm, Smitty, Kaiser, and I sat on the floor of the upper flight deck in prescribed takeoff positions. The pilot, copilot, and radio man sat in real seats. The four men in the back were seated against the rear bulkhead. Smitty held a little stuffed horse with "Crew 71" printed on its neck. Listed were the hometowns of the crew, Brooklyn, "Pitt," Gary, Durham, and the others. Right up under the left ear was "I—Mostar." Smitty was an optimist.

Someone uttered those immortal words from a

World War I movie: "This is it!" The others gravely nodded as the airplane leaped forward on its second combat effort and our first. We were actually on our way to wage battle for our country. Surprisingly, I wasn't too scared. Apprehensive, perhaps, but I felt I was in less jeopardy than on some of those Tucson practice missions, where several war-weary B-24's had blown up in flight. After all, it was only a milk run to Mostar.

The thirty-six planes took off at about thirty-second intervals and began the hour-long assembly into a formation of six boxes, each box containing six planes. Three boxes formed the first attack unit and three formed the second attack unit.

After the formation started its climb, and before we had to go on oxygen, I went into the bomb bay to perform one of my bombardier chores—one that I had been taught but had not yet put into practical use. I carefully pulled the cotter pins from each of the bomb fuses and pocketed them. This pre-armed the bombs. In the event that we did not drop our bombs and had to salvo them, I would then put the cotter pins back in place, disarming the bombs. Bomb fuses pre-armed, I put on my flak suit and crawled on up to the nose section to join Sherman Wood, already at work on his mission log. Neither of us had really important work to do as far as the group effort was concerned.

Only the mission navigator actually navigates. The successful arrival of the entire group at the target is his responsibility alone. Each of the other navigators merely records where he is at all times, in case his aircraft should become separated from the group and he must guide his pilot on the way home. He makes log entries every five minutes as to compass heading, altitude, temperature, unusual occurrences, and other factors. He also plots their course on a large map on his fold-down table. The other navigators in the lead box must also be prepared to take over the mission lead in the event the lead navigator's plane is shot down or must drop out of formation.

When the lead navigator brings the group to the IP (Initial Point), which is an easily recognized landmark such as a town or the end of a narrow lake about twenty miles from the target, he gives the pilot a compass heading and points out the target area to the bombardier. At that point the bombardier takes over.

The lead bombardier in the meantime has been studying the map and target photos and checking approaching landmarks so that he can pick up the target as the plane makes its turn onto the heading requested by the navigator. He then may have to refine the target course heading for the pilot before he actually assumes control of the airplane with the bombsight.

Only the lead bombardier in each of the six boxes operates the bombsight in its entirety. He establishes the "course" over the target and also sights for range. The deputy lead bombardier in each box, whose plane is just to the right of and slightly above the lead plane, sights for range only; he simply lines up his "course hair" with the actual course he is traversing over the ground. If the course is incorrect, there is nothing he can do about it.

This means that out of thirty-six bombardiers, only

six sight for course and range, and six sight for range only. Twenty-four just hit the toggle switch when they see the bombs fall from the lead or deputy lead plane in their particular box.

I was only a "togglier" on this mission but I turned my sight on anyway, just in case, because it would take quite some time for the bombsight gyroscope to rev up to full speed in the unlikely event that I might need it.

At 13,000 feet Charlie Hammett instructed the crew to don oxygen masks. I set the intervalometer for the mission requirement, which was for the first of the ten bombs to hit 500 feet short of the aiming point, and for the other bombs to be spaced 100 feet apart in order to straddle the entire target area. Ground speed and altitude determined the setting.

There was nothing more for me to do until we approached the IP, except worry. I had plugged in my electrically heated suit, which included electrically heated slippers inside my flying boots, so I was reasonably warm despite the minus-sixty degrees outside. The nose compartment was heated by a space heater that burned straight gasoline, something like our tent furnaces, except that it was lit with a spark plug instead of a long torch. When it worked, it did keep the nose compartment fairly comfortable, but often it did not work very well, as we were soon to find out. They said the Btu. output was equivalent to that needed to heat a five-room house, but none of us believed it.

"OK, bombardier, the IP is dead ahead so let's shake a leg," suggested Navigator Wood. I had been reviewing the map and photos, so I stooped down over the sight and looked out my private window to confirm my whereabouts and saw . . . nothing. Nothing but clouds below us. A 10/10ths undercast.

"Yeah, Sherm, where is it?" I replied. He just laughed.

"They'll be taking a heading of seventy degrees at about 0907 hours," Sherm said, "so be ready for the turn, Charlie."

Bomb bay doors began opening on the lead planes, so I opened ours. It was getting exciting. Shortly after we turned at the IP (which no one could see) and were heading presumably for the target (which also no one could see), Sid called out, "We're getting flak!"

"You're kidding."

"No, I'm not."

"This is a *milk run*!"

"Tell it to the Chaplain."

"Where is it?"

"Six o'clock low."

"How close?"

"Not very close, it's way behind us."

About that time the bomb bay doors closed on the lead planes, so I closed ours. We were aborting the mission at the very doorstep of the target. The entire group headed toward the south in a giant U-turn and streaked for home, with its 360 bombs still intact. All we accomplished was to learn that Mostar was to be a milk run no more. They had apparently gotten tired of being bothered all the time and had moved in a couple of AA guns.

Reluctantly I attached a portable oxygen tank to my flak suit with the tank's clothespin-type clamp and went back to the bomb bay to put the pins back in

61

all bombs. Once we were over the Adriatic with a clear view below, I joined the rest of the group in salvoing (some call it jettisoning) my bombs in the ocean. Ten big circles in the ocean, in a straight line, was all I could show for my first combat mission. What a disappointment.

Our first effort was a flop, and we reluctantly headed for Spinazzola and the big welcome awaiting us. As we landed, Danny Smith picked up his little mascot, kissed it, and said, "I knew you would bring us through okay."

The next day it was Bob Holland's turn; they flew to Mostar this time, and Mostar was not to be denied. The few flak guns they now had took aim at the flock of bombers flying over and managed to hit one. Rogers went down over Mostar and the 460th lost its first plane in combat. Just a milk run to Mostar.

Our target the following day was the marshalling yards at Knin, Yugoslavia. We had no fighter or flak opposition, and we managed to get our bombs on the target with fair results.

It began to look easy. On 4 April while Dusty and I were still asleep, our tent mates were a few thousand feet over Altamura. Bob Holland was easing his plane into position right behind the lead plane in his box when somehow he got caught in its prop wash. His plane went into a partial stall and fell over on its left wing and onto Russell's plane. Both aircraft went out of control and plummeted to earth. Only one man got out, but his chute did not open fully because of the low altitude, and his effort was in vain. Twenty more men lost before the mission got under way. A few minutes earlier another plane had crashed on takeoff, killing most of the crew.

The shock of the midair collision had a profound effect on the remaining pilots, new and not yet really combat-tested. The skill acquired from months of diligent formation practice suddenly was not there. Boxes opened up. The formation scattered all over the sky. Discipline vanished. Fifty miles before reaching the target, the group looked like it was on a big Easter-egg hunt, as one man described it. A bomb fell out of one of the lead planes. Tension-filled toggliers saw the bomb fall and began toggling their bombs. A chain reaction ensued. Bombs began falling all over the countryside and *they weren't anywhere near the target area*. The mission was a total disaster. Another flop.

Dusty and I were dumbfounded at the news of the midair crash. The four empty cots sat and stared at us that evening in the stark light of our lamp. The war was right here in our tent.

One of our missing friends had a bottle of Walker's Red Label that he was hoarding for that great day when he could celebrate his fiftieth mission. We took a vote and decided his prize possession would never make it out of the area with his other personal belongings that would soon be sent home. And besides it would only be fitting and proper if we would put it to a use somewhat approaching its intended use.

We weren't so sure, at the rate things were going, that we could make it to fifty either. Three losses just in our squadron, and we hadn't even been to a tough target yet. With very little ceremony we cracked the jug and toasted our fallen comrades, one at a time, several times. Some visitors dropped in and helped us

63

along. It was a good thing that a stand-down was ordered for the next day.

When the plane crashed on takeoff earlier that day, three men, Lieutenant Hester, Lieutenant Morris, and Staff Sergeant Fairchild, had entered the burning aircraft and removed an injured crew member. Intense fire and heat had prevented any further rescue efforts. All three were later awarded the Soldier's Medal for their bravery.

We learned the following afternoon that some of our group's wayward bombs had found a hidden ammo dump and caused considerable damage to the enemy. While not very proud of our serendipitous accomplishment, we did enjoy some amusement at picturing the German high command wondering how the Americans had found their secret hiding place.

The same day, 230 Fifteenth Air Force bombers hit the Ploesti marshalling yards with 587 tons of bombs, inflicting heavy damage to their oil transportation system. Thirteen bombers were lost to flak and fighters. This marked the first attack on Ploesti since the 1 August 1943 low-level assault, serving notice that the eight-month rest period was over. As a result of the low-level attack, Ploesti's monthly fuel production dropped from 400,000 metric tone to 262,000. By the time the high-level attacks began in early April, production had climbed up to 370,000 tons.

While Ploesti was suffering its first high-level bombardment, the marshalling yards at Bucharest, thirty miles or so to the south, were being clobbered by several hundred more heavies as part of a two-pronged attack on oil transportation.

The 460th was not part of either oil strike. It was

sent instead to bomb the marshalling yards at Zagreb. Emphasis on oil and rail transportation was the result of late-March widespread Russian advances along the eastern front. The key to supplying German armies on that long front was the Balkan rail transportation system. The Fifteenth Air Force was assigned a new set of bombing priorities to capitalize on the Russian successes:

1. Destroy the Bucharest and Ploesti railroad facilities.
2. Bomb Budapest railroad targets.
3. Bomb other Balkan targets.
4. Attack rail communication centers on the famed Orient Express route, which ran from southeastern Bulgaria through Sofia, Nis, Belgrade, and Zagreb, and attack the rail lines attaching to it from the south.

The new offensive went into effect as soon as the need became apparent, on 2 April, and by the end of the month the Fifteenth would make twenty-six attacks against major Balkan transportation centers.

On the way home from the attack at Zagreb, a plane from the 761st Squadron had to ditch in the Adriatic and another plane from the same squadron dropped down to check the plight of the survivors. Major Spear, who was piloting the second plane, observed there were no yellow dinghies afloat, but he did see nine men in their Mae Wests in the area where the airplane had sunk. Spear flew low over the survivors and ejected his plane's two rubber life rafts. These normally were for ejection *after* a plane had landed in the water. The life rafts shot straight up into the air and were caught on the radio antenna and the tail section of the airplane. The life rafts were ruined, part of the empennage destroyed, and the radio was put out of commission. Failing in that rescue attempt, Spear continued to circle his buddies until a Spitfire showed up to take over the vigil. We later learned that seven men were eventually picked up.

On Sunday, 9 April, after a day of tough formation practice, many of the men went to evening church service. It was a strange experience. The map of Europe was peaking up over the top of the stage curtain behind the pulpit. The city of Berlin was a stark reminder of our current mission in life, and was in sharp contrast to the spiritual message by Chaplain Dodds. After the service we stayed in our seats and watched a movie entitled, "The Lodger," a psychological murder thriller. It was an unusual Easter for all of us.

A few days later a plane crashed on takeoff and blocked the runway, so the mission had to be scrubbed. The next day, however, we managed to get all the planes into formation and off we went to Zagreb to ruin some marshalling yards. With minimum flak and fighter opposition the planes were able to breeze over the target with excellent bombing results—all except ours. There was a malfunction in our electrical system and no bombs were released over the target. Again, we salvoed over the ocean on the way home and we began to wonder if we ever would accomplish anything.

Replacement crews began arriving with their new

planes from the replacement pool at a base farther south of us. The new planes were different. They were unpainted, bright, silvery creatures of the sky. The omission of paint was said to reduce weight and air resistance, which resulted in an increase in speed of about 10 mph and a substantial increase in range. It would prove to be interesting later on to observe the once darkly toned formation slowly turning lighter as the original drab planes disappeared, to be replaced by the new silver ones. The change in color tone would tell its own silent story.

"H. P. (Horsepower) Whitehead & Co." moved into our tent, and it didn't take them long to get into the swing of things. Whitehead was from Birmingham and liked to kid me in his southern drawl about Pittsburgh being the Birmingham of the north. The other officer members of his crew were from West Virginia, Minnesota, and Wisconsin. They all talked kind of funny, nothing like the normal talk of Pittsburghers. For some reason they all thought I talked funny too.

The Air Force's master plan began calling for stepped-up activity against German oil refineries as well as oil transportation systems. On 15 April, the Fifteenth Air Force sent several groups to bomb Ploesti for its second high-level attack on that target, again simultaneously hitting the marshalling yards at nearby Bucharest. Along with many other groups, the 460th was assigned the Bucharest portion of the dual attack. A few other groups hit the marshalling yards at Nis, Yugoslavia, where many oil tank cars were gathered.

Colonel Crowder believed the most experienced of the group command pilots, staff navigators, and bombardiers should lead the missions. At a previous meeting he had stated this belief and one sincere pilot said, "But I question that. If they were lost the group would suffer too much."

"No," was the colonel's reply, "if the 460th can't find the targets and hit them, we might just as well have stayed home."

Two months earlier, while the group was still in North Africa, Colonel Crowder had gone up to Italy to fly a combat mission to a German target. He would now lead the group's first major mission.

The squadron commanding officer, Maj. Charles Ward, elected to fly our plane. Charlie Hammett moved over to the copilot seat and Dusty flew with another crew.

At the briefing we were told to expect some heavy fighter activity from Goering's Yellow Nose fighters, the elite of the Luftwaffe. Flak would be heavy. They explained the coordinated attack plan and mentioned that we probably would be able to see the action at Ploesti some fifteen miles north of our IP.

I was intrigued by the remarks of the intelligence officer who told us that if we were shot down near Bucharest, we should make our way to a certain address and knock on the door with a special knock code. We would be taken in and hidden for a day or two and then spirited away incognito to Istanbul, where we would be put on a boat with Jewish refugees and taken somewhere to safety.

Our group formed as usual over Altamura and flew to a rendezvous point, where we joined the three other groups from the 55th Wing. Our wing then flew to the key point along the eastern point and joined the four other wings for the full twenty-one assault on the three Balkan targets.

Rendezvousing twenty-one groups of approximately thirty-six planes each is not the same as meeting several friends at the corner of Fifth and Main. Every plane, every group, every wing must be at a precise spot at an exact moment in time; no one can wait around for latecomers. Hammett & Co. was assigned a seemingly innocuous spot in the formation, number 5 in the lead box of the first attack unit. However, if the mission lead, piloted by Colonel Crowder, dropped out of formation for any reason, the deputy lead in the number 2 spot would move to mission lead, and we would then move into deputy lead. In that position we would be next in line to assume the mission lead.

I was properly impressed with the potential responsibility that might come my way, so I studied the target photos very carefully and made certain my bombsight was warmed up long before we reached the target.

About one hundred miles from the target we heard reports on the intercom of fighters in the area. All of a sudden I heard machine guns firing. For the first time our guns were firing in combat. Four fighters made a pass at us, and one was hit as they peeled off early in the face of our firepower, with Howie Thornton getting credit for the "kill" from his ball turret position.

Several more fighters came straight at our formation from dead ahead, cannons and machine guns blazing from their yellow noses. It was suicide. The entire first attack unit of eighteen planes was firing their nose, belly, and top turret guns at the oncoming planes. Over one hundred machine guns firing over thirteen hundred rounds a second. Yet they bore on.

One of the attackers exploded but the others flew right into our formation, like birds flying through a tree. Bullets ripped our plane, but miraculously none of the crew was hit. I had been hearing this drama unfold on the intercom, and looked out my left window just in time to see the invaders sweeping past at lightning speed, swastikas glistening in the sun and one pilot's arm poised in salute. Just like in the movies. He was to be the only enemy soldier I would see in the war.

"Crowder is hit!" screamed the intercom.

I looked over to our leader's plane just a few dozen yards away and had my worst fears confirmed. The mission lead plane, target of the unholy six, had a gaping hole in the nose section where a 20mm cannon projectile had exploded. The cockpit was enveloped in flames, and Colonel Crowder was fighting the control in order to give his crew a few more seconds to bail out. The plane itself was not savable, but his men were. He wasn't.

I watched the stricken Liberator, flames erupting from its sides, slowly roll over on its back to begin its death dive as three lucky bodies spewed from its sick innards. The plane exploded several thousand feet below as the three survivors descended into the clouds. Colonel Crowder, father of the Black Panther spirit, at the helm on all nine missions the 460th had flown, a true leader to the end, had flown his last.

"Get ready bombardier, we're moving up to deputy lead," barked the major.

"Yes sir, I'm set."

The events had moved so rapidly I hadn't really appreciated what had happened. Fighters just don't fly through bomber formations, but we hadn't reckoned with Goering's "Yellow-Nosed Squadron," considered one of the best in the world.

All of a sudden I found myself group deputy lead, about to go over a major target and determined to make good, but facing a serious problem. I couldn't see the ground in the target area. With a 10/10th undercast all I saw below was a solid field of fluffy white clouds.

"Look up north!" shouted someone in the intercom. I had been too concerned about my instant promotion and the coming bomb run to bother looking at Ploesti, not many miles away, due to our northerly course to the IP. I had a few minutes until we would reach the IP, so I stole a quick peek at the target. What a sight it was. The flak barrage over the several targets looked like a huge black sponge in the sky, with the bomber formations being absorbed a group at a time.

Suddenly an earthbound black spiraling line caught my attention, then a second one. I was witnessing two burning bombers in a race for the ground. It was a graphic sign of things to come—the hallmark of Ploesti's antiaircraft defenses.

Navigator Wood alerted Major Ward to be ready to turn at 1006 hours; and, sure enough, at the appointed hour the lead plane began a slow turn to the right at the IP and leveled off for the bomb run, such as it was. I settled into my sight to establish a sighting angle, but it was no use as I still saw nothing but clouds.

"Our orders are to drop on ETA (Estimated Time of Arrival) if necessary, and it looks like that's what we'll have to do today," said Major Ward.

"Sherm, what is our ETA for the bomb release?" I asked.

"1009 hours and 13 seconds."

"Roger."

My disappointment at not being able to sight on the target was replaced by my concern for what I saw outside the windows. Puffs of black clouds began appearing all over the place. Flak! I was seeing flak up close for the first time. Then I was hearing it. The dull thud of the shells exploding outside could be heard over the engine noise. The sound of gravel being thrown on a tin roof was actually little pieces of shrapnel penetrating the thin skin of the airplane. *We are here. We are in the war. We must be near Bucharest to rate this kind of reception. I want to strike back!* Someone once said the black clouds you can see won't hurt you, just like what they say about lightning. It's the ones you don't see that you should worry about. But like ants, if you see one you know there are more coming. And they did come, not in ones or twos, but in dozens. Many dozens.

The flak increased in intensity, so despite the total undercast situation, we knew we must be nearing the target. Our banked turn at the IP was reasonably accurate: we would see the ground through some openings in the clouds during the navigational approach. The accuracy of the bombing would depend upon the accuracy of the lead navigator's course heading, and both his and our navigator's estimation of ground speed on that particular course.

ETA bombing is very inefficient, and it bothered me as a trained bombardier to have to flick a toggle switch at nine minutes and thirteen seconds after ten o'clock and know that all the planes behind me would toggle on my bombs. However, it was better this way than dropping them in the ocean as we had been doing lately. We just might hit some secret oil reserves.

When the second hand reached thirteen, I dutifully hit the toggle switch. Someone reported the lead plane toggled at precisely the same time, and the other planes in our attack unit followed suit. Wherever our bombs may have landed, at least we should have had a good pattern.

We were getting a fair flak reception ourselves, but nothing like the fellows up north. Ours was considered in the heavy flak category, but not in a class with Ploesti. Fortunately, none of our planes was badly damaged, although many did receive some hits.

Leaving the target area, we snuggled up a little closer to the lead plane and headed for home as we turned on the "fighter to fighter" channel on the VHF radio. From the fighter pilot's comments we could tell some exciting dogfights were in progress, even though we could see nothing. When the dialogue died down, we tuned in "Berlin Sally." She amused most of us, even though we realized her intention was to demoralize the American G.I. On the contrary, however, we all enjoyed her great selection of music. Glenn Miller,

Benny Goodman, and the others were a big treat.

The trip home was uneventful, as our P-38 friends mothered us most of the way.

The big push was now underway to cripple the German oil capabilities, and our "one-two punch" in Rumania was just the beginning.

Chapter 3

HANGAR QUEEN

As I looked up, the 500-pound bomb rolled off the truck and onto the hardstand, just ten feet away from me. My jumping, while a reflex action, was rather pointless, because if the bomb were destined to go off, there was nowhere to jump, except into oblivion. It didn't go off, of course, and the bomb handlers were quite amused by my reaction. They apparently did this all the time, as it was easier than using the crane that was provided. A printed warning on the bomb went unheeded.

That was our first trip to the hardstand in an evening when the planes were being serviced for the next day's mission. We were learning what the other half had been doing while we were loafing around writing letters and playing cards or chess each evening after supper. No doubt the bombs were safe enough with the fuses not yet in place, but their casual handling of them made me uncomfortable.

"They say it's a gas hog," commented Dusty. The bright new silver-colored B-24-H was being stuffed

with bombs, ammunition and gasoline in preparation
for its next effort. The big yellow C painted on the
side of the fuselage was its only identification. As
beautiful as it was, it had a bad reputation. All who
had flown it remarked about its abnormally high rate
of fuel consumption.

"*C for Charlie*" was one of the first of the new
NMF (Natural Metal Finish) replacement planes
brought in by the Ferry Command and assigned to the
squadron pool. It was a plane without a crew. We were
a crew without a plane.

"Why don't we ask for it?" someone suggested.
"Maybe it just needs breaking in." The discussion
went on for a few more minutes. "OK, let's do it,"
chimed in Charlie. "After all, it already has part of
my name." He promised to make a formal request for
C for Charlie.

At briefing the morning before, Colonel Harrison
had made an impassioned speech about the importance of shooting down enemy fighter planes. All the
gunners left the room of one mind. Each wanted to be
the first one to get a fighter that day. The colonel's
speech had been effective; the group bagged a fighter
as it came off the target. Unfortunately it was a P-51.

Earlier this day they flew in a P-51, and we were all
invited to come out and take a close look at it. The
colonel gave another speech on fighter planes, and it
shouldn't be necessary to explain the tone or content
of his comments. After that episode we began having
more and more aircraft recognition classes, to be
enjoyed during our free time along with the regular
VD lectures and world situation updates.

The next morning when the stage curtain was

76

drawn, it revealed the blue yarn stretching from the rendezvous point in southern Italy to the Initial Point near Belgrade, Yugoslavia. That wasn't so bad, but the blue yarn went right over Mostar. They had only four guns, but we didn't like them taking target practice on us when we weren't even going to bother them. Someone asked the briefing officer, "Why?" The answer was that we have to fly a straight line to the mountain pass and then a straight line to the target to conserve gas, and the second straight line takes us over Mostar.

"Can't we jog to the left about five miles before Mostar and then jog back and get on course again?"

"No," he replied. "Any more questions?"

By chance we were assigned to *C for Charlie*, so we now would have an opportunity to test-ride the plane Charlie had requested for our own.

The group reached Yugoslavia while still climbing on course over the less mountainous part of the Dinaric Alps, and by the time we were over Mostar we had a 10/10th undercast, so their few futile shots aimed by radar were not very effective. As we penetrated deeper into Yugoslavia, we could see the billowing cumulus clouds ahead raging up to our altitude. Although we reached fairly close to Belgrade, the impenetrable clouds forced our group to abort the mission and return home. More bombs in the ocean. Weather was Germany's best protection against the Fifteenth Air Force.

A few days later we were briefed on Bucharest again. As we got out over the ocean, oil began pouring out of the number one engine, so we had to abort, feather the engine, and return to our base. We shook up some more fish as we again salvoed our bombs in the Adriatic. The problem? Someone had left the oil cap off and the oil had been siphoning out of the engine.

Colonel Harrison was made Group Commander, and the man whom many of us had wanted to choke once or twice was now in command—and we cheered.

Aside from the one daring head-on attack by Goering's Yellow Nose Devils, our group had faced relatively little fighter opposition. We had seen German fighter squadrons fly alongside our group out of machine gun range, look us over, and move on to find a less disciplined group to molest. Colonel Harrison's "preventative medicine" was paying off.

It was mid-April and the Fifteenth Air Force was pounding German oil and transportation systems relentlessly. Germany was paying dearly for the eighteen days in March when the Fifteenth had stood down in deference to the bad flying weather. Add a few days of abortive attempts, and the month of March clearly belonged to Germany. April would be ours!

One beautiful spring evening we were again out at the hardstand where the bomb loaders were kicking 500 pounders off the trucks alongside *C for Charlie*. We tried to ignore the bomb bouncers as we watched the squadron artist draw the large beautiful young lady in the skimpy bathing suit, sitting in a Betty Grable pose, in front of a hangar which was positioned in the background. Then the words "Hangar

Queen" were emblazoned across the tableau that meant so much to us. We, the Hangar Queen crew now had our own airplane. Yellow *C for Charlie* belonged to crew #71.

The next morning the blue yarn went to Bucharest again, and *Hangar Queen* would fly her first mission under her new colors.

A full strike by the Fifteenth was a sight to behold, and twenty-one heavy bomb groups, subdivided into Wings of four or five groups, produced well over seven hundred sets of contrails like a giant spiderweb high in the sky, all heading in the same direction—in this case, Rumania. German oil was going to get it again.

A maximum strike like this brought out the Balkan air force in full. American P-51's flew giant "S" patterns above the maze of contrails in an effort to stay with the relatively slower bombers. When we would arrive at the target, they would turn and head for home, their escort job finished.

When the bomber force was well along on its course, the P-47's would take off and fly, at their much greater speed, directly to the target where they would spell off the P-51's and engage the enemy, or simply patrol in the general target area. After we left the target, they would head for home, and the later arriving P-38's would show up to escort us back to friendly skies. Sometimes, though, P-38's would escort us *to* the target, and P-51's would see us home.

This shuttle deployment of fighter support, each plane equipped with reserve exterior wing gas tanks that would be used on the trip to the target, placed a group of assured fuel healthy fighters at our sides at all times.

A group of German FW-190's drew alongside our very tight formation, looked us over, and went on to the group ahead, which was flying a more relaxed formation. *Thanks, Colonel Harrison!*

The sight of plummeting empty wing tanks from our escort P-51's was another new spectacle in our ever-widening experience. The jettisoned wing tanks were symbolic of barroom brawlers stripping off their coats in preparation for a good scrap. When the tanks fell, action was not far behind. And action is what we saw.

Because the planes were flying at greater speeds than the old World War I Spads and Fokkers, we really didn't see much in the way of aerobatics, but we did see two FW-190's on a one-way flaming trip toward the earth.

" 'Tail-end Charlie' is going to get it if he doesn't move back into formation," warned Tyrone from his nose turret, in reference to the group ahead. This was the designation for the number 6 position in the number 6 box. It was the last plane in the entire formation, located at the lower left, way down at the bottom. This position, even under good formation flying conditions, got the least amount of group firepower protection. If the boxes ahead of this lower box in the second attack unit were in loose formation, it would force the box farther out of position. If the box itself were also loose, it would put Tail-end Charlie that much farther out by itself. No wonder this position was called "Purple Heart corner."

Tail-end Charlie got it. The fighters knew a patsy

when they saw one, so they sent a flight of six in from the eight o'clock position and Charlie didn't have a chance.

Fortunately, the pilot was able to maintain control long enough for everyone to escape. It was gratifying to count ten chutes. Usually we could only count five or six chutes coming out immediately from a downed plane, and could only hope a few more made it out on the way down.

Finally the P-51's came into view and shot down two of the attackers within our sight. Kaiser gave us the blow-by-blow of the action.

We were seeing so much evidence of how right Colonel Harrison was, we couldn't understand why everyone didn't fly in tight formations. The big reason no doubt was because it was physically demanding. Our pilots would come back from a mission so exhausted they could hardly eat a meal. They would simply flop onto their cots and sleep awhile before doing anything else. I always felt a little guilty about being so spry after a mission, as I usually had a little nap on the plane.

"Tyrone" liked to serenade us over the intercom with songs he composed. Some were bad and some were worse, but he actually hit a good one every once in a while. It didn't matter though, because he did help us, lifting our spirits in the midst of battle. As we approached a target, we all knew in the back of our minds that it could well be our last mission, even our last day on earth. No one ever said anything like this out loud, but it ate at us, a little bit on each mission. Bob (Tyrone) Kaiser was good medicine.

His song about the Brown Danube was pretty good.

And that was an apt description of the famous old river: it was no more blue than my army hat. As we listened to him warble about the famous river, we saw a tugboat pushing a dozen oil barges up the brown waters quite a few miles south of where we crossed. It bothered me that no one was bothering them as they moved German oil to war.

Many of the groups were headed for Ploesti—where 290 planes would drop nearly 800 tons of bombs, losing eight bombers—but our wing was going for the marshalling yards at Bucharest again, to pound their oil transportation facilities. About seventy-five miles from the target we developed a serious oil leak and had to abort the formation and head back home. The thought of going home alone was frightening. We knew the fighters doted on such morsels, as one bomber is no match for several fighters. Straggling home alone with engine trouble, or whatever the reason, was certain disaster in most instances.

Apparently the Balkan Luftwaffe was plenty busy with our escort P-51's and the 700 bombers, so none of them were around to bother us. In view of this, several crew members suggested we take care of the tugboat and its oil barges on the way home, rather than jettisoning our bombs in the ocean.

I accepted the challenge. We had dropped down to 15,000 feet so the engine strain would be less critical and the pilots could keep close tabs on the oil pressure. I had never bombed a moving target before, so this would be a new experience.

I lined up the barges in my sight and loosed the dozen 500 pounders on this beautiful target of opportunity. The invervalometer was still set for 100-foot intervals, which was lucky for the boat occupants. My bomb strikes walked across the river right where the barges were passing, but the tugboat chugged along in between strikes. No doubt the concussion of the near misses rocked the boat, perhaps even ruptured the underside of the barges. We'll never know, but we did see the barge formation come apart, so perhaps some may have sunk after we left. Our trip home was without further incident.

The following day our group flew its first mission to the manufacturing complex at Wiener Neustadt, Austria. It wasn't our crew's turn, so we heard about this new "Flak Alley" from those returning.

In addition to extremely heavy flak, and Goering's Yellow Nose Devils who came up from the Balkans, any strike in Austria or southern Germany would have to contend with another adversary. The Central European Luftwaffe was available to attack either the Italian-based Fifteenth's bombers or the England-based Eighth's bombers.

Wiener Neustadt was a brutal target. They made German fighter planes there and they protected it to the best of their ability. Our group lost several planes that day, including Swazey's and Pointer's which contained two more of our original squadron crews. My friend, Dick Fowler from Minneapolis, was on one of the planes and bailed out with most of his crew over Yugoslavia.

The next day *Hangar Queen* went back to Bucharest. This time we made it to the target and were rewarded with a direct hit on our aiming point, a big beautiful roundhouse. The entire roundhouse was well clobbered, thanks to a very tight formation, good aiming, and good toggling. Flames shot quite high into the air. It was like hitting a bull's-eye at a firing range.

763rd Bomb Squadron; 460th Bombardment Group. Note *Hangar Queen*, lower right.

We all knew that this excellent bombing effort would improve our group's standing. From last place early in its career, the 460th was slowly inching its way toward the top in the group standings published weekly. A couple more like that and we could be in first place.

Flak was very heavy, but concentrated behind us, as we banked and turned south for our trip home. Several fighters made a half-hearted pass at us as we leveled out, but heavily concentrated firepower forced them to abort their attack.

This was our eighth mission and by now we all had fallen into our respective behavioral patterns as we left the immediate target area. The first blush of heroics had worn off. Our group losses had been high so far. Six of the original seventeen crews in our squadron had been lost, and we had forty-two more missions to go. The thought of our long odds was sobering.

There was, of course, a certain anxiety on the way to a target. But it was offset by the anticipation of the thrill of battle and a very strong it-can't-happen-to-me attitude. *Scared?* Yes! *Terrified?* No! Our fear was healthy, out of respect to the known possibilities. When the target action started, we put our fear aside, to some degree, and concentrated on our jobs.

Upon leaving the target, I usually would notice a switch of emotions. After the immediate "Whew, I'm glad this one is over!" reaction, I found a strange new anxiety setting in. I had nothing to do from then on except to sit on the floor and stomp my feet to keep them from getting too cold. I found I could stomp and think at the same time. For some reason, with the immediate danger over, my fear level would rise to heights not reached on the way to the target, or even at the target. I would think in terms of the next mission a day or two later, and it would gnaw at me for awhile. My friend so-and-so went down. Do I have to do it again? Why did I get involved in this?

As we left the area this time, I took my usual peek at the smoking target by leaning over the bombsight and looking straight down. Then I climbed into my shell so I could worry the rest of the way home.

"Tyrone" usually burst forth with a love ballad as his post-target reaction. Others just made bad jokes in our ears. Dusty Rhodes, in his calming down process this day, idly unscrewed the hub of his control wheel and discovered a folded piece of paper. A note.

"Hey, what's this?" he exclaimed. "She wants me to call her when I get to Fort Worth."

"Who?" chorused two or three interested voices.

"Peg, the gal who wrote this note."

"Peg who? What note?"

Dusty said, "I guess she is the one who put the hubcaps on these control wheels. I hope she did good work on whatever else she did on this airplane." He went on to explain the note and the fact there was an address and phone number on the other side of the note. Dusty took a Hershey-bar bet that Peg would never answer the letter he said he would write that night. I never did learn who won the bet.

As we crossed the Danube we saw some more boats, but this time all we could do was look, as we had left our bombs at Bucharest.

It was reassuring to see a flight of P-38's fly by and salute us with a dip of their wings. It reminded me of stories we had heard of another group that had just come off a sustained fighter attack, and the gunners were still a little trigger-happy. A crippled P-38 with an engine feathered had tried to sidle up to the distraught formation for a protective escort home. The P-38, with its forked tails, was probably the most uniquely designed airplane in the air. The pilot wisely brought his left wing up so it was perpendicular to the ground, to give the intended host bomber group a clear profile. Then he slowly edged his plane sideways toward his saviors. All of the plane's guns were fixed in the pilot's nacelle, and could only be fired in the direction the plane was pointing. He had done everything humanly possible to prevent the gunners from firing on him in his helpless position.

It was not enough. There is no logical explanation for the burst of gunfire that poured out at the astounded fighter pilot.

"Trigger-happy" was the term everyone used. The gunners must have been so emotionally worked up that they would have shot if it had been an American flag with propellers. The pilot, of course, did the only thing possible: he left the area where he obviously was not welcome.

We also heard of B-24's with an engine feathered, trying to join a group other than their own for a protective trip home, and being driven away in a similar manner. This was more understandable because we were told the Germans had several captured B-24's and had on occasion infiltrated formations and shot down some of our planes.

We made it home safely and then stood down for five straight days due to bad weather. Stand-downs were good and they were bad. Obviously when you were on the ground no one was shooting at you, and that was good. On the other hand, if it weren't for the extended layoff, we could have been two missions closer to the magic "50," and our ticket home.

The ground time was put to good use. We contracted with a local builder to build us a twenty-foot-by-thirty-foot house made of white tufa block and a tile roof. Tufa block was a quarried porous stone about the size of a cement building block.

The *Stars and Stripes* would later run a feature

story on our white house-oriented base and dub it "Bomber City."

The new occupants of our old tent, fresh replacement crews out to show everyone how the war should be run, complained loudly about their "crummy quarters." *Crummy quarters indeed!* If they knew the blood, sweat, and tears that went into that beautiful sagging tent, complete with furnace and tiled floor, they would not have tried to irritate us so successfully. The memory of our departed brethren who had shared it was still with Dusty and me.

Sometimes we were not too friendly with the new crews. We made them earn our friendship. One hotshot rookie looked up at our group flying overhead and asked who they were. Upon learning that they were ours, he seemed shocked that he had been here a day or two and the war was going on without him.

"How come they are flying without us?" he mused. "We came here to fight, not to stand around and watch."

"Take it easy," I said with poorly concealed glee. "Your turn is coming."

While I was talking to him, another veteran came by and raised his right arm, bent at elbow with palm straight up facing me, and exclaimed, "Heil Hitler, shust en caze vee loose!" I responded in kind, with a straight face, and the hotshot just shook his head and walked away. This little greeting was the current fad among many of us. When the C.O. got wind of it, he ordered the practice stopped, so from then on it became a more surreptitious exchange. In the long run, it was this type of offbeat attitude that helped us to keep our sanity and not go off the deep end. Every so often a flying crewman would get a little flak-happy and have to be grounded, or taken away somewhere, sometimes by force.

After a few days the new crews would get their baptism of fire, and it wasn't always a milk run. Some new crews went out on their first mission and never came back. Usually very few of us would even know their names.

Actually, we welcomed new crews, especially if they brought along a new airplane. They had no idea of the valuable cargo they might be carrying with them to their new home. Among other supplies intended for the squadron and stowed aboard their new aircraft was generally a carton or two of toilet paper. An innocuous enough package to them, but gold to us, as it was used for barter and poker stakes.

One day we observed a shiny new B-24 coming in to land, so we grabbed a jeep and rushed out to greet the new crew, with outstretched hands of fellowship, as they stepped off onto the hardstand at their new home. Their faces lit up with surprise. *Here we are arriving in combat and these guys have come out to greet us. How nice.*

After some pleasantries, one of us casually asked if we could carry anything in for them.

"Here, let me carry this big carton for you. Dusty, grab the other one," I said.

"OK, I've got it!" With that we piled the two cartons into the rear of our jeep. That was the last they saw of the toilet paper as they drove off in the G.I. truck, waving goodbye to their kind greeters.

On 30 April we were to make our first visit to an

Italian target, the marshalling yards at Castel Maggiore. The briefing officer told us the flak would be moderate but accurate, and to expect some fighter opposition.

He was half right. There was some flak as we crossed the coast, and it was very accurate. We suffered some damage to our control cables, in that some of the duplicate cables were severed. But as long as at least one cable still ran to each control surface, the plane was controllable. It made me nervous to see the several severed cables flopping around in the bomb bay. These were the control cables going back to the rudders. The one remaining lonely strand just didn't seem enough. *What if it went too?* And we hadn't even arrived at the target.

The formation missed the IP and all of a sudden found itself heading straight west for Bologna instead of the briefed target. When the undercast cleared and the lead bombardier got his bearings, it was necessary to make a left turn into the actual target. This last-minute maneuvering left him less than two minutes for his bomb run at the new heading.

Bombing results were fair, despite the rather accurate flak. No one went down over the target, but several planes limped home with one engine feathered and injured men aboard. Nine aircraft suffered flak damage.

Three cripples, forced out of formation because of being unable to maintain formation speed, formed their own little formation and came home together, at a slower speed than the main body of the group. At least they had company and would dissuade some fighter attacks. One or two roaming fighters would not be likely to take on three bombers. There was no fighter opposition that day, however, thanks to our P-47 support in the target area.

We stood down for several days due to weather, so old *Hangar Queen* was soon patched up and ready to go again. We counted ten flak holes in her sides from our trip to northern Italy. The ten little aluminum Band-Aids were sort of combat badges. It was sobering to watch the ever-mounting number of badges grow, mission after mission. It was a wonder that no one aboard had yet been hit, despite the many opportunities suggested by the badges.

The men were beginning to get a little jittery, and our leaders were concerned about combat fatigue. The group had flown seventeen missions so far and had lost fifteen planes in combat. Our bombing accuracy rating, however, was substantially higher than the Fifteenth Air Force average, and we ranked fourth out of the twenty-one groups for the month of April.

Ploesti fuel production had been cut to 170,000 tons and the 460th had not even been there yet!

Danny Smith became our aerial engineer when Dominic Minitti was taken off flying status due to a chronic ear condition.

One night it finally happened. A loud explosion came from the direction of the hardstands. It was the first and only time I ever heard a 500-pound bomb explode. One of the bomb handlers in another squadron had pushed his last bomb off a truck, an RDX bomb. Something new. Far more powerful than a GP (General Purpose) bomb, and far more sensitive. They *could* explode from a hard jar even without the fuse in place. Evidently the bomb-handling crew did not believe the new handling rules that reemphasized careful handling of RDX bombs.

I never again saw a bomb handler push a bomb off a truck.

PART THREE:
AIR OFFENSIVE—
EUROPE

Chapter 4

ONE THOUSAND GUNS OF PLOESTI

"You Black Panthers of the 460th can expect to see your pretty white houses just piles of dust after the Luftwaffe is through with you," taunted Berlin Sally. She was all talk. The Luftwaffe never came to Bomber City.

On the last day of our long stand-down, we all dressed in Class A uniforms and reported to the drill field. Gen. Nathan O. Twining, Commanding General, Fifteenth Air Force, had come to pin the Air Medal on those who had completed five missions. It was a nice shot in the arm and gave us a running start for the events of the following morning, when the blue yarn on the stage map went to our mecca, Ploesti.

"Gentlemen, today is a milestone in the history of the 460th," began the briefing officer as the impact of the blue yarn settled in. "We make our first strike on Ploesti, the heart of Germany's oil production." He certainly had everyone's attention. We had been awaiting this moment, and all the side conversations and shuffling in our seats came to a quick halt.

He told us that our specific target was the Xenia Refinery on the northwest edge of the city. Xenia was one of the smallest of the important refineries in the Ploesti area, but its tank farms (storage tanks) were a vital cog in the overall oil production for the entire area. It had been virtually ignored in the low-level raid of last August, so it began handling most of the crude from the neighboring oil wells, which could not be put through the larger refineries for awhile due to the damage inflicted on them. Xenia had been rested for the previous few months, but was being pressed back into service again because of the renewed attacks on the big refineries.

He then told us that our job was to destroy the tank farms and the nearby distilling unit—and the 460th could do it! There was no cheering or back-slapping as happens after a pep talk in a football locker room. Our low murmur of appreciation said all that needed to be said at the time.

He told us that we wouldn't be alone up there. About a dozen or so other groups would be hitting various targets in the Ploesti complex at the same time. He continued with more details about the location of the IP, bombing altitude, and other information. Then another officer stepped up to the podium with the "gloom report."

"There are about one thousand antiaircraft guns at Ploesti!" was his opening remark.* Our hearts sank

*While this figure of one thousand guns was used at that time, and we certainly came to believe it, later research by the author indicated there were about seven hundred flak guns at Ploesti during this period.

as we thought of what just four guns could do at Mostar. "However," he continued, "they are deployed in a large circle twelve miles in diameter surrounding Ploesti, so it isn't as bad as it sounds." Pause. "It just means there is no way into the target area without flak activity." He kept our attention. We knew Ploesti was ranked third in the list of the world's most heavily defended targets. Vienna was number two, and Berlin was considered number one. Many contended Ploesti was the most concentrated of the three. (A lot of fellows in our group would place Wiener Neustadt right up there with any of them.)

The officer wouldn't quit. "The German high command is probably aware by now that Ploesti is a prime target for the Fifteenth Air Force, so we can expect not only the Balkan air force to meet us enroute, but a portion of the Central air force too. Fighter action will be heavy, but our fighter protection is getting better, and if we keep up the great tight formation, the fighters will be the least of our worries." We all chuckled inwardly at the word "we" and "our" coming out of someone not planning to come along.

The blue yarn did not surprise Sherm and me, as we had been to a special pre-briefing for lead bombardiers and navigators a half hour earlier. *Hangar Queen* was assigned to deputy lead in the first attack unit. If the mission lead plane aborted or was forced out of formation en route, we would move to mission lead and all the navigational responsibilities would fall on Sherm's shoulders. The target pickup and course sighting would be my full responsibility. Butterflies. I had been invited to one other prebriefing—the first Bucharest mission when the colonel was shot down. Now we were *starting* in deputy lead. One step closer to the lead itself.

Astra Romana Oil Refinery (Ploesti, Rumania); (1) stabilization plant, (2) doctor plants, (3) Dubbs units, (4) boiler houses, (5) new construction, believed to be a catalytic cracking unit

Several target photos were projected onto a screen. First, an oblique shot from twenty miles away, which is what I would see at the IP as we turned onto the target course. Then a second oblique shot from two miles away, which was near the bomb release point. A third shot was from directly overhead. There were also several close-up views taken by P-38 pilots a few days earlier. I was given identical shots. The pre-briefing officer explained that we would be going in on the "thin axis," which meant the thirty storage tanks

98

would be lined up two abreast and about fifteen deep, as we would see them while approaching the target.

Bomb patterns tended to string out, even though the goal was to have the impacts form a circular pattern, so the thin axis was a risky choice. It was like putting all your eggs in one basket, so to speak. When we bombed marshalling yards we usually hit them on the broadside. In that manner there was a better chance of at least cutting the yards in two and slowing down rail transportation for awhile. They were counting on some good course sighting and then just letting the bombs string out a little. We would hit them all or miss them all.

Off to the left of the tank farm was the distilling unit. Our second attack unit was assigned the job of eliminating it. The tank farm was about 900 feet long and 200 feet wide, so the intervalometer setting would be 130 feet. My eight bombs would start at the first rank of tanks and walk right through to the last rank. Now that sounds good: all you have to do is land the first one where it belongs. No one was assured to be that *good*, but we all strived for that perfect strike. Indeed, if the lead bombardiers are reasonably close in their aim, the pilots fly a very tight formation, and the toggliers toggle their bombs just as the lead plane's first bomb comes into sight, the group could make a 100 percent score for the mission. That would mean *all* of the group's 288 bombs would have landed within 1,000 feet of the aiming point, which was the middle of the tank farm in our assignment. This would be like bowling a "300" game.

Although the second attack unit was part of the group flying to and from the target, it was always assigned a different aiming point. The two scores would be combined to determine the group score for the day.

Pertinent weather input data was given to the lead bombardiers. We were also given the target barometric pressure reading, altitude temperature, wind speed, and direction aloft for the estimated time of arrival. This and other information would be fed into the bombsight at the proper time. The navigators were given detailed maps for the entire trip, and briefed on finding the Initial Point and on helping the bombardier to locate the target quickly. This transfer of target responsibility from navigator to bombardier would take place within a period of a few seconds, when the formation reached the IP and started its banked turn toward the target. That would be a very crucial moment, as the bombardier gets only one chance to locate the target and begin his sighting operation for the four- to five-minute bomb run.

After the gloom report, the main briefing continued with specific air traffic and rendezvous information for all the pilots.

We were very good friends with Flight Surgeon Captain Snyder, so we were pleased to learn he would be flying in *Hangar Queen* with us. It wasn't a job requirement, but he felt that if he were to be of any help to us, he should have some idea of what we faced over an enemy target. This would be his first mission. After the briefing I met him under a large poster that read "KILL THE ENEMY." I welcomed him to our crew as we walked out together to the war. "Why did you pick this one, Captain?" I asked. "Well, my old pappy always told me to go first class," he replied. An extra man aboard posed no problem as there were several spare oxygen and electrical outlets on the plane.

While we were tending to our individual preflight chores, John Woodland came running up, hollering, "They won't give us any flak suits!" "How come?" I asked. "Claim they are out of them," came the unbelievable reply. I ran down to the supply tent and asked the dapper young supply officer what it was all about. He shrugged and said, "No more flak suits *today*."

"But we are going to Ploesti!" I shouted. "Sorry, fella," he countered. "When they sank that boat in Bari Harbor, the Air Force lost a lot of flak suits. We've lost a lot of planes lately, too!" I could hardly believe my ears. *When a plane goes down we lose ten more flak suits. Ten parachutes. Ten Mae Wests. What about the ten men?*

At the rear of the tent was a stack of flat cardboard cartons with a band around them. "They look like flak suit cartons to me!" I exploded as I pointed to the stack. "Yeah, but I can't issue them until they have been posted to the records" was the impossible reply. If it hadn't been so serious, I would have laughed. Instead, I shoved him aside and motioned our men to follow me as we attacked the stack of metal aprons. His threats were ignored as we shouldered past him, toting enough cartons to dress our entire crew and guest.

Our new operations officer, Major James was to be our pilot. Charlie was moved to copilot and Dusty stayed home. It was a beautiful clear early morning as our group met the other three groups of the 55th Wing, the 464th, 465th, and 485th. Our line rendezvous was timed to the second, as it was important for our wing to meet the other wings at the keypoint for the mass flight to the target. This grouping of wings was necessary for full protection deployment of the P-51's who would be escorting the bomber force to the target.

The 55th Wing met the others at the keypoint (a coastal landmark) and began the 500-plane invasion of Lt. Gen. Alfred Gerstenberg's Ploesti defenses, the fifth such test within a ten-month period.

About a year before the low-level attack of 1 August 1943, thirteen early model B-24's took off from Khartoum at night to bomb Ploesti. None of the airmen had ever heard of Ploesti until the day before. How they got involved with Ploesti is a little-known milestone in U.S. military history.

In early May 1942, the U.S. high command, still smarting under the attack on Pearl Harbor, dispatched twenty-three B-24's from Florida on a 9,000-mile trip to Tokyo for a retaliatory bombing attack. It was to be a one-two punch coupled with General Doolittle's carrier-based Tokyo raid. Col. Harry A. Halverson led this strike force, which was appropriately named the "Halverson Project No. 63," or "Halpro" for short. Each plane carried bomb bay gas tanks and had room for just six 500-pound bombs.

While the secret attackers were en route, the Japanese captured Chekiang on the east coast of China which was to be their jumping-off place for the actual Tokyo attack. This forced a change in plans as Halpro cooled its heels at Khartoum. The American War College was well aware of Ploesti as a potential bombing target, but up until that point it was considered out of bomber range for existing bases. Now the United States had a few bombers loaded with bombs, just thirteen hundred miles from Hitler's most important oil supply. The "taproot of German might," as Churchill so aptly described Ploesti. General "Hap" Arnold ordered Halpro to bomb Ploesti from its Sudan base. To make the attack legal, the United State Congress declared war on Rumania, Bulgaria, and Hungary on 5 June. Rumania had declared war on the United States several months earlier, but we had ignored the action. Now we answered in kind.

The twenty-three planes had dwindled to only thirteen capable of such a flight. On the night of 11 June, those few bombers embarked on the first combat mission of the B-24 Liberator under American colors, and on the first U.S. combat air strike on Europe—an historic moment. Only twelve of the bombers reached the cloud-covered Ploesti area, and did very little damage to the oil refineries themselves, but they made an impact that led to the making of aerial bombardment history. That little token slap-on-the-wrist retaliatory strike at the gathering momentum of the Axis war machine was to set in motion two powerful opposite forces—*offense* and *defense*. Both centered around one target. The battle of Ploesti was on!

The world was not aware of what was happening; the Allied press didn't even mention the raid directly. Some oblique mentions were made of a mysterious Black Sea air strike, and Ploesti was not identified.

The German press ignored it completely, and it wasn't even reported in official U.S. communiques.

Enter General Gerstenberg, for the *defense*! Gerstenberg knew that it was the beginning. His main problem was that Hitler wasn't as impressed with the importance of the incursion as he was. Although Hitler had placed Gerstenberg in charge of developing the Ploesti defense, he gave it a lower priority than the general thought it deserved. He fought a constant uphill battle to get the necessary equipment to build the defenses he knew were needed for the day that certainly was coming.

He erected a trunk pipeline around Ploesti, linking all the refinery units. His plan was that, if some storage tanks were hit and the refineries themselves were intact, neighboring tanks could be used on a pool basis. The same would hold for destroyed refineries with intact storage tanks. The key to all this was in positioning the exposed pipeline above ground so that it could be easily repaired. This proved to be very successful. One problem, though, was created by the objections of the various plant managers to sharing their facilities. Allied Intelligence knew nothing about this pipeline arrangement until the capture of Ploesti! Circular cement and brick walls up to twenty feet high and nearly four feet thick were erected around sensitive areas within each refinery. Each oil tank had a wall around it to contain the contents of the tanks if they were ruptured by bombs.

Two dummy "Ploestis" were constructed to try to fool the bombers, one about thirteen kilometers northwest and the other about twelve kilometers east of the real Ploesti. Gerstenberg's flak defense is a story in itself.

Enter President Roosevelt for the *offense*. While Gerstenberg was preparing for the coming battle, the American Commander in Chief was formulating his own plans, which called for a joint Eighth and Ninth Air Force Attack, unprecedented and low level, from a North African base.* The code name was TIDAL WAVE.** Three experienced heavy bomber groups from England's Eighth Air Force came to the North African base to join the local bomb groups in low-level practice missions against a "Ploesti" that had been built in the desert.***

Gerstenberg would experience two surprises in the first test of his defense structure. He never expected a low-level attack, in view of the dramatic successes of the U.S. high-level bombings. The high proportion of Eighth Air Force bombers in the attack force astounded him. He recognized it as a very special effort.

As a matter of interest, it can be mentioned that while the three Eighth Air Force groups were in North Africa, they were pressed into service to bomb some

---

*For an exciting, well-told account of that attack, read *Ploesti*, by James Dugan and Carroll Stewart.

**See Appendix B, p. 222; *Air Objective Folder*.

***From the Eighth Air Force, Col. Leon W. Johnson led the "Eightballs" of the 44th BG: Lt. Col. Addison E. Baker was the CO of the "Traveling Cirus," 93rd BG;and Col. Jack W. Wood headed the "Sky Scorpions" of the 389th BG. The host groups were the 98th BG "Pyramiders," led by Col. John R. "Killer" Kane, and the 376th BG "Liberandos," whose CO was Col. Keith K. Compton.

Italian, Austrian, and southern German targets, flying some eighteen missions before returning to England.

In June 1944, we had one advantage over the first thirteen B-24 crews that struck at Ploesti: we had certainly heard of the place. As we headed for our first joust with Ploesti, none of us, though, had ever heard of Gerstenberg and his defense. All we knew was that, from the reports of the low-level mission and the three high-level raids that preceded our maiden venture, someone down there knew something about antiaircraft guns.

While flying high above the clouds, I found the sight from my side window so dramatic, I forgot about Ploesti for a few moments. I was struck by the contradiction of the beauty of 500 four-engine bombers in orderly formation, a thousand contrails streaming behind, forming a spectacular skyscape on a peaceful morning, with the purpose soon to be revealed.

When my bomb-pin pulling detail was completed, I began calculating the input data for my bombsight. I checked my bombing tables for the type of bombs aboard, plotted the target temperature and barometric pressure reading, and read off the information to be entered into the bombsight. After setting the bombsight drift angle for the expected "crabbing" angle on the bomb run, I sat and waited for the moment to turn on the sight. The heater that was supposed to be able to heat a five-room house was not working. The higher we climbed on course, the colder it got, several degrees about every thousand feet. The temperature was expected to be minus-sixty at the target, and it seemed that cold inside the drafty nose compartment—but I knew it would become warmer once we arrived. Finally I turned on the sight. Although I had previously double-checked all my figures, I rechecked them. All seemed OK.

It bothered me that we had a solid 10/10ths undercast so far, and no signs of it breaking up. The intervalometer was set for 130-foot intervals. All the switches on the bombardier's control panel were in order. I kept reminding myself not to forget to arm the bombsight about ten seconds before "bombs away." Failure to do so by a lead bombardier would result in a "no-drop" and would be both embarrassing and potentially disastrous, as it could ruin a mission. A ruined mission meant not only the needless exposure of hundreds of men on that mission, but the need for hundreds of men to come back again to do the job right.

The evening after a mission, a lead bombardier was either a hero or a bum. If he lined up the run badly, and the entire target was missed and perhaps a plane or two went down, he would not be looked upon very kindly. Nasty words were sometimes spoken—and not in jest. On the other hand, if he did a good job and the target was clobbered, his compatriots couldn't buy him enough drinks and say enough nice things to him. *Would I be a hero or a bum tonight, providing I got back?*

Someone spotted fighter planes about three thousand feet overhead, and after a few anxious moments we were assured they were P-51 Mustangs. That little exchange reminded me I had not yet put on my flak suit and flak helmet. Neither had Sherm, so we helped each other into our flak suits—not really that difficult a task, but much easier with help.

A flak suit always reminded me of a "sandwich board" carried by a "sandwich man." I used to see these men roaming around the streets of downtown Pittsburgh, with their advertising signboards hanging front and back, hinged at the shoulders. Ours, of course, were made like a canvas apron hanging front and back with many overlapping sections of metal, smaller but thicker than a playing card, sewn into individual pockets. This gave protection against spent flak, which was just as deadly as fresh flak if it hit your body.

Flak* is the same as shrapnel, which is simply fragments of the antiaircraft projectile after it has exploded: small pieces of jagged steel, perhaps the size of your little finger. Flak from a nearby fresh explosion, not impeded by the metal of the fuselage, has the force of a bullet and can pierce a flak suit. However, much flak is actually spent flak and, by the time it has cut through some airplane metal or Plexiglas, the flak suit will generally stop it from entering your body. Even though the flak is stopped, the effect is like being hit with a baseball bat. A flak suit also will not stop a fresh bullet from a German machine gun if it is a direct hit, although you may survive a glancing blow.

*From *fl(ieger)*, or "aircraft," plus a *(bwehr)*, or "defense," plus *k (anone)*, or "gun."

The flak helmet looks like an infantryman's steel helmet and fits over the regular leather flying helmet. Big hinged ear cups covered the earphones, which were built right into the flying helmet. A flak hit on a helmet would usually leave you with a headache, if it didn't knock you out. No one ever left his helmet off in battle.

By now the undercast was breaking up and it looked like about a 5/10ths undercast dead ahead. Not good, but not as bad as 10/10ths. We might luck into a good sighting.

Sherm was making log entries every five minutes and I knew he would tell me, at some point about ten minutes from the IP, if there were any appreciable changes in the target weather figures so that I could refine my bombsight data. I was far more nervous about my upcoming *performance* over the target than I was about the danger itself.

"Newb, the weather data looks OK to me," Sherm finally said. "Roger," I replied with much relief. *No changes; all I have to do is find the target.*

"Lead bomb bay doors are opening," called out Bob Kaiser. (He didn't do much singing with the brass aboard.) I immediately opened our bomb bay doors and flipped on the bomb "train" switch, and eight amber lights lit up on the board overhead, one for each bomb position. Sherm nudged me. I arose and he pointed out the right window. I stood transfixed as I gaped at the incredible sight of Ploesti. *My God, I'm here!*

There wasn't a natural cloud at our altitude, but it was cloudy high over Ploesti. Not over the city proper, but the groups of black polka-dot clouds formed a protective ring around the city, reminiscent of the circled wagon trains of our Wild West days. Two miles above us were several white polka-dot cloud formations. The Fifteenth was simultaneously attacking all of the refineries encircling Ploesti. At least this would spread the flak around. The black clouds were from German Flak 37 guns that fired 88mm shells weighing over twenty pounds, at a rate of fifteen to twenty rounds per minute. These could reach 26,230 feet and were intended for our B-24's. The white clouds were from Flak 39 guns that fired 105mm shells weighing over thirty-four pounds. These were for the B-17's that flew at 30,000 feet. The B-17's were also favorite targets for the relatively new Flak 40 guns that fired a 128mm sixty-two-pound five-ounce shell and were mounted on railroad cars.

The black and white clouds came in various sizes and shapes. Small, sharply jagged clouds were the fresh ones, and they were potentially harmful if they were too near you. If you saw the red flash that occurred just before it was surrounded by the sharp cloud, there was a good chance you were close enough for some of it to hit your plane. Seeing a red flash was a relatively good sign though, because it meant you were still alive. Larger, more rounded puffs were past history. They had done their damage but were mute reminders that there were more from where they came.

The really startling sight was the nearest huge block of black puffs in the sky—at our altitude, and off to the right. We weren't there yet and they had already set up a barrage of flak! Then I saw why. *Somebody's* target was ablaze. The distinctive narrow column of black smoke that always identified a burning refinery target was pushing up through the low natural white clouds that seemed to be trying to protect the cluster of targets. High above the smoking target, bomb bays empty, thirty-five B-24's were turning southeast, heading for home, their crews thankful to have made it through the most concentrated flak barrage of their experience so far—although they had left one crew behind at Ploesti.

The principle of the barrage, as opposed to predicted fire, was to establish a large box in the sky consisting of bursting flak at or about the bomb release point. This huge flak box was much larger than the mass of a bomber formation, in order to make certain the formation entered the living box of streaking steel. The flak gunners, each firing a round every three or four seconds, would simply keep it filled with flak bursts. They knew the formation of bombers could not actually be stopped. Their only hope was to hit a plane or two and cause the formation to split open in order to avoid the careening aircraft, thereby reducing bombing efficiency.

Our instructions were very clear. Fly into and through the box of flak. No evasive action; just get in and get out. A straight line is the shortest distance . . .

This preview had me sweating, and we were only spectators so far! You had to see the spectacle to appreciate the enormity of Ploesti as a bombing target. The cloud cover below us only added to the drama. Some fifteen bomber formations were moving relentlessly toward their respective targets, and most of the bombardiers were having difficulty finding their targets through the clouds. They would only get one shot at their target in a situation like this.

The conspicuous groupings of black or white puffs at our altitude, in an otherwise cloudless environment, were like giant neon signs pointing to the several oil refineries surrounding the city. I really did not know which cluster of flak clouds was trying to signal our target. Or had our hosts not yet begun their flak activity?

Fifteen miles northwest of the city was another sky sign, indicating the whereabouts of Steaua Romana, the second largest refinery in the area. I began to see why it took many hundreds of bombers to make a dent in this massive oil-producing arena, and why we would no doubt be back here many times before it was completely subdued.

Twenty miles seems far enough away, but I could see the trip up to the bomb release point was going to be a busy one. The sought-for target checkpoints would not yet be seen, and the 5/10ths undercast didn't help in trying to orient ourselves. It's funny how your mind works in moments like this. I had a mental picture of people hiding in basements, and I said a little prayer for them. Actually they were fairly safe as we had no intention of hitting the city proper, and very few bombs were likely to land in residential areas unless they were located right next to the refineries. Of course, with this nearly solid cloud cover things could be different. In the great land-air battle of 1 August 1943, very few homes were hit by American bombs.

"Major James, get ready to make a turn to a

seventy-seven degree heading at 1416 hours," announced navigator Wood. At 1415 hours the lead plane dipped its wings and began the turn onto the bomb run. They turned a minute earlier than Sherm had calculated. By then I had left the side window and leaned over the sight to locate the target through my own private front window, my oblique photo in hand. Glancing back and forth between the photo and through some cloud holes to the target area, I finally saw what looked like oil tanks, and settled my eye into the eye piece of the bombsight.

The function of the bombsight, while intricate in its working detail, is relatively simple. For a given set of circumstances including altitude *above the ground*, course over the ground, ground speed of the aircraft, weight of the bomb, barometric pressure, wind direction, wind speed, and temperature, there is a precise point in space where the bomb must be released for it to hit the aiming point. A skillful bombardier with a properly functioning bombsight can find that infinitesimal point in space. Once he puts the plane on the proper course, all he has to do is find the point along the longitudinal line where the bomb is to be released. He never really *knows* where that point is, but he can manipulate the bombsight so that *it* knows and responds by automatically dropping the bombs at that precise point.

The bombsight telescope is held perpendicular to the earth by the gyroscope. The telescope will hold that position, despite the undulating and rolling motions of the bombing platform (the airplane). If you were to look into the eyepiece from several inches away during turbulent weather, you would see the top of the telescope seemingly oscillating within the bombsight. Actually, the telescope is stoutly maintaining its position perpendicular to the ground, and it is the bombsight itself, attached to the airplane, that is wobbling around. Sometimes the air is so rough you have to literally hold onto the bombsight with two hands to keep your eye snugly against the eyepiece. When you do that you see an astounding sight. The cross hairs are serenely glued to some point on the ground (providing, of course, you have completed the snychronization).

Attached to the bottom of the telescope and about an inch below it is a mirror on a horizontal pivot. By pivoting the mirror, the bombardier can visually sweep an area from directly in front of the plane to twenty or thirty miles forward. Superimposed on the telescope lens are two cross hairs, one *fore and aft* and one *lateral*. These etched-on "hairs" are one hundredth of an inch wide, but when they are placed on a target some twenty miles away, the cross point covers an area perhaps a square mile or so, and yet covers only a few square yards at the bomb release point.*

My first job as deputy lead on this bomb run was to line up the course hair with the actual course we were on, as determined by the lead bombardier. Right or

*For a more detailed explanation of how the bombardier uses the Norden Sperry bombsights to solve the course and range problems, see Appendix A, p. 333.

wrong, I had to make my course hair agree with his established course. Not being the lead bombardier, I disengaged my bombsight from the autopilot so that any course hair adjustments I put into the sight would not affect the airplane controls. They did reflect on a PDI (Pilot Director Indicator) dial on the pilot's control panel. If a lead plane's bombsight was not engaged with the autopilot, the pilot would make manual course adjustments from this dial.

I first displaced my course (fore and aft) hair so as to make it run generally through the target area some twenty miles away. Then I displaced the rate (lateral) hair toward me so the cross hairs were on an area just a mile or two in front of our plane. This procedure magnified any course hair alignment error and permitted more effective course hair adjustment than if the cross hairs were on the target twenty miles away. Luckily the clouds were breaking up directly in front of me and my visibility was good enough for the purpose of synchronizing my course hair with our actual path across the ground. My course hair was sliding to the left of the ground objects in its path, which meant my sight was not lined up with the actual course of my airplane, over which I had no control. I then disengaged the bombsight course control and rotated the course hair on its axis until it stayed right on every object in its path. Then I locked the course control, knowing my sight was aligned with the lead plane's course.

When I displaced the rate hair back up to the aiming point, I found the course hair was a quarter mile off to the left. No problem. I merely displaced the course hair back onto the aiming point. Displacing either hair did not enter any information into the sight. Displacing was merely a follow-the-facts sort of maneuver.

Up until now I had done nothing toward establishing range with my rate knob. So before I got too serious about establishing my rate of approach, I tried to locate the actual aiming point. It was then I got the shock of my life. Instead of a two-abreast tank farm running generally east and west, the tank farm in my bombsight eyepiece was *square* shaped. I checked my target photo and had my worst fears confirmed.

"Sherm!" I hollered, "Did we turn early?"

"Yeah," he answered. "A minute early. Why?"

"This is the wrong target!"

"Right or wrong, this is the one we are going to bomb," interjected the pilot. He wasn't going to be a hero.

"Yes, sir!"

Not only was the tank farm the wrong shape, but there were a lot of strange-looking structures immediately to the right of the cluster of oil tanks. This certainly was not Xenia, because their tank farm was all by itself. However, we had a straight shot into some target, so I decided to make the best of it.

At least we had one thing going for us: the group that was assigned to this target had not yet shown up, so we did have it all to ourselves. I would not have liked to be racing someone for it. Being first in meant you would not have the target obscured by bomb bursts from a previous group. Usually it took awhile for the smoke to clear from a first attack, and if they had hit some oil tanks the smoke would not clear at all.

116

I went back to my sight and chose a new aiming point—the large tank at the center of the farm. We would be attacking the tank farm on the diagonal, so our intervalometer setting wasn't too far off. It was too late to change the setting. I had no idea what the lead bombardier had picked for his aiming point, and it didn't really matter, as the others would toggle off the first bombs to be released from either plane.

The intervalometer was keyed to the bombsight. Based upon the distance in feet that the first bomb was intended to land short of the aiming point, an adjustment was made in the bombsight prior to the bomb run. This caused the first bomb to be released a split second earlier than if the bomb had been intended to hit the aiming point. In this instance, I would be aiming at the middle of the tank farm, but the first bomb would be released early, so it would hit 455 feet short of the aiming point. The second bomb would be 325 feet short, and so on. If the aiming was accurate, the eight bombs would walk from the leading edge of the tank farm right through to the far edge. Sounds good. That of course would be perfection.

The cloud umbrella was over the target and extended about five or six miles in front of the aiming point. *I will not be able to see the aiming point for the final twenty or thirty seconds of my bomb run!*

I set the course hair so it generally covered the center of the tank farm, and then ran my rate hair back down again to a point three miles in front of us. It was this racing up and down with the rate hair that made it mandatory to keep the sight unarmed during the early sighting operation. Otherwise, the bombs would be inadvertently released the moment the sighting angle index pointer subtended the dropping angle index pointer. That would be fifteen miles short of the target, and very embarrassing. The reason for bringing the rate hair down to the area in front of us this time was to magnify the rate hair movement along the ground when I engaged the rate clutch. Any rate hair adjustment would then enter dropping angle information into the sight. This would specifically be ground speed information, which is what I and the bombsight were seeking.

Prior to the bomb run I had entered an estimated dropping angle into the bombsight. This was calculated from expected winds aloft, bomb run compass heading, and anticipated ground speed, all figured out on my trusty E6B computer. By doing this, I reduced the amount of rate hair corrections necessary during the actual sighting operation. The rate hair tended to hang on any object on which it was placed when I moved it down directly in front of the airplane, because of this preset dropping angle—it was almost synchronized. I moved it onto a farmhouse that happened to be on the course hair line and popped in and out of view through the clouds. It slowly moved off, away from me. That meant the telescope mirror drive mechanism was running too slowly for our rate of closure, or ground speed. I speeded it up with a slight movement of the rate correction knob. Then I displaced the hair back onto the farmhouse. It slowly moved off again. Another small correction, and there was displacement back onto the unwitting "sighting target." Now the hair drifted toward me. I had overcorrected. Finally I homed in on the house and the cross hairs were synchronized, glued to the "target." If that were the real target, I would have hit it, or come very close, but I still had several more miles to go.

It struck me as funny at the time—I was thinking about a farm family having a quiet breakfast in the house as the cross hairs of my bombsight were synchronized on their ham and eggs, or whatever they were eating for breakfast, oblivious to their unwitting role in a major military effort. Then I noticed two unusual things that I had never noticed before. I was breathing heavily, as if I had been running, and the air I was breathing seemed a little dusty. I was too busy, though, to give it more than a passing thought.

By now we were less than a minute from the bomb release point, so I displaced both the course and rate hairs back onto the real aiming point, the central oil tank, which was looming quite large in my eyepiece. Looming also was the specter of the cloud lid over the target that definitely extended well this side of the expected dropping point for our bombs. Even though I could still see my oil tanks, I knew they would soon slip under the clouds. This situation called for the special technique of "offset aiming."* The object of this method of aiming was to monitor the synchronization of the rate hair up to the last possible moment before "bombs away," even though the actual aiming point may no longer be seen because of the clouds.

*"Offset aiming" involved finding a *reference* rate aiming point off to the left or right of the actual aiming point, and one that could still be expected to be seen at or much nearer to the dropping point.

Now the course hair began drifting off the target to the left, and when I lined it up with our actual course we were several hundred yards off the aiming point. I hoped the lead man was aware of this. He was. Just then I felt the plane bank and turn slightly to the right as my pilot followed the lead plane's course correction. A quick check, and we were now perfectly on course. I breathed a deep, dusty sigh of relief. A change in course meant any previous rate synchronization was destroyed, so I brought my rate hair back down in front of our plane; I picked out a crossroads that happened to be on the course line, and "killed" my rate hair again. When I displaced both hairs back to the center of my "farm," they stayed there. What a thrill! *I am going to lick Ploesti!—at least part of it.*

But first a word from the defenders. They had other ideas. I had been hearing the muffled bursts right outside our plane, and had been seeing the flak in my bombsight telescope. Their accuracy was emphasized when a piece of flak came through our nose compartment side window and narrowly missed Sherm's head. I felt the plane rock from the nearby explosion. One of our planes received a flak hit, and an engine caught fire. I couldn't see it and I was just as glad to be spared the sight. Knowing it was there was bad enough. Some described a flak barrage as "standing out in an open field during a severe hailstorm." There was nothing you could do about it. No place to hide; just pray a lot.

The cloud lid bothered me, but I ran my eye across the rate hair to the left and locked onto an excellent offset aiming point—a cluster of large white buildings about one mile away from the target. They, too, were in a dark cloud-covered area, just like the actual aiming point, the difference being that there was a sunkissed area about two or three miles in front. This suggested I would be able to peek under the target cloud cover and continue to reference sight on the white buildings, at the edge of my scope of vision, right up to the dropping point. What luck! I picked out a distinctive corner of one building that was right on the left portion of the rate hair when the cross hairs were on my aiming point. This corner was to be my new offset aiming point when the center of the tank farm disappeared under the clouds. I focused my attention, however, on "my" tank, checking occasionally on my savior, the white building, to make certain it would hold up as the alternate aiming point.

As we approached the release point, the flak intensity increased, as did my anxiety. My rate hair was very slowly drifting toward me, and a quick glance at the sighting angle index pointer creeping up toward the dropping angle index pointer told me I was only about twenty seconds away from the release point. Failure to stop the hair and stick it back on the oil tank or on the white building before that point was reached would result in the bombs falling well short of the target. I quickly made a final adjustment that looked pretty good as the center tank went out of sight under the target clouds.

In my concentration at locating the target and synchronizing my cross hairs, I had inadvertently pulled my oxygen mask hose out of the hose connector on the hose coming from the "Auto Mix" on the wall.

My oxygen mask hose was dangling on the floor and I had been breathing floor dust. I was also breathing rarified air, with a low oxygen content, hence the deep breathing. My system was reacting to something of which I was not aware. I was in the early stage of anoxia, an oxygen-deficient condition that would soon lead to loss of consciousness, followed in a few minutes by death. The insidious thing about anoxia is that you do not know it is happening to you. Thin air is just like normal sea level air: you can't tell the difference. My next stage would have been a state of euphoria that steals away any sense of impending danger. You just don't do anything about the problem because you do not know there is a problem. Sherm took good care of me. He kicked me in the butt and pointed to my dangling mask hose. Then it all made sense—the dusty breathing, the heaving chest. *I was running out of oxygen.* I quickly hooked up as Sherm turned my Auto Mix to "PURE OXYGEN."

Head back in the sight and fully alert again, I looked to the left. My white building was still there, with the rate hair bisecting and *holding* on the important corner that was my new rate aiming point. I looked down my course hair, toward me, and it too was hanging on all the course reference points along its line. Everything looked good so far. The intersection of the cross hairs was of course on a cloud.

During the next several seconds I made some minute rate corrections on the white building corner, and by that time the little warning flag had popped into view. It was about eight seconds until bombs away, and even though I could no longer see the target

122

I was certain we would hit it, or come very close. Satisfied that the cross hairs were permanently glued to the invisible center of the tank farm, I came out of the eyepiece, sat back on my haunches, armed the bombsight with a flick of my finger, and took one more peek at the white building as it too disappeared under the clouds. I looked up at my buddy Sherm and gave him the Ballantine's "OK" sign. We both watched as the sighting angle index pointer closed in on the dropping angle index pointer. When the indices met, I heard a click within the sight as the electrical contact was made and, simultaneously, the louder sound of the bomb releases and bomb shackles expelling the bombs from the bomb racks.

"Bombs away!" I reported, with a trace of pride in my voice. I tried to play it cool but I couldn't, as I knew I had done well. The eight amber lights on my control panel winked off one at a time, so fast that they all seemed to extinguish at once. It was my final confirmation that the bomb run was over.

"Bomb bay doors closed," I added, this time more matter-of-factly, as I flipped the appropriate switch. Despite the minus-sixty outside, and not much warmer inside, I was soaked from my waist up. Even my feet were warm. As I crawled over the bombsight to watch the bombs fall, Sid told us from his rear turret, "Beautiful release. Everyone toggled on time. We have a great formation, so if the world's greatest bombardier got a 'shack' we'll have a perfect mission."

Now I really began to sweat because soon everyone might know how we made out. I could follow the group's bombs for about twenty of the thirty-seven-some seconds it took the bombs to reach the ground, and watched the pinpoints disappear into the clouds, hopefully headed for the cluster of oil tanks. As we banked away from the target, Major James came on the intercom with "We've been working for the government up to now, but from here on in we are in business for ourselves!" I don't believe it could have been stated better. *Our sole job now was to get home.*

The flak was the most that I had ever been exposed to and I really hadn't seen too much of it, so the rube in me took over for a moment and I climbed up and looked out the side window. It was awesome. In between some old, soft black clouds a bright red flash would appear, to be immediately surrounded by a sharp, jagged black shroud which would soften into the familiar flak cloud. Then another, fifty yards away. And another, and another. This ubiquitous display of death's calling cards begged the question as to why none of it had hit me.

I was so enthralled by it all, I innocently pushed my face up against the window like a kid in a candy store. Nothing but a thin section of Plexiglas and my flying goggles between the potentially hot steel and my face, a foolish move on my part. A smarter move would have been to "climb inside my flak helmet." Howie Thornton, from his orchestra seat in the Sperry ball turret, broke the spell when he said, "Captain Snyder, I hope you brought along some Band-Aids."

By now we were in a fairly steep bank for formation flying, as Major James followed the lead plane to a southerly heading toward Bucharest. Actually, we continued in a giant U-turn that covered eight or ten miles. As we left the immediate target area, I looked down again but was unable to see the bomb impacts because of the cloud cover over the target. I also wondered what refinery we had bombed. We had a tight formation and the lead man had done a perfect course sighting, both keys to good bombing. Our rate sightings probably were both good, as we dropped simultaneously according to Kaiser. We never did learn what refinery we sighted on. Many returning crews thought it *was* Xenia, but it really wasn't. It may have been Columbia-Aquila or possibly Astra Romana.

Somebody hit Astra Romana, the largest refinery in Europe. It would be shut down for nearly a month and not get back to any significant production level for another month. It never again achieved more than 39 percent of its previous peak performance in the fall of 1943. Phoenix-Orion, which was entirely surrounded by Astra Romana and was the fifth largest refinery at Ploesti, was destroyed. It would never reopen. Xenia lucked out that day.

As we turned off the cloud-protected target, we could see the ground below us. While the visual contact with the ground was too late for us, it was just in time for a group of people on the ground. They were the gunners of the flak batteries. They were now using the continuously pointed fire technique and tracking us visually.

I could see the flashes as the guns were fired. There were usually five guns to a battery and sometimes more, so when you saw one flash you could expect several more from the same area a few seconds apart. Then the surprise. *I could see the shells coming up at us as they neared our altitude.* Five black spots quickly growing larger. It was spooky. I couldn't take my eyes off them, even though I knew they might be set to explode at our altitude and quite near us. *Would one piece of flak have my name on it?*

Our group lost one plane over the target, twenty-eight had flak damage, and two planes later made crash landings at the base. Of those returning, only one man was injured. The Fifteenth lost nineteen planes, the worst of the high-level raids so far, as 1,257 tons of bombs were unloaded on Ploesti by the 465 planes that made it to the target. It had been a classic confrontation between offense and defense. Both were effective, but each had some innovations still up its sleeve, to be revealed in the coming months.

"Let's have a check by stations," requested Major James. With that, each crew member, in a prescribed sequence, reported he was OK and had no significant battle damage in his area. No injuries and no known battle damage, but the Band-Aid boys would be busy that night patching old *Hangar Queen.* Our nose compartment had that Swiss-cheese look. Sherm and I later counted eight holes and wondered how we were spared.

The action over, no more flak, no more worry about performance, only about survival till we got home. I sat on the floor and got the shakes. No doubt my soaked underclothing was beginning to reduce my body temperature. After a while I settled down for the trip home, stomping my feet occasionally to keep them warm.

I removed my oxygen mask for a moment to dump out the pool of perspiration in the chin section. I was

126

startled to see the water bounce when it hit the floor. It had become ice on the way down. For the last six or seven minutes of action, I had been operating with my gloves off, as I could not get the feel of the control knobs with gloves on. A bombardier's touch on his controls is not unlike the deft caress of a safecracker as he fine tunes the dial with ear cocked for significant sounds. At least that's how they seem to do it in the movies. Surprisingly, my hands, while quite cold, still functioned and were not frostbitten. In between knob refinements I did tuck my hands inside a bath towel I had stashed behind my flak vest, so it wasn't as bad as it could have been. My sheepskin gloves were now a welcome addition to my strange wardrobe.

Most everyone by now was in need of some bladder relief. The only problem was that the relief tube was reported to be frozen. The relief tube looks quite like the mouthpiece of an old-fashioned dictaphone with a rubber hose running from it into the wall. It was relatively easy to use, but if it froze while in use, the user became the object of high comedy, as he needed an extra detachable hand in order to extricate himself from his predicament. Lacking the solution, he either handed the filled relief tube to a buddy and made his way to the bomb bay to complete his job, or he dropped the tube and its contents on the floor and departed. The latter was an unpopular move.

When the community john was out of commission the bomb bay became the men's room, which was the case this day. That may not have been the most sanitary procedure, but somehow, at 20,000 feet over Rumania and after having survived the most savage flak exposure of our lives, none of us could think of anything of less interest than the propriety of what we were doing. All except one of us. Sid Woods in his tail gun turret thought otherwise.

You may have noticed that when an automobile drives along a leaf-strewn street in the fall, all the leaves swirl in its path and tend to fly up toward the rear of the car. This is because the moving auto creates a slight vacuum immediately behind it and the light leaves are sucked into the vacuum. The same principle applies when a liquid is sprayed out of an airplane traveling over two hundred miles an hour. The end product of our bladder relieving became atomized and frozen as it trickled out through the loose fitting bomb bay doors, and when it got to the tail section it was sucked into Sid's compartment through its many cracks. Sid didn't like the arrangement very much and mentioned it over the intercom. In fact, the men in the next plane probably heard his comments, as his goggles were covered with the frozen yellow mist. It permeated his exposed neck area and every place imaginable. The more Sid complained, the more guys lined up to torment him. It was just the comic relief needed to bring us all down from our emotional high. I hope Sid appreciated how much he helped us. I'm sure it even helped him. We loved Sid and he loved us, although his love for us was put to the test at that moment. Tyrone couldn't resist singing a little song about Sid's plight as we headed for home.

After we got down from altitude and could remove our oxygen masks, I made my usual trip to make a more thorough inspection for possible battle damage in the bomb bay. I also wanted to make certain all the

128

bombs had left the plane, even though the indicator lights were all out. Bombs have been known to hang up even with the lights out. I even went back to the tail turret to help Sid clean up. He was smiling by now. After all, he *was* alive.

"Well, Captain, how was your maiden mission?" I inquired when I arrived back on the flight deck.

"I guess I'm not a virgin anymore," he replied. He vowed he would fly some more missions, and he did. He flew at least five combat missions that I knew of, all to tough targets. He was a man's man, our flight surgeon.

As we pulled up to our hardstand, who was standing there trying to look nonchalant but Dusty Rhodes, our grounded copilot. He said it was one of his roughest missions yet, to be on the ground with his crew at Ploesti. I hadn't thought about it up until then, but I guess it would be rougher sweating it out at home when your crew is out on a tough one. Actually, you haven't really avoided anything, because you still have to fly that mission you missed, so you might as well fly with your crew.

Meanwhile, back in Rumania, where our bomb run and departure from the target area had been within sight of two German POW camps, ripples of excitement from our attack still lingered, Prison de Lagrel No. 18, located at Timisul de Jos, a swanky ski resort deep in the heart of Count Dracula country high in the Transylvanian Alps, was the home of about one hundred surviving participants in the low-level attack. By the very nature of that attack, very few residential structures had been damaged, even though the many refineries circled the city proper just on the outskirts. There was little animosity on the Rumanians' part toward these men. The occupants of this camp were called the "Africans," in reference to their home base. The "Africans" had been waiting a long time for their countrymen to return and finish the job they started.

The job they had done was remarkable. In one daring low-level attack, bombing the targets at *below* chimney-top level after a 1,100-mile treetop flight from Benghasi, Libya, they had cut Ploesti's then-current oil production by one-third and totally destroyed all of Ploesti's excess production capabilities. They flew through fire and bombs exploding from preceding aircraft, ambushed en route by point-blank AA fire from innocent-looking haystacks and railroad cars with the sides lowered to expose the depressed flak guns.

In stark contrast, the airmen shot down on Bucharest/Ploesti high-level attacks were imprisoned in an old schoolhouse within the city limits of Bucharest. We were blissfully unaware that any day we could be joining them in the old schoolhouse, and that then our buddies would continue to rain bombs all around the area, as we had done on occasion. These prisoners were called the "Italians," and not looked upon as kindly as their fellow captives at Timisul. They were also called the *murderers*, since the high-level attacks, although briefed on military targets such as oil refineries and marshalling yards, had resulted in some bombs landing in nearby residential areas of the two cities. German smoke-pot defenses also contributed to many bombs missing intended

130

military targets.

Our Bucharest POW's were never touched by Fifteenth Air Force or RAF night bombs. Ron Meyer, a bombardier POW from the 463rd Bomb Group in Foggia, later said they were especially concerned by the night bombing, since it was more spectacular, as well as our bombing on overcast days or when the smoke pots were used.

With the fall of Ploesti imminent, Hitler ordered the bombing of Bucharest on 24, 25, and 26 August. Meyer said this was the most frightening period of their internment. Thirty Junker 88's and Stuka dive-bombers flattened the POW schoolhouse, and then started on the nearby hospital. Five American POW's were killed in the bombings and four other died later when a German soldier entered a restaurant and machine-gunned them as they dined. When some Americans from Timisul entered Bucharest, they found dozens of American POW's lying around, wounded and unattended. The able-bodied POW's cleaned up several wards at the hospital and obtained food and medical supplies.

While Ploesti had been able to return to near previous production levels within a few months after the low-level attack, it had never been able to go beyond that level. We "Italians" were trying to do something about lowering their current daily production rate.

The coffee and doughnuts served by the Salvation Army tasted extra good after this mission. The shot of Old Overholt hit the spot too; we each were entitled to one shot of whiskey after a mission.

Tomorrow was our turn to stand down. So I thought.

Chapter 5

ANZIO BREAKOUT

One of the other bombardiers was ill, so I was notified early in the evening that I was to fly with another crew as deputy lead in the high box of the first attack unit. I would get to use the bombsight again, so I would have to attend the pre-briefing half an hour earlier.

This time it was the Rumanian oil transportation system at Craiova, about 125 miles southwest of Ploesti. We had fair results on the marshalling yards, and the highlight was watching a locomotive explode from a direct hit. Flak was moderate and inaccurate. While we were at Craiova, the Fifteenth also hit Ploesti with 165 heavies and dropped some 329 tons of bombs. Six planes were lost over the target.

We did not fly any missions for several days after that, due to bad weather and a welcome two-day pass to Bari. The day after our Bari leave, Colonel Harrison called a meeting of all officers at 1400 hours at the site of the nearly completed Officer's Club. No one suspected what it was all about, but we soon learned.

Someone had stolen all the nails from the project, and nails were the most difficult of all building materials to come by. Actually, most of the nails involved were reclaimed nails that someone had straightened with a hammer. That's how scarce they were. It wasn't the cost but the near impossibility of replacing them that upset the colonel.

He then stripped off his shirt and invited whoever took them to step forward. He stated he was out of uniform and had no rank insignia on him, and if the culprit would do the same there would be no questions asked or action taken afterward. F/O Steve Goode was a big six-foot four-inch super physical specimen, so several of us tried egging him on to accept the challenge. No thanks. For one thing, the colonel had been an intercollegiate boxing champ while at West Point, and besides, Steve hadn't taken the nails anyway. No one stepped forward, but we all got the message. The next day the bag of used nails showed up at the building site, and construction continued.

Colonel Harrison was tough. He flew nothing but the rough missions, and did not put up with any sloppiness around the base. We were required to be clean-shaven, have our hair cut, and be dressed in clean uniforms at all times. We were supposed to run the two-mile obstacle course on days we were not flying missions. It was not that tough a course, but it was a bit of a grind. The colonel ran it almost every day, so I figured if an old man of about thirty or so* could do it, so could I. Actually, I rather enjoyed

---

*Group records later showed that he was only twenty-seven years old at the time.

it—to be up there getting our butts shot off.

On 10 May, while we had been loafing around Bari, our group suffered its worst loss to date. There were no fighters at Wiener-Neustadt where they went to blast an aircraft factory, but the flak was uncanny. Three planes were lost over the target, two were missing in action, and two made forced landings elsewhere. One of them landed at the Island of Vis in Yugoslavia. Another plane received a flak hit at the IP and an oxygen bottle exploded, causing a fire. Six crewmen bailed out, but before the pilot and the others could jump, the fire went out. The remaining four went back to their stations and continued on the bomb run. They returned home safely. The Fifteenth lost twenty-eight planes that day.

After our rest leave, our first mission to Modena, Italy, to bomb some marshalling yards was a bust. Twenty minutes before the IP, we lost the super-chargers on two engines and could not hold altitude to stay with the group. We had to drop out of formation and salvo our bombs in the mountains of central Italy, and were all a little nervous about coming home alone. As stragglers, we were sitting ducks for any wandering band of fighters.

While still at fairly high altitude, we heard a lot of commotion coming from Sid back in his tail turret. I thought the Yellow Peril had struck again, but that wasn't it. Sid's electric suit had a bared wire which shocked him in the crotch area, where one tended to be a little moist from perspiration. While any empathetic thoughts made us cringe, it *was* humorous, especially so because it was Sid, the object of earlier misfortunes. We needed our occasional comic relief, and Sid was coming through again. He was yet to produce his masterpiece, a classic probably unequaled in the annals of aerial warfare.

The Officer's Club and mess hall finally opened. Over the bar was a painting of a very drunk, shaggy-haired Black Panther leaning on one elbow, eyes blotto, tail tied in a knot, tongue hanging out, a good conduct medal on his chest, captain's insignia on his shoulder, and smoking a big cigar. His testicles were bright red. Beside him was an empty whiskey bottle with only part of the two-word brand visible. The partial words, "Pant," and below it, "Pis," could be read. New recruits did a double take when they saw it the first time. We told them that's what everyone looks like after fifty missions.

The opening night was a memorable occasion. With no mission scheduled the next day, things got just a little wild. The highlight was when a group of free-spirited young men threw Colonel Harrison out of the window. It was only a couple of feet down to the ground, so he didn't get hurt. Man that he was, he took it good-naturedly, knowing how important it was to let the fellows blow off a little steam. We had lost quite heavily that day. The house specialty drink was one called "No Mission Tomorrow," and would only be sold when a stand-down had been declared for the following day. It was almost all rum.

Rome was still occupied by the Germans, and our

small ground force at Anzio, imprisoned on the beach since mid-January, was getting ready for its breakout to assist in the taking of Rome. Anzio was located some thirty miles south of Rome. The Fifteenth was also being pressed into service as tactical support in preparation for the taking of Rome. This was a new role for the heavies. On 17 May, the 460th was assigned the task of bombing the dock installations at Piombino, north of Rome. We were part of a ten-group attack on these and other docks located at San Stefano and Porto Ferraio harbors. On the way up along the western coast of Italy I saw Anzio for the first time, and I felt a sense of pride in knowing that those men down there had stormed ashore on that bloody beach and had held their position for four cruel months. I couldn't see any of them, of course, but I am sure they were waving and cheering us on. As we passed over Elba, I could almost see the ghost of Napoleon grinning up at us. Someone else, however, was watching, because they had a couple of AA guns down there and were taking a few potshots at us. Bad aim though, so no problem.

That flak was light at the target, so flak was no excuse for our poor bombing results. A ship in a harbor is a lot smaller target than a big oil refinery or marshalling yard. We did some damage to the docks but did not sink any of the several ships docked there. Smoke from an earlier group's efforts did make our sighting difficult. Although the flak was light, it was fairly accurate as there were virtually no clouds, and we were a good target for the "Ack Ack" boys. They could do visual sighting that day, which was generally more accurate than the radar sighting that had to be used on overcast days.

One piece of flak hit part of the ball turret support mechanism, rendering it nonretractable. Howie Thornton could not climb out and back into the airplane, and we could not hoist the ball turret. We tried everything, but we could not bring Howie and the turret back into the plane. This posed a new problem, as the plane could not be landed with the ball turret extended and the guns hanging straight down. During landing, even with the turret retracted, the clearance between the belly of a B-24 and the ground was minimal.

Landing with the turret extended was possible, but the guns must be held up so as not to ram into the ground and rip the turret out of the plane. Howie, with his great sense of humor, "volunteered" to hold the guns up against the underbelly of the plane.

When we got back to the base area, we radioed our problem and were told to land last so that the others could get in before a possible crash. This was to be a difficult maneuver because the normal landing attitude of a B-24 is with its nose slightly up and its tail down as it settles in for the touchdown on the main landing gear, quite similar to any large multi-engine aircraft. A normal landing approach in this instance would have ripped off the ball turret and split open the fuselage, so Charlie had to make an unorthodox three-wheeled touchdown with the body of the plane parallel to the ground. Howie's back would be just inches off the runway as he held the guns up against the plane.

One danger inherent in this landing attitude was the relatively weak nose gear which was not intended to be part of the landing mode. It was only to be used for taxiing after the aircraft was completely on the ground and rolling along on the main landing gear. The pilot and copilot normally would apply the brakes gingerly so as not to put too much downward force on the nose gear. Heavy braking could result in a collapsed nose gear, and a nose-down crash landing. This could be dangerous on the steel runways, because giant sparks would be created which could ignite leaking fuel, a distinct possibility on a plane returning from a combat mission. Charlie and Dusty had to thread the needle in their landing and braking on this one. It was a masterful tour de force on their part, and a moment of high peril for Howard Thornton. The rest of us just sat in our crash landing positions, closed our eyes, and prayed.

The following day, the group went to Ploesti without us and joined five other groups for a mighty rough day. The attackers lost fourteen planes for the second highest loss ratio of the entire high-level Ploesti campaign. Visibility at the target was poor due to intervening clouds, and overall results were not worth the high price. There were several fighter attacks, and our gunners shot down at least one FW-190. As the group left the target, Lieutenant Stevenson's plane, with both inboard engines ablaze, was forced to drop out of formation. The others watched in horror as the fighters swarmed around "Agony Wagon" for the kill. Steve, one of the charter members of our squadron, lowered his landing gear in surrender and all fighter activity ceased. The fires then seemed to be under control, so he retracted the landing gear in a vain attempt to regain the protective custody of the mass bombers. But it didn't work. The fighters bore in again and inflicted more damage to the stricken aircraft. The crew was forced to abandon ship. According to all reports, the German fighters did not strafe the parachuting men. Twenty of our planes were damaged by flak or fighters, and seven men were wounded.

Next day it was our turn, and we drew Bologna. On the way up we heard Berlin Sally warning a specific bomb group that they had come close to a hospital the day before and if they kept it up, the Luftwaffe would take retaliatory measures against them. This meant the named group would get the full force of the entire German fighter force on a given mission. No one liked that. Every group would like the German air force to spread it around a bit. The 460th of course had it made, as the GAF rarely bothered us anymore. It was a welcome compliment when a fighter group would pull up alongside our group, look us over, and move on to another group.

For a little diversion, Charlie turned on the fighter-to-fighter VHF channel so that we could hear the interplay between the pilots of the "Red Tails," the famous Negro fighter group. This was perhaps the best fighter group in the Air Corps. They flew P-51's as escort for the heavies on the way to the target, and did an excellent job of keeping fighter attacks to a minimum. They mounted a particularly high kill score on the GAF. These men really knew how to stay loose, but their method had a familiar ring to it. As a youth, I had enjoyed the annual local visit of the Homestead Grays and Pittsburgh Crawfords, perennial greats of the Negro National Baseball League. I saw Satchel Paige, Josh Gibson, Buck Leonard, and others who were better than the best players of their day in the Majors. Mostly, I looked forward to Josh knocking baseballs over the poplar trees located beyond the 450-foot center field fence as if they were just behind second base. Then, after the Grays or Crawfords had built up a good lead over the local Church League All Star team, they would start their comedy routines, with patter and comments that broke up the crowd. It was always a fun evening, especially when Paige would call in the outfield and infield, and then strike out the side while the seven fielders sat around the mound.

Now we were being treated to the same kind of carefree dialogue, but it wasn't a game.

"Blue Angel, Blue Angel, I'm in trouble down here," would be the plaintive call. "I have two Messerschmitts on my tail!"

"Who's in all this trouble?" came a reply.

"Red Rover, *that's* who!"

"Where are you, Red Rover?"

"You know very well where I am. You come down here and help me this minute!"

A third voice chimed in with "You're on flight pay just like the rest of us. You take care of yourself."

Despite all this nonchalance, we knew of course "Red Rover" was getting the best help possible and that the two Jerries would soon be dispersed. These men didn't have a tail gunner to torment, as we had, but they sure stayed loose with their chatter. We were glad they were on our side.

No one was very proud of the bombing results at

Bologna. We hit some marshalling yards and knocked out some rolling stock, but it was the wrong target. We were actually after troop concentrations on the highways.

The trip home was a memorable one for me. Charlie let me fly the plane for about ten minutes. We were in the "slot," which was directly behind the lead plane, but below. We were the middle plane of a six-plane box. This was the easiest spot for a novice to take the controls, as there were lots of reference points to help keep the plane straight and level. I was able to keep it fairly straight, but I had difficulty keeping it level. There were a lot of complaints from the rest of the crew about getting airsick from the roller-coaster effect of my flying.

Most of the past few missions had been tactical in nature rather than strategic. That is, we were bombing in support of ground troops, rather than hitting oil refineries, marshalling yards, and factories. We were helping out the Twelfth Air Force's medium bombers by extending ground support beyond their normal range, and were softening up the resistance for the forthcoming Anzio breakout. The Fifteenth blasted the Castel del Monte Casino, one of the most famous of all monasteries, when the Germans insisted on using it as an artillery spotting post and causing terrible casualties among American soldiers in the valley below.

Then on 22 May, as the Anzio breakout began in earnest, we were briefed to bomb a small Italian village by the name of Valmontone, located about thirty miles southeast of Rome, and not far from

Anzio. We had never before been briefed to bomb a city proper as a primary target; always it had been industrial targets, usually on the edge of a city. The reason for this attack was that Valmontone was a key German headquarters for the ground forces that had been holding off our ground troops in their efforts to take Rome. It was a small isolated town in a mountainous area, with about six major roads converging on it; one being Highway 6, a major north-south artery. A total wipeout of Valmontone would seriously impair German transportation and hopefully eliminate some key officer personnel, as well as help the Anzio breakout. It was a rush call, and there were no photographs available for bombardiers, just maps. It no doubt was a good idea, but when we got to the target area there was a 10/10ths undercast. We never saw the ground from the time we turned in from the Tyrrhenian Sea. No bombs were dropped over land, so we killed a few fish again as we salvoed into the ocean. Seven aircraft received flak damage at the coast.

We had been flying two missions a day during the Anzio breakout activity, which meant that each crew flew every day instead of every other day. While we were helping out tactically, the Anzio forces joined the Second and Sixth Army Corps on their march north, which culminated in the capture of Rome two weeks later.

The next day, we were briefed again for Valmontone, and I was scheduled to fly second attack lead, but with another crew. I was pleased at this opportunity, but wished I had more to go on than just the equivalent of a road map with a small village in the middle of it. While we were prepping our plane for takeoff, a jeep came steaming up and an intelligence officer leaped out, handed me a photograph, and shouted, "Here's your target!" It was a twelve-by-twelve photo of barren land taken from 30,000 feet. Located in the middle of it was a small spot shaped like a peanut, but about a quarter-inch long, and with six whitish lines, or roads, emanating from it like spokes on a wheel. "There," he exclaimed, "is Valmontone," and pointed to the speck. "Thanks a lot," I said.

The weather wasn't much better than the previous day as we swept up the coast with the 10/10ths undercast again. The lead navigator of the first attack unit made the turn inland strictly on ETA. Our navigator then told me the ETA for the target, based purely on "dead reckoning" navigation, the only kind possible under the circumstances. I kept looking out ahead, hoping for a break in the clouds, with both the photo and map in front of me. Suddenly, the extra navigator who was riding in the nose turret said, "There's a break in the cloud, and I think I see the target. We are right on ETA." I looked and saw the big hole in the clouds—the only hole for miles around, and right in front of our target. What a break! *Look out, German Command Post, here we come!* There it was, the peanut-shaped city among all the mountains, several roads spoking out from it. A novice could spot Valmontone from where I sat.

Both the first attack lead bombardier and I did a good job in our sighting. Of course there were no flak or fighters. A creampuff milk run if I ever saw one. Our formation was a little loose, but the toggliers were

144

on the ball. The result was that we generally saturated the center of the town, and it appeared that the junction of the several highways would be impassable for awhile. I hoped the people had left town, as I felt badly about purposely hitting a city. "But," I rationalized, "if we mess up the German ground forces, our guys can escape from Anzio and we can take Rome."

An astounding thing happened on the way home on one of the other planes. A gunner was in the bomb bay with the bomb bay doors open when the plane lurched, throwing him out. But on the way out, one flying-boot zipper caught on a piece of the bulkhead, and he found himself hanging outside the airplane with no parachute, with just one foot inside, powerless to pull himself in. The zipper, however, held long enough for two of his buddies to retrieve him. Several men gave up their whiskey rations to the lucky one, and suggested he write to the Talon Zipper company and give them the best testimonial they could ever hope for.

As we sat around our house in the early afternoon, I was quite pleased with my performance. The deputy group commander had even congratulated me during the debriefing session. We knew the Jerries were being run out of Rome, thanks in a small way to our efforts.

Then a messenger came to tell me I was to come to group Intelligence headquarters at once. *Probably going to give me a medal.* When I walked in, someone handed me a bomb impact photo, showing the beautiful bomb pattern I had just seen for myself a few hours earlier. My grin faded fast and my heart sank when I saw the caption at the top, "Unidentified Target." We had hit a city twelve miles southwest of

Valmontone. The lead bombardier of the first attack air unit was already there, looking as embarrassed as I felt.

They placed the Valmontone pre-mission photo next to the bomb impact photo, and they were nearly identical. Both cities were peanut-shaped and had six roads converging at the center. The lead navigator, with the 10/10ths undercast, had turned several miles too soon on ETA and we flew parallel to the intended easterly course. The similar-looking town unfortunately had the hole in the clouds overhead at precisely the wrong time and place for its own good. We were all told there would be no criticism for anyone involved. It was an honest, unavoidable mistake under the circumstances of the minimal briefing and target information available, as well as the urgent need to effect this road blocking effort.

Officially, we had not done anything wrong, but I had a difficult time sleeping that night, thinking about the people in that town who had no reason to believe anyone would drop nearly one hundred tons of bombs on them that day.

Chapter 6

MILK AN EMPTY TANK

"Your mission: destroy the Luftwaffe *in the womb, in the nest, and on the wing!*" The words sent chills up my spine. "Today," the briefing officer continued, "we destroy them *in the nest!*"

Some of us knew very little about Wiener-Neustadt, Austria, before the blue yarn of that briefing map went to the western edge of Neusiedler Lake and on over to Wiener-Neustadt. It then turned south and stretched on back to Italy. All we knew from earlier reports was that it was a mean place. We had never heard of the west edge of Lake Neusiedler either, but they had heard of us! While our bomb group had only been to Wiener-Neustadt once, the Fifteenth had been there several times. They had even bombed it the previous fall from North African bases, when sixty-five B-24's attacked this important aircraft factory complex, inflicting considerable damage while losing two aircraft.

The Germans were determined to protect the Wiener-Neustadt Messerschmitt aircraft factory with everything they could throw at the attackers. The 500

Messerschmitts per month from that factory were important to an air force that was being hunted and shot down in ever-increasing numbers by fighter escorts and bombers of both the Fifteenth and the Eighth—not to mention the medium bombers of both the Tenth and Twelfth Air Forces.

The west side of the lake happened to make an excellent IP from which to start our bomb run. It was easy to find, but even more important, at our bombing altitude the prevailing winds generally were from the east. Normal winds at that altitude could run as high as 50 mph or more, so a fully loaded B-24 flying at a true air speed of, say, 220 mph with a tail wind could have a ground speed of about 270 mph. If it were bucking that wind, its ground speed would be reduced to about 170 mph. That 100-mph difference, converted to time, represents about two minutes in the flak zone, and nobody needs an *extra* two minutes in the flak zone.

Our problem was that the Jerries knew the lake was an appropriate IP too and they did something about it. They set up additional AA guns at the IP where we predictably would have to make a relatively sharp turn in mass formation. Our entrance into "flak valley" would now be made with considerably more fanfare than at other targets. The flak would not be as intense as at Ploesti, but it would last much longer. Since our entire route was also known, they lined the bomb run with flak batteries that used continuously pointed fire techniques. This is the most accurate, and therefore the most dangerous, type of AA fire. Enemy flak gunners use it whenever your course is predictable.

It takes from ten to twenty seconds of tracking to

enable the fire control instruments to compute the lead for the first rounds, and pass along this initial firing data to the guns. After that, it takes from fifteen to thirty seconds for the first bursts to reach your predicted position. The time of flight varies with your altitude and with the distance of the battery from your ground track. Once he computation of firing data has begun, the enemy guns are continuously pointed; that is, they are given a continuous lead based on your speed and direction of flight.

Our target was a supply of recently manufactured ME-109's, not yet delivered to the Luftwaffe. Our bomb load would be forty 100-pound napalm bombs. I had never seen one of these bombs before, and wouldn't have minded if I were never to see one again. It made me nervous, just being in the same plane with them. *What if the gasoline-impregnated gelatinlike substance leaked out?* What if a piece of hot flak went through the very thin sheet metal skin? Our regular 500-pound GP's had thick steel jackets and could take a lot of flak, but these things didn't look very substantial.

The lake people certainly were ready for us, and peppered our formation as we started the turn at the IP. This was indeed a first for us. Ploesti had so many targets in the immediate area, they could not afford the luxury of meeting us at every potential IP. They just set up their big barrage and dared us to fly through it.

It was a 10/10ths undercast at the IP; we weren't sure at first that it *was* the IP, except for one significant clue—the flak reception. Then began about twenty-five miles of continuous flak pecking away at

149

us. The flak gunners were aiming by radar, and we were countering with "window," or as the British called it, "chaff."

"Window" was nothing more than Christmas tree tinsel. A strand of tinsel floating down would be picked up by ground radar as a "blip," or signal, quite like the blip reflected from a B-24. An entire group dispensing hundreds or thousands of these blips would distort the exact whereabouts of the group's aircraft. It was remarkable that a few strands of tinsel could defeat the tremendous power of radar. Window saved countless men and planes in the war.

The waist gunners had several cartons of window, each carton containing many smaller boxes of the tinsel strands. The idea was to scatter it out in very small quantities, separating the strands as much as possible, somewhat like decorating a Christmas tree. A single strand twisting and turning did more to foul up the radar signals than clustered handfuls of the stuff. So the message was one of "Go slow, fast." Throw out a lot of the window quickly, but *one* strand at a time.*

*When Betty Wachowiak of Albert Lea, Minnesota, read the manuscript of this book, she found the answer to something that she had wondered about for years. When she was a small child in Yugoslavia and Austria, she and her friends used to see tinsel floating down from the air when the American bombers were flying over, and no one knew just what it was. The children were told not to touch the strange things, as they might be poisoned. It was a nice try on the parents' part, but the kids soon learned the tinsel was harmless and began gathering it on a competitive basis.

Try telling that to a frantic window tosser who sees flak bursting all around him. If one strand is good, two must be better. Four is better than two. Twenty is better yet. As the flak intensified, various men reacted differently. Some simply increased the speed of their operation, becoming more productive because of the excellent incentive plan under which they were working. Others panicked and began throwing it out by the handfuls. A handful was nearly useless as it would plummet to the earth and not really perform its intended task. As the panic increased, full boxes could be seen coming out of some planes. Someone once reported seeing an entire carton coming out of one distraught gunner's plane. *I'll show them!* The human mind works in strange ways under stress conditions.

The Jerries occasionally would counter our window with a spotter plane. An ME-109 would park at our altitude, just outside of our machine gun range. We knew exactly what he was doing, and could imagine his radio conversation with the Ack-Ack boys. "Fritz, cut the fuses for 21,400 feet." Just as often, though, our great P-47 fighter support would chase them away.

As the flak became more intense, we figured we must be nearing the target area. I found myself wondering, on these totally overcast days, why they didn't hold their AA fire. With the entire bomber force turning on the IP by ETA, and all bombing by ETA, we could well miss the target area by several miles if they would just play possum with their flak guns.

151

With flak this thick, we had our customary sweats, but as concerned as we were, our concern was nothing compared to that of Maj. Charles Ward, our Squadron CO, who was in another plane. At the height of the flak, he happened to look down at his chest pack parachute on the floor and noticed that instead of the two snap fasteners that were to be snapped over the "D" rings on his parachute harness, there were *two D rings on the chute pack*! A quick glance at his parachute harness confirmed the two "D" rings there. Obviously you cannot hook up two female connectors, whether it be electrical connections, hoses, or whatever. One must be a male connector. The major just about died on the spot. Here he was high over one of the worst flak zones in the world with a useless parachute. He then just shrugged and went back to work.

Meanwhile, the commander in the group lead plane closed his bomb bay doors before the expected bomb release point was reached, as he had no idea where the target was, and decided not to waste the bombs on an ETA release. We always had the option of seeking a target of opportunity, and usually one was suggested at the pre-briefing.

Just as we were turning out of the flak zone, nose gunner Bob Kaiser electrified everyone with "Red Flak at twelve o'clock even!"

"Red flak?" questioned several who were not in a position to see it. We knew about black flak and white flak, but this was a new one.

"It's getting on my goggles and all over my clothes!"

"What getting all over your clothes?" asked Dusty

152

Rhodes.

"Red stuff. Some sort of a powder. It's staining everything." Regular flak never left a dust residue. We had flown through a fresh red cloud and, since our nose turret was not airtight, the red smoke penetrated into the nose turret and deposited its red dust. We were all concerned. Was it some sort of poison gas? No one seemed to be dying, or acting any funnier than normal.

After the red flak episode we headed south toward home, and the overcast opened up as if by magic. The city of Nuncherchin loomed ahead, with some sort of a factory right on the edge of town. This seemed like a potential opportunity. The lead plane reopened its bomb bay doors and the others did likewise. The bomb run on the unsuspecting factory was a good one and the bomb pattern excellent, leaving the factory a flaming mess. I don't know what they made there before we came, but they weren't going to make many more the next day.

I noted all the bomb indicator lights had gone off, so I closed the bomb bay doors and sat down for the trip home. As I prepared to relax, something kept nagging at me about the bomb bay. One of the lights had blinked momentarily. I had never seen that before. I was so glad those fire bombs were out of our plane, I wanted to shout but something told me to take a look before I celebrated. I hooked up a walk-around oxygen bottle, clamped it to my flak suit, and crawled along the tunnel to the bomb bay to look around. Was I glad I had followed my sixth sense! There, hanging by one of its two hooks and pointing straight down, was one lone napalm bomb, its little wind-off propeller turning idly in the ever-present draft. The movement was probably a long way from the 600 rpm's necessary for the propeller to come off to arm the bomb, but I didn't know the count.

I opened the bomb bay doors with a lever shaped like a bicycle handlebar. As the hydraulic-powered doors rolled open, the incoming air caused the propeller to spin rapidly. What to do? If I closed the doors to stop the arming process, I wouldn't be able to get the bomb out of the airplane. If I left the door open, the bomb might become armed before I got to it, and it was swinging around back there rather menacingly.

I decided to go after it, so I started down the narrow catwalk. I could see four miles straight down on either side. The leftover bomb of course was in the last position in the rear bay. By the time I reached it, the propeller was spinning quite fast. Releasing it was easy, and since I arrived before the bomb became armed, it turned out to be a big sweat over nothing. No one else even knew there had been a problem. That incident did not increase my love for napalm bombs. As time was beginning to run out on my walk-around oxygen bottle, I hurried along the catwalk, closed the doors, and went back to my station.

I'm glad I wasn't the squadron supply officer when Major Ward got back to the base and went to the supply tent. We had brought our parachute harnesses and chest chute packs with us from the States, and upon arrival we put our chest packs into the squadron pool. Before each mission we drew a chest pack, which was later (hopefully) returned. No problem up until that day. It seemed the new replacement crews were also depositing their chest packs in our pool, and that would appear to be no problem either. However, the new chutes were significantly different from the ones we brought over. Ours had snap fasteners on the chute and D rings on the harness. The new recruits had D rings on their chutes and snap fasteners on their harnesses. As the major found out, the new chutes were not compatible with the old parachute harnesses. Either no one thought to advise us of the change, or the supply officer had failed to read a bulletin. Either way, it could have been a catastrophe for someone. Maybe it already had been, and no one but the luckless victim ever knew it. Major Ward quickly resolved the parachute mix-up. He had all of our harnesses and the pool chutes color-coded, red or yellow.

They say communications was one of the most difficult problems of the war. This incident was a hint of a far more serious breach of communications yet to come.

"I'm not worried about all the bullets or flak being fired at me; I'm just worried about the one with my name on it" goes the old cliché. However, one nose gunner in another squadron had a harrowing experience that put the lie to this brave attempt at unconcern. A piece of flak about three inches long and a half-inch thick came into his nose turret, bounced around like a pea in a pod, and came to rest on his lap. After the jagged piece of projectile casing cooled off enough for him to pick it up, he looked it over and saw a portion of the serial number embossed on it. The visible portion was the *same as his laundry mark*—his last initial followed by the last four digits of his serial number! What a souvenir to take home.

155

Red flak was the subject of discussion that evening. Every crew had reported it, and no one had a ready answer. The Air Force had already heard about it, so we soon had our explanation. Red flak was merely a signal to the fighter planes that the flak was over and they could come in for the attack on the bombers. The Jerry fighters didn't care for the flak any more than we did. No poison gas, no secret weapon. Just a simple signal. What a relief.

Our deepest penetration into France took place the following day when we went to Lyon to hit the marshalling yards. With little flak or fighter opposition, we had an excellent bombing score again. With the Anzio breakout and the taking of Rome behind it, the Fifteenth Air Force had gone back to its primary duties of strategic bombing. Oil got a little breather, as most efforts were concentrated on Austrian aircraft factories and marshalling yards in southern France.

A plane from another squadron ditched off the coast of Corsica on the way home. Five men were lost.

While the rest of my crew rested the next day, I was scheduled to fly back up to France with Major James. We were to lead the second attack unit of eighteen planes. Our plane that day was a brand new replacement B-24J, the latest model, fresh off the production line. The "J" was the second model with an electric Emerson gun turret in the nose. It looked just like an "H," but with some internal differences. This would be its first combat mission. It was so new it didn't even have the group or squadron markings painted on the tail section.

Our target was the marshalling yards at Nimes. This time there were some enemy fighters in the area, and our group shot down two of them. Our tight formation was paying off again. The navigational plan at the target generally was to follow the east-west railroad tracks, located some twenty miles south of Nimes, to a junction where some tracks went north and on into Nimes. That rail junction was the IP, and we were to follow the northbound tracks right to the target. It had looked easy at the briefing and in a study of the target maps.

As we approached the area, I was checking closely to try and find Nimes even before the navigator announced its location. I was certain we were some distance short of the IP, when all of a sudden I heard over the intercom, "Bombardier! Get ready to turn because the first attack is turning onto the bomb run!"

I was positive it was the wrong railroad junction, but a colonel was flying the lead plane of the first attack unit and a higher ranking bombardier was also in the plane. Who was I, a "Second Looie," to challenge them? But I felt so strongly, I said, "Major James, I think they are turning early, and the target is not at the end of the railroad they are following."

"Are you sure?"

"Yes, Sir! Our turning point is the next railroad junction about twenty miles ahead."

"Positive?"

"Yes, I'm positive," I said as I looked to the navigator for some support. He nodded.

"You better be right," said the major tersely, as he kept the plane on a straight course west.

That was a very important moment in my life. I had stood up for something I thought was right and had gotten the support of someone who counted—the number two ranking officer in our squadron. As he said, though, I better be right. Then I got the butterflies. *Was* I right? Too late to back out. We were committed. I looked out the right window and saw the first attack unit heading merrily for the wrong (I hoped) target.

"OK, Newby. Here's your junction. We're turning onto the bomb run." "Roger," I replied. When he leveled out, I called for three more degrees to the right in order to cut down on my sighting corrections.

It was a piece of cake, providing it was the right target, as I followed the railroad tracks to the big marshalling yards on the edge of the city. The closer we came, the more certain I was that I was right, because the photographs indicated key landmarks that were showing up on schedule. I now was feeling a little sorry for the other unit leaders, as they were going to have some explaining to do when they got home. Better them than me, I felt. However, they did find the target.

Flak was moderate and fairly accurate, but no planes seemed to be seriously hit as we reached the bomb release point, and my Sperry did its job. "Bombs away," I reported and reached to flick the bomb bay door switch. Something was wrong: one bomb station light was still on. A bomb had hung up on me, and I wasn't anxious to have it aboard any longer than necessary, since flak was still coming up and fighters were in the area. I flicked the toggle switch and the light stayed on. I reached for the manual salvo lever and yanked it. Still nothing.

The salvo lever was connected to the bomb racks by

cable. A yank on the lever would turn a long bar that ran the length of the bomb bay near the ceiling. This torque action would physically open all the bomb shackle latches, and any bomb still in the airplane was supposed to fall out. The safety wire would go with it so that the bomb should not go off on impact. RDX bombs were temperamental, though, and could go off even when they were unarmed, as some of our recently departed ground crewmen had found out.

After two or three frantic pulls on the salvo lever, I saw the light blink off. Then I leaned over the sight to watch the lone bomb's descent. Later one of the crewmen cried out, "Beautiful pattern, right on target." As much as a bombardier likes to hear those words and see the results of his handiwork, I had eyes only for the single bomb I had sloppily kicked out.

All French cities were "open cities," and we were forbidden to drop bombs on them. Florence, Rome, and Venice in Italy were also open cities. Most other cities within our bombing range were available targets, and we could drop on them at any time, no questions asked.

I had committed a grave error. I had loosed a 500-pound RDX bomb on an open city. In the several seconds it took me to finally get the hung bomb off our property, we had turned from the target and toward the city. I watched in horror as the bomb headed for a large amphitheater that looked somewhat like Pitt Stadium. I had no idea what it was, but I had a feeling it was something that had been there awhile.* The trajectory was as good as any I had ever

---

*The amphitheater at Nimes was 2,000 years old.

hoped to see. Right straight for the stadium. Talk about "body English" by a bowler. I was twisting and grimacing and pleading for the bomb to change its course, but to no avail. All that saved me was that it overshot its mark by several stadium lengths, and it *did* explode.

"Fifteen hundred feet at twelve o'clock," I reported, matter-of-factly. And under my breath, "From the world's greatest bombardier."

"What was that?" asked the pilot.

"Just a little private joke, Major," I replied.** When I told the major what had happened, he said, "Let's hope the photographers didn't catch it." We never did hear any more about the incident.

I was feeling pretty good about this mission, as one who has been recently vindicated should feel, when I heard a disturbing bit of dialogue between the flight engineer and the pilots. Major James was of the school that believed in not transferring fuel from the Tokyo wing-tip tanks until after leaving the target, mainly because empty fume-filled tanks are more

----

**My crew called me the "world's greatest bombardier" because of an early training mission when I missed the target badly on my first attempt with a Sperry bombsight. All my training had been on a Norden. I was forced to call out, "Fifteen hundred feet at twelve o'clock." When I began showing any improvement at all, they pinned the nickname on me, and later any bad sighting would elicit "Fifteen hundred feet at twelve o'clock by the world's greatest bombardier" from someone.

dangerous than filled tanks if an incendiary bullet rips into them. Now that we were leaving, it seemed the fuel transfer system would not bring the 400 gallons from the two wing tanks into the main gas tank system. The fuel transfer pumps were not responding, for some unknown reason. Here we were on one of the longest flights our group had ever flown, and it looked like we would be denied 15 percent of our fuel. Our Ploesti and Bucharest flights usually ran about eight hours. This one was scheduled for about nine, so we really needed all the gas we could get. It was a fact that under normal flying procedures we could not make it back to Spinazzola on what was left of our basic 2,300 gallons. So what to do? The engineer tried everything he knew. The regular transfer pumps seemed to be working but the ones from the Tokyo's weren't.

"We'll have to redline it all the way home," announced Major James. "If an engine doesn't blow up, we might make it." By "redlining it," he meant he would permit the cylinder-head temperature of each engine to rise above the red line placed on the temperature gauge at the maximum safe temperature mark. By reducing the gasoline-to-air ratio in a carburetor, two things would be accomplished. It would conserve fuel and make our meager gasoline supply last longer. In addition, it would increase the power output of each engine, and thus increase our speed—big pluses in our quest for increased range. But there was a price to pay for this seemingly free gift in our time of need. The more powerful lean mixture

161

would cause a significant rise in cylinder-head temperature. How high can the cylinder-head temperature be permitted to rise above the red line? How high is up? How long can an engine accept this abnormally high temperature before it responds? Its response, of course, would be to explode. Would the added range from this risky procedure equal the loss of range because of the fuel shortage? All good questions. The answers were academic. It was this or get out of the plane over the ocean, or perhaps over enemy-held territory.

Major James established a lean fuel mixture that pushed the four engines' cylinder-head temperatures quite far, I thought, above the red line. I had no idea where the critical point was, but I presumed he knew what he was doing.

Our navigator was now in a position to show us how good he was, as we immediately dropped out of formation and headed home alone. We could not afford the higher rate of fuel consumption required by formation flying. We also established a slow descent on course to conserve our fuel even more. About every ten minutes, it seemed, our pilot asked the navigator for the fuel status. He kept relating our ETA for Spinazzola to our ETA for an empty tank, and they seemed to be running neck and neck. I didn't relish the idea of a tie.

As we approached the Italian shore north of Rome, still in enemy territory, we dropped to about three thousand feet. The inevitable overcast was blanketing the mainland, so we ducked under it and started down a valley at about five hundred feet, with a ceiling of clouds above us and tree-lined mountains on either side. Our engines seemed to be surviving the extra high temperature, even if our nerves were near the breaking point. How long would either last? I had no idea how far we still had to go as I grimly watched the trees passing by the side window, and noted the four cylinder-head temperature gauges with their indicators well above the red lines. I recalled one of the nicknames for our Liberator, "The Flying Time Bomb," and thought it was sort of funny—but I didn't laugh.

The fuel gauge on a B-24 consisted of two long vertical clear glass tubes, with calibrations along the sides of each tube. One tube was for the port engines and one for the starboard engines. The gasoline level of each engine's tank could be read visually with a flip of a switch, two tanks per glass tube.

The engineer took a reading on our gas supply, by tank. *None* of the four glass gauge readings showed *any* gasoline at all. He looked at me and shrugged. I asked, foolishly, "What does that mean?" He said, "When the gasoline drops out of sight on a gauge, it means we have less than fifty gallons in that tank. All four have been out of sight for quite some time." With that, the red warning light on the pilot's control panel lit up. "That's our final warning that our fuel is about gone," he explained without my asking.

Finally, I looked at my parachute; then I looked out the window at the mass of trees below us. What to do? We couldn't possibly land in this, and we were too low to jump. It was the most frightening moment of my life. We had had it. I just knew it.

"Hang on, men, I think we might make it," Major James said reassuringly. I had so much faith in him, I believed his words, and despite the fact that I *knew* I was going to die, I suddenly felt very calm. A few prayers helped a little, too.

Suddenly we broke out of a pass and there was our field, a few miles ahead. The navigator had known what he was doing, and had done an excellent job of low-level pilotage navigation over strange mountainous terrain. The radio at Dolly Tower was doing its bit, too. The red light was glaring at all of us. What was its real message? How much longer? Musical chairs. When the music stops, will there be a chair for us? I was hypnotized by it all. Not our pilot though. He made a straight on, no frills landing. No traffic pattern this time, as the group had not yet arrived.

At the end of the runway he turned onto the perimeter taxi strip, and was headed for our hardstand when one engine sputtered. Then another. Finally all four engines choked and quit. We were out of gas. What an ignominious ending to a bombing mission, having to be towed to our hardstand, with 400 gallons of gas still in our Tokyo tanks. We weren't complaining, though, as Major James's gamble and skill had finally paid off.

The ground crew chief, after hearing we had flown some four hours with the cynlinder-head temperatures above the red line, ordered all four engines replaced in the brand new aircraft. Further investigation about why we could not reach the reserve tanks in our plane revealed another case of poor communications. This brand new J model had a different fuel transfer system than the H's we had been flying. The manufacturer of this plane had installed a fuel transfer "on/off" switch on the bomb bay side of the bulkhead that separated the bomb bay from the upper flight deck. The fuel transfer controls were still located on the flight deck side of the bulkhead, as they were on the H model. The new switch was secured in the "off" position with a piece of wire, which meant the fuel transfer system could not be operated until the toggle switch was flipped to "on."

There was nothing wrong with the designers making improvements in our aircraft, but it would seem logical for them to put a warning label in the vicinity of the fuel transfer controls, for the benefit of flying crews who had been flying planes without a switch that was locked in the "off" position. A bomber crew, fresh from a briefing at 0500 hours, should not be expected to be up on all technical changes on every aircraft assigned to them. That oversight nearly cost ten lives.

The official photographs were kind to us. They showed we did hit the right target, with fairly good results, and they did not reveal our little secret about the wayward bomb. Only the ten of us and some people on the ground knew about it. A stand-down was ordered for the next day, which was the signal for a relaxed evening at the Panther's Lair. The navigator and I couldn't buy Major James enough drinks that night. I also learned why a "No Mission Tomorrow" was so named.

By now I had twenty-one missions under my belt and was beginning to feel the effect of the pressure. I was having difficulty sleeping and getting a little jumpy. I began looking forward to our "flak leave," the R&R week at Capri that we had been hearing about. Our vacation was supposed to come at about the midpoint in our tour of duty. Some of the fellows had already cracked, and had to be taken off flying duty. In the spirit of all this, I said to the flight surgeon, Capt. Dean Snyder, as he walked by our house, "Hey, Doc, I'm coming down with a little cold. How 'bout grounding me for a few days?"

"Why should I ground you?"

"Well, you know, high altitudes. My ears fill up and I could be a detriment to the crew, and perhaps the whole group. I'm not thinking of myself. I have all the others' interests at heart."

"Come on over to my tent and I'll fix that."

"How?"

"I'll just puncture your ear drums and that will equalize the pressure. No problem with high altitude then."

He went on to explain that the German Stuka bomber pilots all had their ear drums punctured so their ears could survive the drastic change in air pressure during their dive-bombing activities.

"Maybe I'll just take an APC tablet and forget it. Thanks anyway, Doc."

We didn't talk much about the morality of our killing people. We all thought about it once in a while, but the advice of our friend, the chaplain, helped us keep our sanity. He pointed out one night over a couple of beers at the club that the smartest thing we could do as individuals was to put what happened on the ground below us out of our minds. Keep it impersonal. We were primarily there to drop bombs on military targets. We didn't start the war. Our efforts would have a direct positive effect

166

on shortening the war and, in the long run, save more lives than we might take in the performance of our duty. If any of us would falter and let it get us down, there would be someone to take our place the next day.

They were comforting words. I did manage to keep the personal aspect out of my mind, but the unidentified target episode nagged at me occasionally.

The next morning we awoke to a beautiful day—fog all over the place. It was funny how our viewpoints on the weather changed. Fog and heavy overcast skies meant you were guaranteed to live one more day. As much as we acted as if we were glad to see overcast days, we knew deep down that we were just staving off the inevitable. Fifty missions were fifty missions, no matter how you sliced it.

By noon the sky was clear, so a couple of us hiked halfway up the mountain that ran parallel to the airstrip and looked out over the airfield and tent area. Beyond the tent area about a mile or so was a deep ravine that we always flew over on the downwind leg of our landing pattern. And to the left was the flat farm field that one day would be so important to our crew. About three miles away was the centuries-old village of Poggiorsini, where the women lived who did our laundry.

On the way back we stopped in the orderly room, located in a pink tufa block building that had been the railroad station at one time. There it was on the bulletin board: the weekly standings of the twenty-one groups of the Fifteenth Air Force. Just like the major league baseball standings. The 460th was in third place! From a poor last about two months ago, we went to near the top of the list. This was a dramatic testimonial to the terrible week we had spent in aerial close-order drill. Both Colonel Crowder and Colonel Harrison had told us we would be the best, and we were starting to make them look good.

An accompanying article in the official weekly publication, *Straight and Level*, was headlined "ORCHIDS TO THE 460TH," and went on to cite the group for scoring over 80 percent on a particular mission the past week. A 50 percent score was considered excellent bombing. It was nice to be with a winner. We knew our side was going to win the war. There was no doubt in any of our minds about that. But being among the best on a winning team was a great feeling.

After the free day, we were briefed on and sent to visit Wiener-Neustadt again. About two hours into the mission, as we were climbing on course, a spent shell from a plane in the front of our formation struck the pilot's windshield and cracked it badly. It was a freak accident, but was the result of a normal procedure. Every gun position on every plane was test-fired as the group gained altitude and the temperature dropped. This was to make sure the guns would not freeze from the low temperatures.

A situation like this called for an abort, because a broken windshield would make it nearly impossible to pilot the airplane. Our abort, however, left us with mixed emotions. It was first an embarrassment. You felt as though the others thought you were dogging it; yet it was the right thing to do. No one could rightly say they would miss the trip to Wiener-Neustadt

168

and its long flak valley. Yet we might have traded it for a milk run and still have been shot down. One really cannot control his destiny in these situations.

Those who made it to the target were treated to a surprise: parachute flak. After a flak burst, a large triangular-shaped, kitelike object with lengths of cables hanging from it appeared—sort of a balloon barrage in the sky. None of our planes became enmeshed in the traps that day.

The next day we again were briefed for Wiener-Neustadt, as the Fifteenth continued its pursuit of the GAF *in the womb* and *in the nest*. This time our tail turret was inoperative in the preflight test. It would not rotate. The ground crew checked the hydraulic system and could not find what was wrong. We reported it and were told to abort the mission. Two aborts in a row to Wiener-Neustadt invited funny looks and snide comments. This was really embarrassing.

The group got together again without us and had good bombing results. General Acheson, CO of the 55th Wing, telegraphed the 460th Bomb Group:

THE FOLLOWING MESSAGE RECEIVED FROM COMMANDING GENERAL FIFTEENTH AIR FORCE COLON QUOTE THE TERRIFIC DESTRUCTION INFLICTED ON THE ENEMY BY UNITS OF THE FIFTEENTH AIR FORCE ON TWENTY NINE MAY AND THIRTY MAY IS A RECORD WITHOUT PRECEDENCE ANYWHERE

PD LET US KEEP THIS HIGH STANDARD OF ATTAINMENT AS OUR GOAL PD THE HUN CANT TAKE IT PD UNQUOTE IT MAY BE ADDED THAT THE PUNISHMENT DEALT OUT BY THE FIFTY FIFTH WING OVER THE PAST WEEK HAS NOT BEEN EQUALED ANYWHERE PD CONGRATULATIONS PD END ACHESON

Chapter 7

PLOESTI HIDE AND SEEK

The 460th had been in battle for two months, but our individual views of the war had been very limited. We would go to early morning briefing, receive our marching orders, and fly off to wherever they sent us. Oil one day, marshalling yards the next, perhaps an aircraft-producing complex or an airfield the following day. No doubt they knew what they were doing. We of course knew one of the overall objectives was to destroy the Luftwaffe *in the womb*. We knew because they told us, and we had noticed where we had recently been going.

The attack on the womb had actually begun in 1943, with modest efforts averaging about five hundred tons a month. (A B-24 normally carried about two or three tons of bombs.) In February 1944, the Eighth and the Fifteenth engaged in what was known as "big week," during which aircraft complexes were hit on six consecutive days by 3,800 bombers. In that one week, nearly 10,000 tons of bombs were unleashed on aircraft production facilities. This tonnage was equal to that dropped in the Eighth Air Force's first year of operation. Bomb tonnage on these targets dropped to 2,400 tons in March with the poor flying weather, but zoomed up to a record high of 12,000 tons in April, when the 460th joined the effort, and was about 6,200 tons in May.

The Germans had begun dispersing their aircraft complexes early in the year, so despite our increased bomb tonnage, their production rate stayed at about 1,400 planes a month. However, we and the Eighth Air Force were getting to them *on the wing*. In the fall of 1943 and the first half of 1944, some of the most ferocious air battles of the war were fought in European skies. Bomber losses of 50 to 60 in a given day were offset by GAF fighter losses of 150 to 200. Both the bomber gunners and their escort fighters were taking their daily toll of the GAF. Coupled with this double-barreled assault on the Luftwaffe, we were also bombing airfields and catching quite a few planes *in the nest*. We of course were not privy to these facts at the time, but in retrospect they do help to explain some of the things we were doing then.

Back in 1940, when the Luftwaffe was blitzing London, the world thought it was witnessing the greatest concentration of bombing it would ever see. The newsreels, newspaper accounts, and radio reports were breathtaking in their own way. In the Luftwaffe's biggest month against England, it unloaded 11,172 tons of bombs. But in just the two months that the 460th had been in the war, the Eighth, Ninth, Twelfth, and Fifteenth Air Forces had dropped 164,000 tons of bombs on Germany. In the month coming up, June, they would be dropping 122,000 tons! An eye for an eye—and then some!

While the bomb tonnage on aircraft complexes would drop steadily in May and June from the record high of April, the tonnage on oil refineries would zoom from about 6,000 tons in May to some 14,000 and 16,000 tons in June and July. Although the tonnage figures were in themselves not great, the yield per bomb was tremendous in the oil campaign.

Within the scope of the Fifteenth's bombing range were twelve occupied countries. Also within its scope were fifty-two oil refineries, which contributed nearly 80 percent of all German oil. Ploesti's nineteen square miles of refineries represented about 25 percent of Hitler's oil production. No wonder our summer plans would include more emphasis on oil.

On the last day of May, the 460th was sent to Ploesti as part of the increased oil activity. Hammett & Co. was invited to go along on this trip. Our squadron commander, Major Ward, again chose *Hangar Queen* and its crew to support him as leader of the second attack unit.

Our target was the Concordia Vega refinery, the third largest in Rumania, and the second largest in the cluster surrounding the city of Ploesti. It was to be the first attack on this target since the low-level raid of the previous August. Although hard hit on that day, Concordia Vega had recovered to about half its pre-attack capacity by the time it was our turn. Normally the middle of their city would have been as safe a place as any, because we did not knowingly bomb the city proper on clear days. With ten targets surrounding it, the city itself was somewhat like the eye of a hurricane—usually, that is. This day, however, would be different. There would be no assured good place to hide.

This was to be a major Fifteenth Air Force effort. Twenty-one bomb groups with full bomb loads, over seven hundred planes, were assigned to hit most of the refineries. Only six hundred made it to the target. Weather and mechanical problems were still taking their toll.

There had been some evidence of a renewed defensive technique for Ploesti, developed by General Gerstenberg. Smoke generators, similar in effect to the smoke pots used in the California and Florida orange groves, were dispersed in the target areas in an effort to hide the refineries from the searching eyes of the Sperry and Norden bombsights. A smoke generator consisted of a smoke storage tank, a pressure tank and a nozzle. Each assembly was located in a shallow trench. They usually had a forty-minute warning of our arrival, and it took only twenty minutes for the system to effect total coverage. The system worked best under high humidity and low wind conditions. The higher the wind velocity, the less effective and shorter lived would be the coverage. One of the side effects of this defense was that the ground smoke made the flak gunners "seasick." We would have enjoyed knowing this, but unfortunately we were not privy to the information at that time.

Experimental smoke pot attempts earlier in May had been ineffective, but they had planned a big surprise for the Fifteenth on the last day of May. About two thousand smoke pots were deployed in a manner that would form a giant irregular circle about six to eight miles in diameter. The ten refineries were located within a four- to five-mile-diameter circle within this larger circle. This subterfuge could throw most of the various groups' aiming efforts off by a mile or two.

I was pleased to lead an attack unit again to a major target, for two reasons. One of course was a matter of personal pride, somewhat like that felt by a pitcher when he is chosen to pitch an important game. The other was that it was less nerve-wracking to go over a heavy flak target as a "working" bombardier, because it kept your mind off the reality of what was going on all around you.

Although the target area was always exciting, the trip to the target was a long, lonely, and boring one for the bombardier. All he could do was sit on the floor and stare at the four walls of the small nose compartment and at the navigator's legs. He could review the target photos and maps just so many times in three or four hours. He couldn't stand up and look out the window, as he would be in the navigator's way.

I would often think about the war itself. *What was I doing here? I chose THIS? I could have been stateside.* Not really—I actually *wanted* to fight in the war. We were on the right side. We were the good guys. I could be slogging along the Italian mountains, or through steaming jungles. I could be storming Pacific island beaches. I could be below the ocean, or on the ocean. Where do you go when they sink your ship, or sub? I could be in a tank racing through Europe. No thanks. Who of us had the best duty? The worst? I figured it was just the luck of the draw. Here I am and that's it. Let's win the war and get it over with.

I did like the idea of our having sort of a contract. Fly fifty missions and go home. I don't think any other branch of the service had it cut and dried like that. However, when the flak hits for that five to fifteen or more minutes, there are no foxholes to hide in. When our day's work was done we could relax and sleep in reasonable comfort, and our C rations were better than the foot soldier's K rations. Even though we all had the intense desire to help defeat Hitler, and we put all we had into each mission, there is little doubt that our number one concern was to survive—fifty times.

As we neared the IP, Sherm laughed and said, "There's your target," as he pointed out the side window. All I saw on this beautiful clear day was a big glob of white on the ground, where Ploesti was supposed to be.

"I see a big white cloud on the ground, but where is Concordia Vega?" I asked.

"Follow that group ahead; they may be going to the same place."

I knew the location of the target in relation to the city—due north—so I had a general idea where it should be under the white ground cloud. By now the flak was beginning to seek our altitude, and as we turned at the IP, it was showing signs of being accurate. This was a frustrating moment. Here I was, leading an eighteen-plane attack unit about four or five minutes from "bombs away," and I couldn't even see the target, let alone the aiming point. I called for the pilot to level out so that the course hair in my sight would intersect at a point about a half mile in from the northern edge of the circle of white. That would do for openers.

Our first attack unit just a few hundred yards ahead of us was going for the same general target area, so I had some company in my misery. I brought my cross hairs down to right in front of me where I could see the ground, and established my course. And while I was there I established my rate hair synchronization. It was a helpless feeling to relocate my cross hairs on a nebulous section of white nothing, hoping my target would somehow be at that spot. The bomb release point was by now less than three minutes away, and I was beginning to learn a fact of life. No decision *is* a decision under certain circumstances, and this was one of them. *No decision* would mean a possible fly-by, unless my wing bombardier decided to let the bombs go, and triggered a fusilade of toggling by the others. A fly-by meant a return trip to the target, and nobody wanted it.

The flak was frightening. We could hear it exploding, and feel pieces hitting our plane. Some reported that a plane from another box in our attack unit had just blown up from a direct hit. I was sweating profusely, partly from the normal flak sweats, but mostly from my frustration as the bomb release point was fast approaching—and I didn't know where it was. I knew the group a few miles ahead of us was a sister group from our 55th Wing, and was assigned the same general target but a different aiming point. I knew too that the lead bombardier would have the same problems to face before I did. When Kaiser announced that the first group had just dropped its bombs, I wondered what they really aimed at.

All of a sudden I saw a familiar sight. A thick column of black smoke began rising from just about where I had guessed the target should be. Great! The first guy in had lucked onto the target and hit something. What's good enough for him was good enough for me. The first attack unit of our group was now a half-mile to my right, as their aiming point was on the southern section of the same refinery; but I didn't let that influence me. I was going to stick with a winner.

One of the facts of high-altitude flying was that the lower pressure at 21,000 feet tended to cause us to pass gas more frequently than under normal conditions. It so happened that when I knelt over the bombsight, my rear end was right next to the Auto-Mix control for Sherm's oxygen supply. The Auto-Mix control was designed to mix the existing thin air with pure oxygen from the airplane's central supply, in a ratio that would deliver air to the user's oxygen mask at sea-level oxygen-to-air proportions. Now, right in the midst of all the high tension of the moment, I passed a considerable amount of gas that found its way into Sherm's Auto-Mix.

"The bombardier just farted in my Auto-Mix," shouted Sherm over the intercom, as he gave me a boot in the rear. "Aim it to the left the next time."

"Great, great!" shouted Sid from his rear-end prison. "Do it again!" I guess misery loves company. It wasn't very nice of the bombardier, but the more Sherm complained, the more he invited succeeding attacks. It was a rather ludicrous situation. We were all seconds away from possible death. Our friends were falling out of the sky around us, and we were on a very serious mission to drop fifty-four tons of bombs on one of Hitler's largest oil refineries, and here was the navigator kicking the lead bombardier in the rear end, for whatever good cause. It did serve to break the tension, and it was just this sort of thing that kept our crew loose and, at least so far, free from combat fatigue.

The situation struck me as funny. I got to laughing so hard, tears welled up in my eyes and I couldn't see the cross hairs. We were less than thirty seconds away from the bomb release point, and my cross hairs had been perfectly synchronized at the base of the column of black smoke where the other group had apparently struck oil. I could afford the luxury of a few seconds away from the sight. I sat back on my haunches, removed my oxygen mask and flying goggles, and wiped my eyes with the towel stashed behind my flak suit. As I shook the perspiration out of the chin section of my oxygen mask and turned to wave to Sherm, there was a loud explosion just outside the nose section. A large piece of flak tore through the right side of our compartment and across, just above the top of the eyepiece of the bombsight and out the other side. Two gaping holes told a graphic story. *If I had not lifted my head from the sight, the piece of flak would have gone right through my head—or at least would have hit my helmet.*

I thought immediately of the gunner from another squadron who, a week or so earlier, had taken a piece of flak through both eyes and the bridge of his nose. He would live. *Would I?* In that brief moment the muscles in my lower abdomen relaxed for a split second, and I suffered what would continue to be an

179

embarrassment all the way home.

Those two related events erased all the frivolity of the previous moments. I got back to work and refined my cross hairs at the base of the tower of black smoke that was spiraling its way toward our altitude. It was a snap. When the bombsight released the bombs, I hollered "bombs away," closed the bomb bay doors, and peered over the sight to watch the results of my handiwork. The flak was now worse. The loud bangs were happening more frequently and the familiar sound of gravel thrown onto a tin roof never seemed to stop. Another of our sister ships peeled over on one wing and went into its death dive. Before the wings came off due to its inverted dive, seven men escaped. A B-24's wings were not designed to withstand such a strain.

My bombs seemed to disappear into the general area of the smoke column, but I didn't see any new smoke. Strange. What I did not know at the time was that the column of smoke was from a dummy fire the defensive team had lit in an open field about a mile north of our target. Most of the attacking groups were fooled in the same manner. There were dummy fires all over the place, everywhere but on any of ten refineries. The defensive signal-caller, General Gerstenberg, had caught up with the seemingly unstoppable Fifteenth Air Force offense. It was a total victory for the Germans, even if their flak gunners got a little seasick. Several groups had chosen not to drop their bombs and had gone on to secondary targets. However, over a thousand tons of bombs were unloaded into that sea of white smoke. The flak gunners claimed sixteen U.S. heavies. Twenty-seven of our group's aircraft received flak damage.

As we left the target, I got a call to go back to the waist section: Howard Thornton had been hit in the head with a piece of flak. I grabbed a walk-around oxygen bottle and headed back to help out. After the bombs were dropped, I was the least important person aboard; all the others were manning guns, piloting, or navigating. Howie was conscious, lying there with a piece of flak sticking out of his head through his leather helmet. It was about the size of a one-inch section of an ordinary lead pencil.

First, I carefully removed his helmet. I was afraid that if I dislodged the piece of flak, blood would squirt out. Then I took a bandage from the first-aid kit and held it in one hand while I attempted to remove the flak with the other. I really expected I would have to slap the bandage over the hole fast, to stop the onrushing blood when the metal was removed. It was nothing like that at all. I worked the metal loose and it came right out, and there wasn't a drop of blood in sight. I was amazed. I poured sulfa powder into the hole in his head and taped the bandage over the wound; he seemed to be all right except for the considerable pain. We had a long way to go, so I gave him a shot of morphine and he was at least comfortable. I stayed with him the rest of the way home to make sure he had enough oxygen and was indeed surviving the ordeal. We both survived. I was rather scared by the experience, since I wasn't sure I was doing all the right things.

The next day we were furious when we heard how we had been outwitted. We all wondered what could be done to combat this new defensive wrinkle, but our top people were not asleep, as we would soon learn.

I gave my old buddy, Sherm, some of the great Kraft caramels my Aunt Effie had sent me, so we were still friends. It must have been a ten-pound box, because it fed half the squadron for nearly a week.

May had been a busy month for the 460th. It flew nineteen missions, with 607 aircraft reaching the targets. Fourteen of our bombers were lost that month, and we moved into third place in the Air Force in bombing accuracy for the month of May. Ploesti had been busy also; the Fifteenth sent 1,307 heavies there to drop 3,195 tons of bombs, and cut their monthly production to 160,000 tons. The relatively minor drop in production, despite the heavy onslaught, was due to the tremendous resiliency of Gerstenberg's recovery teams who patched up refineries that were not hit in May—that, and his crossfed pipeline network. Ploesti's defenses accounted for fifty-five heavy bomber losses in May.

After the recent Ploesti visit, a two-day pass to Bari seemed like a good idea. On the afternoon of the first day in Bari we rode around the beautiful waterfront area on bikes, and stopped in at the Red Cross canteen for some good homemade ice cream. While there, I met some of the Negro flying officers from the Red Tail fighter squadron. It was a thrill for me to talk to them, because I had always been an avid reader of "G-8 and His Battle Aces," a pulp magazine of my high school days that had been devoted to World War I aerial battles. I knew all about Baron Manfred von Richtofen and Captain Roy Brown, the Canadian Ace that shot him down. These were real

182

fighter pilots I was talking to, and I was like a kid outside a ballpark, talking to a big league baseball player. I told them how much I enjoyed their radio chatter and how it reminded me of the Homestead Grays, and the great Josh Gibson and Satchel Paige. They laughed and said something to the effect that you had to stay loose if you wanted to survive. Sherm told them about the Auto-Mix incident, and I thought they would die laughing. One of them said, "Now you're getting the picture. Stay loose, and the flak won't get to you." Later that evening, we went to the local officers' club and enjoyed some dancing, real hamburgers, and too much champagne.

Returning to our hotel was a real challenge, since it was a cloudy night with absolutely zero visibility. We got home by the Braille system. We sidled along the fronts of buildings, back to the walls and walking sideways, hands pressed against the wall. When we reached a corner, we walked like blind men across the street and up the curb onto the sidewalk, and again slipped along the wall. We navigated by dead reckoning: down two blocks, left a block, and then right a block to our hotel. We made it, but it was an experience. I'm not sure if the champagne helped us or hindered us.

For some reason I missed the truck back to the base, and had to start out hitchhiking. I *had* to get back because I knew I was scheduled to fly the next day. If I didn't make it home I would be AWOL, and that would be a serious matter in a combat zone. I made it to Altamura without incident, but it was getting dusk and I was let off in the middle of this town of about 70,000. As I walked down the street, I saw some chickens flying out the window of a residence; I began to feel that anything could happen. Someone had earlier reported seeing a horse being led out of a house in Spinazzola. Why not?

Soon it was dark, and I hadn't seen a single jeep or truck coming through town heading for Spinazolla. Walking down a side street just by chance, I saw a jeep sitting in front of a house, unattended.

Driving out of town, I wondered how the owner of the jeep was going to get to wherever he was going next. The fear of being AWOL had transcended my normal sense of right and wrong. All's fair in love and war, I rationalized. Besides, I knew the war needed me the next morning and I didn't know about the other guy.

I had never driven a car before, but I learned as I went along. Arriving in camp, I abandoned the jeep in front of headquarters and walked to my house, where Dusty and the others were relieved to see me. They were beginning to worry about my making the morning briefing.

In another house the fellows were still sweating out two of their buddies who were also scheduled up the next morning. When wakeup came at 0330 hours, the men still had not arrived. Just as we all were entering the briefing room, the near-AWOL fliers hopped off a GI truck, bleary-eyed and unshaven, still in their class A uniforms and looking somewhat like Bill Mauldin's Willie and Joe. Their last-minute entry saved them from a peck of trouble. I was glad someone that bent out of shape wasn't on my crew; then I realized I had almost been in their shoes. Maybe someone borrowed their jeep.

Fortunately for all concerned, the mission turned out to be a super milk run. No fighters and no flak. Bombing was good, with a tight pattern on the busy marshalling yards at Feanza, Italy. At least we fattened up our bombing average that day.

Berlin Sally began twitting us about the "Cotton Tails" of the 450th Bomb Group. It seems they had done something to earn the ire of the Germans. We didn't know just what it was, but she vowed that they would destroy the 450th for their evil deed. Later we heard what happened. It seemed that one of their bombers was a straggler coming home from a mission with a couple of sub-par engines and was not able to keep up with the rest of the formation. The pilot of this bomber, with its two big rudders painted a cotton white, was well aware of his slim chances of survival as a flight of enemy fighters approached. When the fighters began positioning for the kill, he dropped his landing gear in surrender, resorting to the unwritten law of the war skies. At this sign of surrender, the fighters began flying a loop circle around the cripple in an effort to escort it to a landing spot. A bomber taking this action is supposed to do one of two things: bail out the crew, or land the plane in the nearest available field or clearing. The fighters are supposed to refrain from shooting at the airplane or its parachuting crew.

After dropping his landing gear, as the story circulated all over Italy went, the pilot decided he could correct his mechanical problems. He reportedly ordered his gunners to pick out specific fighters who were within machine gun range but flying parallel to the bomber, and, upon command, fire at them. His ruse was successful, to a point. They shot down all but one of the defenseless fighters. On the next mission after that one, the entire German Air Force went for the Cotton Tails. They never even looked at any other group. The attack resulted in the worst losses from fighters that any group had ever experienced. It was so devastating, they had to ground the Cotton Tails for awhile. They later painted out the white tails and tried to look like someone else, but the GAF wasn't fooled. They still paid more attention to the 450th than anyone else for quite some time. The rest of us, while basically feeling sorry for the Cotton Tails, were sort of like a funeral director trying to look sad at a $20,000 funeral. We knew that as long as they kept attracting the fighters, the fighters would leave us alone. This was a fight for survival and their tough luck was our good fortune. We wouldn't have minded if more groups had pulled some dumb stunts like that.

We heard later reports that the turnover in commanders of the 450th was so great that at one time the CO was a second lieutenant. That may not be true, but it was a popular story at the time. Aside from this error in judgment by one man, the 450th was an excellent bomb group and had an otherwise good record. Sally continued to chide them from time to time.

The 6th of June 1944 was destined to become the "longest day." The Allied invasion in northern France had begun. Our men were told that, through the great efforts of the Fifteenth and Eighth Air Forces along with those of our brothers in the fighter medium and

186

bombing groups, we had destroyed a considerable portion of the Luftwaffe in the air and at their production facilities, and as a result, resistance to the invasion by the GAF was not expected to be very significant. This later proved to be true, as the GAF never even showed up at Normandy!

As our invasion forces hit the Normandy beaches, the 460th joined nine other groups for a 310-plane assault on Hitler's oil at Ploesti. (Our crew wasn't scheduled that day.) Nearly 700 tons of bombs were dropped, with a loss of fourteen bombers. It was on this momentous date that I predicted my fiftieth and final mission would occur on 10 August, and so recorded it in my mission diary. It was an open secret that there would soon be another invasion, this time in southern France. We sensed this from the increased bombing activity in southern France and northern Italy.

The following day we were to try our luck again on some ships at dock. We loaded up with five 1,000-pounders this time, instead of the usual ten or twelve 500-pounders, and the target was the harbor installations at La Spezia, Italy. We never did find La Spezia with the 10/10ths undercast, so we went after the alternate target, the harbor installations at Leghorn some fifty miles south. Our IP was a town about twenty miles north along the coast, and as I started down the bomb run it was pretty quiet, no fighters and no flak, yet. About halfway along the run, Sherm kicked me in the butt and said, "Hey, look! The Leaning Tower of Pisa!"

"Where?" I inquired, as if I had been interrupted reading a newspaper.

"Out the left window."

"I'm busy."

"But you may never get to see it again!"

"You're right," I said, as the rube in me again took over and I got up and rubbernecked out the window for a few seconds. There it was in all its glory, just a mile or two away.

I was flying lead in the low box of the first attack unit, so I did have my sight turned on and was sighting for range and course. I was able to sneak the short look without risk, since the cross hairs were well synchronized.

The flak at the target, while only moderately heavy, was surprisingly accurate, since it was all around us at our level. Seventeen aircraft had flak damage, but there were no injuries. Our bombing was very good, since the pattern covered the entire dock area. We didn't see any ships sink, but we shook them up a little—one transport received a direct hit, and some others a near miss.

Chapter 8

GREEN FLAK AT
FOUR O'CLOCK LOW

He was one embarrassed young man—the aerial photographer who climbed out of the jeep with a sheepish grin on his face and a rolled-up parachute tucked under one arm, most of it dragging behind him. He had forgotten his oxygen mask and reported it to the pilot soon after takeoff. The pilot simply told him to get out. Most of us "old-timers" were in our early twenties, some not yet twenty. By this time in our brief combat career none of us had ever been kicked out of an airplane, but a few of us were getting a bit edgy. Not quite flak-happy, but close to it. Some got a little shaky; some began to twitch; some just couldn't sleep. The pressure was beginning to build. I for one was losing weight. The polite word for our condition was combat fatigue. Our enlisted crewmen had invented an expression to describe this ailment. When someone started to get too far out they said he was "seeing green flak," which of course did not exist.

* * *

Munich, Germany was one of the few targets shared with the Eighth Air Force, and on 9 June we were to find out what the Eighth had known for some time. Munich was bad! It was bad not only because of its heavy flak concentration, but because it was in Germany and the central German fighter force could join the Balkan force and double up on us. On this particular day, Sherm Wood was assigned to one of the mission lead planes and we had a substitute navigator. I would get to use my bombsight again, as we were the lead plane in the high box of the first attack unit.

The new navigator told me, just prior to the IP, that he hadn't seen the ground for awhile and we would be turning at the IP on ETA and probably bomb on ETA. It was another 10/10ths undercast situation.

We made our turn onto the bomb run, and all I saw in front of me and below were white clouds. This was a bomb run? I soon found out it was. *A black puff here; a black puff there; everywhere a black puff.* Yes, we were nearing the target. The boys in the waist were shoveling out "window" as fast as they could. It was beginning to get mean out there, when over the intercom we suddenly heard Homer Luke, who had taken Smitty's place in the waist gun position, saying, "I see green flak!"

"Where?" asked Charlie Hammett excitedly. Obviously he was not up on our special catch phrase. After a brief pause came "Four o'clock low," which, of course, was the one location the pilot could not see from his left seat position. The game was on. Sid joined in with "There's another one!" Dusty from his copilot seat helped out by lifting himself up and looking out the right window to confirm the phenomenon. Charlie was overly concerned about the green flak.

In the meantime, the real black flak was tearing up some of our sister planes. No. 5 in the lead box had a gaping hole in its right rudder, but seemed reasonably airworthy and stayed in formation, bomb bay doors open and ready to deliver its load. (It even made it home in that condition.) Two other planes had feathered engines, one with smoke pouring out of No. 3. Another in the group ahead began erupting parachute-clad bodies, and soon peeled over and went on in.

I felt powerless. My bombsight was useless over these clouds. I was told by the navigator the precise time I should toggle my bombs, and when the second hand reached ten seconds to the hour, I hit the switch. It was all done with a compass, a watch, and the navigator's trusty E6B computer. The E6B had some of the properties of a slide rule, and provided useful information on wind, vectors, and the like, but it was no substitute for a bombsight.

Who knows where the bombs landed. They could have been five miles from the target. The factory we were gunning for was probably the safest place in town.

I didn't think any more about the green flak episode, but I also didn't realize the substitute navigator had recorded the green flak sighting in his log. He was supposed to note any unusual incidents en route. He knew about black and white flak, and had had the brief scare of the red flak, but this new green flak got his attention.

We had no further incidents and returned home safely. After piling out of the plane and returning our checked-out gear to the squadron pool, we headed for the refreshment stand and some doughnuts and coffee, compliments of the Salvation Army, and then on into the debriefing tent. The bored debriefing officer began his usual questions.

"Any of our planes shot down?"

"Yeah, one from the group ahead."

"Any chutes?"

"Seven that I could count," replied Woodland.

"I thought I saw another one way down low," added Sid. "Hope the other two got out."

After hearing us grumble about all the flak and the target that could not be seen, he asked wearily, "Anything else of interest?"

"Yeah," said the navigator excitedly. "We saw green flak at the target!"

"GREEN FLAK?" the debriefing officer shouted. "GREEN FLAK?" He sensed a scoop on his hands.

"That's right," echoed the navigator, getting into the spirit of the thing. "Lots of it . . . all around us."

I looked at Dusty and he rolled his eyes upward, piously. Sid glanced at me and turned away. Charlie, still not sure if we were putting him on or not, looked at each of us for some answers. No one faltered, but there were a few ill-concealed mischievous grins.

With that, the debriefing officer, thoroughly excited, leaped up and rushed out of the tent to be the first, and only, one to report this new weapon to headquarters.

None of us could explain why we didn't stop him.

The moment was so magical, so priceless, that each of us felt someone else could be the one to spoil the sport with Charlie. Charlie, however, had begun to smell a rat and wasn't quite sure, but all the emerging full-fledged grins on the way to our quarters confirmed his suspicions, too late. When the orderly came an hour or so later and told Charlie he was wanted up at Group Intelligence, we knew we had gone too far. We wished him luck as he started up the path through the olive orchard with its symbolic signs of peace hanging all around. He knew there wouldn't be much peace where he was going.

"Tell us about the 'green flak,' Lieutenant," said the stern-looking major.

"Well, sir," Charlie choked out, "I don't believe there was any green flak."

"Why did we get such a report from your navigator?"

"He isn't our regular navigator, sir."

"So?"

"Sir, he didn't realize what was going on."

"What was going on?"

"It was a joke, sir."

"A joke!" he bellowed. "Why do you permit those kind of jokes to go on among your crew?"

"I didn't know it was a joke until I got back to our quarters, sir," replied Charlie from his stiff brace position, his crimson chest meeting his equally crimson chin. It was just like cadet days.

"Why didn't your crew speak up at the debriefing?" The major wouldn't let up.

"I guess they didn't want to spoil it for me, sir."

The major looked at the captain, who would not

meet his eyes. Then the captain, with his face buried in some papers, said, "That must be a pretty bad crew you have there."

"No, sir, it's the best crew in the Fifteenth Air Force!" retorted the red-faced plane commander.

"I suggest you straighten them out. Dismissed."

We learned later that both the major and the captain had a difficult time keeping a straight face during the obligatory chewing-out session. Especially so with the two other high-ranking flying officers in attendance. They understood what was behind the green flak caper. They all knew the strain we were under and the value of a safety valve for our emotions and tensions. This was a new one, and they had silently applauded our crew during Charlie's ordeal.

The crew of *Hangar Queen* was a good crew. We had survived so far, and that in itself was good. And we were determined to make it all the way. *They can shoot down all the others, but not us*. We had Thornton's ball turret landing that really jelled our crew; Sid's Yellow Peril and electrified crotch; Kaiser's crazy songs; and Sherm had his green flak over Ploesti. We had been experiencing green flak all along. Every crew had its own variety, even the Red Tail fighter pilots with their lighthearted banter.

While we were trying to keep our spirits up and stay alive for our fifty missions, the planners of our overall strategy were trying to find ways of outwitting our common enemy—the defense efforts at Ploesti.

The following day Ploesti was host to its second low-level bombing attack, this time by the "Italians." In an effort to combat the new smoke screen defense, our leaders tried a new offensive ploy. They equipped each of forty-six P-38 Lightning fighter planes with a single 1,000-pound bomb, and sent them in on a dive-bombing attack at treetop level to catch the defense by surprise. But their only real surprise was an ambush by a swarm of GAF fighter planes who came in and shot down twenty-four of them while they still had their 1,000-pound millstones around their necks. The bombing was effective, but the price was high.

A few days later, our group went to a small oil refinery at Petfurdo, Rumania, and at the first sign of flak a waist gunner on one of the planes snapped on his chest chute and jumped out. There was no immediate danger and none of the flak ever got close. There wasn't a fighter in the sky.

Why did he jump out?

Combat fatigue was showing up in strange forms. At least that was the best explanation anyone offered at the time.

The next day's trip to Munich was different, at least for me. It seems bombardiers and navigators were the most expendable people on a crew. Sherm and I flew with other crews from time to time as their men were indisposed, or in some cases killed, with a replacement not yet on board. Sherm was loaned out to another crew who was flying a lead spot, so I was to be the "bombigator" for this mission, as we would fly with a man short.

I knew nothing about taking "sun shots" or celestial "star shots," but I had had a smattering of navigation at Victorville. I knew how to keep a log and how to plot a course on a map. My only function would be to keep track of where we were at all times, in case we got separated from the group and had to find our way home alone. If that situation would ever occur we would be in deep trouble, because it would have been my responsibility to give the pilot the proper heading that would bring us back to Italy and to our base. It was an interesting challenge. I took it very seriously and kept my log religiously. Every five minutes I recorded the compass heading, altitude, and indicated air speed. I looked for checkpoints along the way, such as peculiar shoreline shapes, cities, rivers, railroads, and so forth. It was fun to plot our course ahead and then, by calculating speed and time, determine an ETA for a given checkpoint and see how close I would come.

Arriving at the IP I located the target, a big factory and warehouse, and then put on my bombardier hat for the big job of toggling my bombs on cue. We were so far back in the formation, there was no chance whatsoever of my using the bombsight, so I never even turned it on.

The flak was much heavier and far more accurate than it had been a couple of days earlier; mainly, I suppose, because there wasn't a cloud in the sky over the target. Just my luck to draw togglier duty on a clear day like this, and a lead spot on a bummer like the other day. Fighter activity was heavier than normal. We even had a few passes made at us, which was a rarity. The Cotton Tails must have been to another target, or perhaps were still grounded. We missed them.

Our briefed target, a warehouse, was buried under

196

an excellent bomb pattern. As we left the target, one of our squadron planes feathered a propeller and was unable to keep in formation. We watched it slowly fall behind, to become a straggler. Our hope was that one or two other stragglers from another group might join it. Sometimes three stragglers flying tight formation will scare off fighter attacks if there aren't too many fighters involved. Janoiak, the plane's pilot, never made it back to the base, and was listed as missing in action. They were pecking away at the charter members of the 763rd Squadron. Janoiak was the eighth loss from our original seventeen crews that had left Chatham Field, and this our twenty-ninth mission. We were heading for a near wipeout.

My navigation suffered some while I was away from my duties over the target, and I had a little trouble getting my bearings as we left. Adding to my woes on the way home were a few clouds under us that made it more difficult to locate our position from ground checkpoints. About an hour later, after much kibitzing over the intercom, I was busying myself with this task when Charlie came on with "Navigator, how about an ETA for the shoreline?"

"I'll have a reading for you in a moment," I replied in my best navigational tone. (Much laughter.) My bombardier vocabulary had consisted of such profound statements as "Bombs away," "Bomb bay doors closed," and "Where's the target?" I then engaged my E6B computer, and at 1148 hours announced triumphanty, "Navigator to pilot, our ETA for the shoreline is 1153 hours."

"Take a look out the side window, Mr. Navigator," came a chuckled-filled voice.

I did, and I saw nothing but water. We were well past the shoreline and out over the Adriatic. The intercom was filled with boo's and comments like "That was even worse than 1500 feet at twelve o'clock."

Despite my navigational efforts, we did make it home safely, and on time, mainly because Charlie made sure he stayed with the group. As we were coming off our downwind leg and turning into the landing approach, a plane from another squadron fired a red-red flare and cut in front of us. We of course pulled up and went around the landing pattern again. The red-red flare indicated an emergency on the plane, such as being low on gas or having a seriously wounded man aboard, and gave that plane an undisputed right of way. Sometimes it got a little hairy when two planes fired red-red flares. They would race for the landing strip in a frightening game of "chicken," each pilot feeling *his* emergency was the most important. The plane with the red light shining on the control panel usually would win.

We later learned why the flare-firing plane had cut in front of us. The nose gunner had taken a 20mm cannon projectile in his chest and was still alive when they landed. It had gone through some metal which slowed it down somewhat, and then through his flak suit, which slowed it some more, before entering his chest just under his shoulder, and lodging under his armpit. As it was an armor-piercing type it did not explode on impact. It also missed all his vital organs. He was rushed to a hospital in Bari, and the last we heard, he was expected to recover with no permanent damage. It was his ticket home, making him luckier than some of those he left behind who would not be going home at all.

Some of the replacement flyboys came on pretty strong at first, but after a few missions would usually come down to earth and become one of us. The ground officers I knew were regular Joes—all but one. This new spit-and-polish major came out of the woodwork one day and proceeded to see how unpopular he could become in the shortest possible time. He was quite successful. He knew it all. The evening of the second Munich mission we were all feeling low because of the heavy losses sustained, when this major called down F/O Steve Goode for failure to salute him outside of the Officer's Club.

"How long you been here, Major?" Steve asked innocently.

Taken aback, the major replied, "Two days."

Steve's answer was a classic. Towering a foot over the major, one hand patronizingly placed on his shoulder, he quietly said, "Major, you better grease yourself real good—you've got a long way to slide."

Steve got a lot of free drinks that night, the major a lot of smirks. "No Mission Tomorrow's" were selling like hotcakes, and we all had a good night's sleep for a change.

As mean as all the other rough targets were— Ploesti, Wiener-Neustadt, Bucharest, and Munich— the waltz capital of the world, Vienna, was still considered the second most heavily defended target anywhere; and I hadn't even been there yet. Not that I missed it, but I felt I hadn't really seen it all.

The Germans soon took care of any slight I might

have felt. Two days later, on 16 June, I was on my way to the Lobau Oil Blending Plant at Vienna, but they seemed determined to keep me away. On the way to the target, what looked like the entire GAF came after the Fifteenth, which had mounted a 600-plane attack on the area.

It was most gratifying to watch the parade of fighters marching past us, looking for easier marks. Due to our tight formation, we were largely ignored in their search for patsies. However, to the flak gunners, we all looked alike in the sky, and they picked on us as much as any of the others. We were flying in the slot position of the high box, so I didn't have too much to do except open the bomb bay doors, toggle the bombs on cue, and notice what was going on.

The AA's picked us up just off the IP and quickly found our range. They had an altitude spotter sitting off to our right who got the word to his ground buddies before the P-47's drove him off. Flak got heavy fast, and right at our altitude.

Since I didn't have my head buried in the bombsight, I had lots of time to rubberneck and see what I had been missing at a busy target. In order to get a better view, I stuck my head up into the astrodome, a large Plexiglas dome in the ceiling of the nose section. My head was outside the confines of the airplane and I could see everything. What a sight! I saw far too much for my own good. As I gazed around I saw a plane from another group explode. No one got out. A few seconds later another B-24 slowly rolled over on its back and began falling out of formation as its nose pointed toward the earth. Two men came out of the right waist window. Then two more. One . . .

two . . . three bodies tumbled out of the bomb bay, chutes erupting from two of them. One chute caught fire and collapsed.

Watching the several planes going down in flames, emitting bodies on the way, some blossoming into cotton puffs, some not, I felt a strange mixture of emotions; a cross between guilt and relief. I felt guilty that there were men going down, some to die, and I was standing there, in relative safety, watching them as if it were some spectator sport. Superimposed on that emotion was another frightening one: I was *relieved* that it was someone else and not me. I knew our losses were statistical to some degree, and therefore everyone I saw going down meant one less chance for me to go down. If the statistical quota was filled by someone else, I needn't be the one to go. All so logical. I was consumed by a feeling of superiority. *I'm alive and safe, and you are not.* I was transfixed by the death dives. Then I felt guilty again, for being in fact thankful that it was someone else and not I. These fluctuating emotions were difficult to wrestle with. This was the second or third time I had found myself experiencing these contradictory feelings. I would always end up rationalizing my position by recognizing that I was going to have plenty of chances in the coming months to become one of the statistics, and by so doing I would extend someone else's tenure as a surviving combat flier, until their turn would come. It sounded good.

A particularly close explosion shook me out of my reverie and I went back to my job, watching the lead plane's open bomb bay and waiting for it to give birth to a dozen 500-pound eggs so that I could hit my

201

toggle switch. Just as I hit the switch, the astrodome shattered into a thousand pieces as a large chunk of jagged metal crashed through it. *What if my head had still been in the dome?*

I didn't mind the drafty nose compartment on the way home, figuring it was better to be a little drafty than to be headless. At least we were going home. Fourteen other bombers of the Fifteenth were lost on this mission and would not be flying home with us.

We had seen some of the parachute flak again. Not much and not effective, but something new like this always concerned us. Then, while flying over the Adriatic, someone reported green blotches on the still surface of the ocean.

"There are several of them," pointed out Howie from his ball turret.

"There's a life raft, I think."

"You're right, and those green spots are men in the water."

It was a chilling sight, several men floating in the ocean out of sight of shore, their plane at the bottom of the sea. The green spots we saw were signals from the downed fliers. Each Mae West life preserver had a packet of green dye marker powder affixed to the front section. The procedure was to rip down the marked flap when friendly aircraft were approaching. The dye would spread into a large circle and last for several hours, and could be seen from quite a distance. We also saw a yellow life raft as we drew closer, with several men calling it their home of the moment. Their plane had been ditched; otherwise the life raft would not have been available.

Ditching a B-24 was reported to be quite an experience. If it didn't break in two, it would usually float only about ten or fifteen seconds. You had to get out fast if you survived the water landing. One pilot told me that when he ditched his plane it went right down. All of a sudden he was under water, with just enough time for a deep breath. He had to swim from his seat and up through the top escape hatch, which had been opened by the escaping crew, and then swim some more in order to reach the surface.

We all felt rather guilty passing them by, but there was nothing we could do to help them except record their location to report upon our return. There were several other bomb groups passing by, so they would not lack for reporting of their plight and they were in relatively little danger at the moment. The dye was supposed to contain a shark repellent too, but I don't think there were any sharks in that area.

Major Martin, the CO of the 760th Squadron, led the second attack unit this day, and his plane was severely damaged by flak over the target. Both rudders had their control cables shot out. Rather than abandon ship over the target, he steered his crippled craft by the use of the A-5 autopilot and headed for home, a marginal straggler. This was challenge enough, but to attempt a B-24 landing on autopilot was virtually unheard of. Martin offered his crew the chance to bail out near a friendly field but none took him up on it, even though there was only a slim chance the plane could be landed safely.

Why didn't his men accept the opportunity for a relatively safe parachute escape? Very simply, one of their buddies had a bleeding flak wound in his knee and couldn't jump with them. They all chose to face possible death together rather than leave a helpless buddy behind with the pilot and copilot, who had already made their decision. There was no combat fatigue on this crew!

Major Martin landed his plane successfully at the Bari Air Field, where the wounded man was rushed to the hospital.

The B-24 Liberator bomber was an excellent aircraft, but one thing that was missing was a lavatory. As there were occasions when one or more crew members had a touch of dysentery, this lack of facilities was conspicuous. When one so afflicted had a sudden urge to have a bowel movement at 20,000 feet, and no men's room in sight, he had a problem. If this problem occurred while in the midst of a heavy flak barrage, it sometimes solved itself. The solution was called "browning out." A "blackout" is an aeronautical term for the condition that may result when you dive a plane and suddenly level out. The blood rushes from your head and you lose consciousness. A "redout" is a rarity, but happens to a pilot at the bottom of an outside loop, as the blood rushes to his head and into his eyeballs, causing everything to have a reddish glow. Blackouts and redouts were generally limited to pilots in fighter planes. All bomber crew members were eligible for brownouts.

If a person in need of a comfort stop chose to handle his relief in an orderly manner, he had merely to (1) remove his flak suit, (2) remove his Mae West, (3) remove his parachute harness, (4) zip down his flying suit and drop it to the floor, (5) drop his pants, (6) drop his shorts, (7) somehow push all the dropped items between his legs and out in front of him, (8) position a receptacle in the appropriate spot, (9) squat, and (10) perform—all the time hoping the bailout alarm wouldn't ring.

There was no specific receptacle for this operation, but a popular target was an oxygen mask box. This green waxed cardboard box was about five inches square. It was well equipped for its occasional special calling, as it was watertight and would properly contain its contents until such time for disposal. On this memorable mission, several crewmen had had occasion to use one particular oxygen mask box in the manner just described. It was quite full, lid closed, and sitting there quietly on the floor. There is a fact of B-24 life that is as resolute as any of Newton's laws. You cannot throw a small object out of the waist window opening while the plane is flying. The actual window itself had long since been removed to reduce weight. You must first hold the object outside the airplane, and then let go of it. If you stand a few feet away and throw the object, it will hit the airstream and bounce back in.

On the way home, we got out over the ocean and were then reasonably safe from enemy attack; we were down from altitude to non-oxygen-required levels where it was also warm, so crew members would often walk around and visit each other. I was back in the waist section when Bob Kaiser came back and spied the previously busy little oxygen box, and decided to dispose of it in the ocean. A commendable enough plan. Before anyone could stop him, he picked it up and pitched it toward the open window from his position in the middle of the waist compartment.

There have been many famous, important, and

significant coincidences in history. There have been many funny incidents in real life, movies, and stories. There have been many unforgettable experiences in people's lives the world over. But what happened on that June morning over the Adriatic in a bomber named *Hangar Queen* will forever be etched in five minds: mine, Sid's, Bob's, and the two guys trying to keep Sid from throwing Bob out of the airplane. At the precise moment that Bob threw the box, Sid in his cramped tail turret had decided he could safely leave his post and stretch his arms and legs in the comparative warmth and safety of the waist compartment.

The loaded missile had hit the airstream and did just what the law said it should do. It had not only failed to penetrate the airstream, but it exploded on impact, spraying and painting everything from the window on back a distinctive brown color.

Sid was in the midst of his well-earned stretch, big smile and a great-to-be-alive look on his face—but just for a split second. In his new brown coating Sid looked like a stop action photo, arms outstretched and mouth open in a big frozen grin. Then in classic silent movie style he pressed both palms to his eyes and rotated them. The stop action changed to slow motion as the hands were slowly lifted from the eyes to reveal two large pinkish white spots at the top of this grotesque brown figure. It was Stan Laurel performing live, right in front of me.

It had been a tough war so far for Sid. He really didn't deserve this, but it was funny all the same.

The "Black Panther" at Home

460 BOMB GROUP (H)

Officers' Club of 460th Bombardment Group

Sid Cohen patting his
"prison," the tail turret

Bombardier Newby on graduation

Newby and Rhodes after a mission

Gilber, Kaiser, Woods, Thornton, and a friend

Newby and Rhodes lived here
. . .   And here.

Chapter 9

KILL HITLER!

The base was abuzz with reports of a happening over at another airfield.

"He what?"

"He shot him in the head!"

"What happened?"

It seems a B-24 had crash-landed and all but the pilot had managed to climb out before it caught fire. The pilot was pinned and could not extract his foot from where it was crushed by the caved-in understructure. Flames began licking all around him in the cockpit as he struggled and screamed for help that was not available. Several of his crewmen were gathered around just outside his window, which was at about head level because the entire substructure was caved in. The flames became intense, and his plight was obviously hopeless; he pleaded for someone to shoot him. His buddies were dumbfounded. What to do? One young man made probably the most soul-searching decision of his life. He drew his .45 revolver and, with tears in his eyes and a prayer for forgiveness in his heart, pointed it at the pilot's head just inches away and pulled the trigger of peace. He turned, took two steps, and vomited.

Was he right or wrong? It was the main area of discussion that night around our house. The consensus was in his favor. Almost everyone said if they were in the pilot's shoes they would expect a buddy to save them from being burned alive.* I for one was in agreement. We heard later that a court-martial was held, and the flight surgeon testified the pilot died from smoke and flame inhalation before the gun was fired. The best friend the pilot ever had was charged with disorderly conduct and found guilty. He paid for that bullet that was fired, so we heard, and was given a suspended sentence. He could never be brought to trial in a civilian court over the incident.

*A remarkable incident involving somewhat the same ethics was reported by Paul Magness in the *Arkansas Democrat* on June 29, 1981. Magness was a pilot in the 97th Bomb Group, and he reported how time had stood still during a battle. A B-17 in the middle of a formation was mortally hit and was on fire. The crew bailed out, but one man's parachute caught on the bomb bay and he was left hanging and whipping in the wind, doomed to die a horrible death. None of his comrades could help him. The surviving planes were scrambling to avoid the inevitable explosion that sometimes took another plane down with it.

Then the war kind of hesitated, as Magness put it, when a German ME-109 flew right into the belly of the enemy—the middle of the formation of bombers. They were amazed that he had the guts to fly into the center of all those guns pointing at him. The war halted as everyone quit shooting. The German gently eased up to the helpless airman and shot him. Not another shot was fired as he peeled off and went on his way. They let him go, and the war started again.

The next day we gained a new crew member: Clyde Gilbert replaced John Woodland who, we presumed, was a prisoner of war. John had been subbing on another crew when their plane was shot down over Bulgaria earlier in the month. No one knew what happened to them. They were stragglers coming off the target and fell behind the formation. They had been reported missing, and all we could do was hope the crew members had at least become POW's, or better yet, were able to evade capture and were still roaming around somewhere. Perhaps they were "refugees" on a boat from Istanbul.

I was to learn later that when John's plane was attacked by Bulgarian fighters, he made a successful parachute jump. The Bulgarian fighter pilots, brave men that they were, shot at John as he hung in his parachute and hit him in the leg. He was picked up by Bulgarian soldiers and taken to a POW camp, where he spent the rest of the war. Unfortunately Bulgarian POW camps were the most brutal of all. They did not respect the rules as well as the Germans did.

Clyde came along just in time for a chance to be a hero, along with the rest of us. We were alerted one night that crew 71 was "up" the next day, so we got to bed about 2000 hours and were awakened at 0230 hours, a little earlier than usual. *Wonder what's up?*

When we arrived at briefing there was a low-level murmur pervading the room. There for all to see was the familiar blue yarn, except the curtain had not yet been drawn! The yarn poked up over the top of the curtain and stopped a few inches below Berlin.

Berlin! Berlin! It isn't even in our territory! At least it hadn't been until now.

The most significant aspect of the blue yarn going to a point near Berlin was that there was no *return* yarn! The yarn to a target usually formed a long rectangle. It would stretch from the wing rendezvous in Italy to the Initial Point, then to the target some twenty miles away, and then straight back to Spinazzola, a quite familiar pattern. But this yarn stopped near Berlin. There had to be an explanation. Perhaps it was just a little joke on us. (We hoped.)

It was no joke. The curtain was pulled and there it was. The yarn went east halfway across the Adriatic, and then turned sharply north to a little town about sixty miles south of Berlin. It was a strangely shaped yarn pattern. We awaited the explanation—and it was a good one.

"Gentlemen, your mission today is to kill Hitler."

This electric announcement sent chills up my spine. Maybe they went down; I wasn't sure. Kill Hitler! This was fantastic. We would go down in history; we would not be just a bunch of guys who flew a lot of bombing missions like thousands of others. We were going to do something that could have an immediate effect on shortening the war. There had been plenty of reports that Hitler was looney and that most of his generals knew the war was lost and wanted to quit, but Adolph plodded on.

The plot was this: the entire Fifteenth Air Force would start out on a full 750-plane maximum effort to a deep Balkan target. This would keep the Balkan fighter force in the Balkan area. Simultaneously, the Eighth Air Force would mount a 2,000-plane raid to some major targets in western Germany to draw the north German fighter force. The central German fighter force would be expected to go to meet either or both of the twin American major efforts.

Our group was scheduled to be the last one in the Fifteenth's trail of twenty-one bomb groups heading east. Just like a delayed line buck by a football team, the 460th would suddenly veer north after we were out over the Adriatic, and head straight for the Berlin area some three hundred miles north of Munich. Munich had been one of our farthest targets to date. It was staggering. Over 2,700 heavy bombers flying decoy missions so our thirty-six planes could move onto center stage, perhaps at potentially the most crucial moment in the war. We were to fly at a relatively low altitude, just enough to clear the mountains en route.

Our target was a group of houses in the center of a very small village where Hitler had a secret hideout. He supposedly had moved his headquarters here because of the heavy bombing he was being subjected to in Berlin. It was so secret, no one knew he was there (except for our intelligence people).

The plan *was* exciting, but we were all curious and concerned about the lack of a blue yarn trail back to Spinazzola. The explanation was simple. There was no blue yarn back to our base because we weren't going to make it all the way back to our base.

The hero part of the mission didn't look as inviting as it did at first. The briefing officer went on to explain that we would not have enough gas to return home, but would probably make it back to northern Italy or northern Yugoslavia. Some might make it out over the Adriatic, but no farther.

We were assured the entire Allied underground force was alerted to watch for us. We would have lots of friends waiting to help us evade capture and eventually make it back to our lines. There would be a large fleet of PT boats spotted along our expected course. It was comforting to know they cared.

We left the room with mixed emotions. Perhaps the most frequent expression was "Why us?" Someone answered, "Why not?" I guess that said it all.

We performed all the pre-mission chores and were about five minutes from start-engine time, when the "red-yellow" flare shot up from the control tower. STANDBY. Everyone climbed out of his plane and stood around wondering what was up. The sky was reasonably clear, so it shouldn't be a weather problem. Most of us weren't too sure if we wanted the mission to go on or be aborted. No one wanted to come out and say he hoped for a cancellation, but no doubt most of us really did feel that way. It was one thing to go out every day in a big game of Russian roulette where a certain percentage of us would not come back. The odds of not returning were from one to four out of a hundred, sometimes higher, sometimes lower. We understood those odds and each of us believed that someone else would be the losing two or three percent, or whatever. But to face a shot where your odds were 100 out of 100 of not coming back was a bit much. This wasn't quite a kamikaze mission, but it certainly came close. When the red-red flare went up, you could hear the cheers from all over the place. Someone else can be the hero.

The cheers of that morning turned to wails that evening, for the same crews were alerted for another

0230 hours wakeup call.

We knew.

In a flurry of letter writing that night, guys who never wrote, wrote. No one involved slept very well.

Our concern was well founded, as the same yarn arrangement appeared on the map at briefing the next morning. A bank of cumulus clouds over Austria and Yugoslavia had made it impossible for us to fly the mission as planned the previous day, but the plan was on again for this day. Resigned to our fate, we accepted our challenge and made ready once more. But just as we were about to leave the briefing room, they announced the mission was scrubbed. Strangely, no one cheered. Relieved at the stand-down, perhaps, but not elated. I think this time we were *ready*.

The plan for the 460th to kill Hitler, however, was scrubbed forever. After two days of aborted efforts, the powers-that-be decided that the enemy probably knew of the plan by then, and it would have had little chance for success. We had no idea how many of the Italians working around our base were spies. Even the goat's-milk ice cream tasted pretty good that afternoon. Now we could get back at odds we understood.

By mid-June, the Fifteenth Air Force had inflicted heavy damage on twenty-nine oil refineries within its assigned range. About the same number of refineries had not yet been touched, but their day would be coming. Beginning 23 June, the Fifteenth's heavies would strike for oil for six consecutive days.

While there was not an oil strike on the 22nd of June, it was a big day for me. One of the replacement planes had a Norden bombsight in it, the first one

216

ever in our Group. Colonel Campbell, the Group Operations Officer, knew I was a frustrated Norden man, so he assigned me to use it in flying with Major James to bomb the marshalling yards at Castel Maggiore again. *Hangar Queen* was in for an overhaul, but our entire crew was along, except for Dusty.

We flew up along the eastern seashore of Italy and turned west. As we crossed the coast, we experienced a little flak, light and inaccurate. Flak at the target was another thing. It was light, but very accurate. We caught several pieces, but no damage was done, and no one was hurt.

A surprising thing happened over the target. An ME-109 came in from 11 o'clock high out of the sun, and began firing rockets at us. One rocket exploded in the nose turret of a plane in the low box of our attack unit, killing the nose gunner. The plane, however, made it back to the base, even though the front of the plane was torn off.

This was a strange mission. Our two attack units were to hit the marshalling yards broadside. The second attack unit, which I was leading with my trusty Norden, was to hit an aiming point on the *left* side of the general target area. The first attack unit was to hit a point on the *right* side. For some reason, the first unit approached the target on our left side and behind us. Our positions were exactly reversed from the plan, and I was not aware of it.

I enjoyed using the Norden and thought I had a reasonably good sighting. I felt the bomb pattern would be pretty fair, since we had a tight formation and the rest of our group did a good job of toggling. The other attack unit had overshot the entire marshalling yards by 1,000 feet for a conspicuously botched-up job of bombing. Because of the reversed positions of the two attack units, we all thought *ours* were the bad bombs, and I was unable to explain the snafu to the pilot. Actually *our* bomb pattern was right on the mark.

Leaving the target, we flew straight south over the German-held mainland to conserve gas, since our Tokyo tanks were not filled for this trip. For some reason we felt relaxed. There were no more fighters reported in the southern area, and of course no more flak. All of us had doffed our flak suits, and some of us were sitting on the upper flight deck with oxygen masks removed, mentally chalking up another mission. Smitty was asking how to spell "Castel Maggiore." He was penciling in the name of this latest target on his little stuffed horse. He would ink it in later at home, where it would join the impressive list of other targets where the faithful little good-luck mascot had taken us safely.

Suddenly Sid broke into our peaceful little worlds with "Flak at seven o'clock." Then he followed with "My Gawd, they hit a plane." We looked out the window and saw that one of our planes was starting down in flames. Six chutes were reported. We were only at 10,000 feet and the last thing we expected was antiaircraft fire, but it was AA fire designed for the medium bombers of the Twelfth Air Force, and we were in their altitude territory. By the time we hastily put on our flak suits, we were out of danger—but we learned a lesson about complacency.

Then an odd thing happened. During the short flak attack, one of the planes in our squadron had its No.

3 engine hit, and flames shot past the right waist window. This was moments after the other plane had been shot down. It was a known rule of thumb that when a B-24 caught fire, you could barely count to ten before it blew up. One of the waist gunners, seeing the wall of flames outside his window, decided not to test the ten-count rule. He just put on his chest chute and went out the other window. The flames never made it to ten. They went out. The engine kept on running, and the plane continued on as if nothing happened. We watched the lone parachute float down behind enemy lines, its hasty passenger hanging below. I'm not sure, but I thought I could see him shaking his fist at his departing plane and crew. We couldn't quite hear what he was saying, but we had a pretty good idea of his commentary on the situation.

Sixteen aircraft received flak damage at the target, including one that had its nose wheel shot out. The pilot made an excellent landing on the dirt emergency runway, keeping the tail down until the plane slowed down. As it slowed down, the nose of the plane dropped and the aircraft plowed up the dirt runway for a hundred yards or so. No one was injured.

The following day we worked again. We joined nearly five hundred other heavies and went deep into Rumania to Giurgiu on the Danube River, about seventy-five miles south of Ploesti. Our bombing that day was superb, with a very high score of 74 percent. The lack of fighter and flak opposition no doubt helped the cause.

Leaving the target, one of the planes in another squadron had a propeller rip off the No. 2 engine. They of course had to drop out of formation, since they could not maintain formation speed. On the way home alone they were attacked by five ME-109's and, instead of being shot down, they managed to shoot down one of the attackers and limped back on three engines. A remarkable tour de force.

Meanwhile, four other groups tested the growing smoke pot defenses at Ploesti, hitting selected oil targets, and suffering a loss of six planes. Gerstenberg was getting his pound of flesh.

Ours was an easy Rumanian trip and we had an uneventful flight home. After lunch, Major James asked me to go with him to wing headquarters for a critique on the previous day's mission. I had been to several of these sessions before when I had been an attack unit leader, so I had an idea of what to expect. We would be getting a good chewing-out for the bombing on the marshalling yards at Castel Maggiore, where I thought I had done a bad job.

Just before we went into the meeting, someone met us in the hallway, patted Major James on the back, and began saying nice things about the mission. We were puzzled. It seems that the official photos showed that ours were the good bombs, and the other attack unit had overshot their mark and hadn't landed a bomb near the target. At the briefing, Major James and I were singled out for some nice words by the meeting leader. The other lead pilot and bombardier were treated less kindly. They had a difficult time explaining the poor results. One striking thing about these wing meetings was to see a lowly second lieutenant sit there and watch a full colonel from another group standing in a brace and getting his tail chewed out by Wing Commanding General George R. Acheson. I felt embarrassed for him, but it did sort of make full colonels seem more human.

Colonel Campbell, as a matter of fact, sent for me after we had returned from the wing critique and told me we had a special plane on the field with a new kind of bombsight, basically a Norden, but equipped with radar. It was officially called H2X. Unofficially it was called "Mickey." Planes equipped with H2X were called "Pathfinders."

He asked me to go along with him and see what I could learn about the device while he flew the plane. This was quite an experience. It was a fairly cloudy day, so we flew up to Foggia, where there was a 10/10ths undercast. The "Mickey" operator stuck his head in the sight and went to work. I was impressed that he was sighting on a target when all I could see was clouds—normally a bust situation. Finally he motioned me to look into the eyepiece. I didn't really see anything. Just a single white spoke turning slowly on its hub. In front of the turning spoke there was nothing; but following it were several globs of white and black that looked like clouds. Years later I was to see this same thing on the nightly TV weather news.

"What am I seeing?" I asked.

"The white irregular spot is Foggia."

"Can you see the river running east and west, north of the city?" he asked. "If it's the white thread going across, I guess I see it," I replied. Even though I wasn't too sure I could be effective with this newfangled machine, I could see its possibilities in the hands of a trained operator. Here was the answer to the smoke pots of Ploesti! Each group would later be assigned one of these Pathfinder planes for use against Gerstenberg's latest defensive ploy.

On 24 June, 135 heavies hit Ploesti again, in the running battle for oil, with a very heavy loss ratio of 10.4 percent as fourteen bombers fell to the flak guns.

The 460th did not make the Ploesti run that day, but our group went back to France the following day to bomb the oil tanks at Sete, on the coast not far from Spain. It was a long flight, with no flak or fighter opposition. We flew in the number two spot in the lead box, which meant I got to sight for range. With no opposition, we had tight formation and the bombing was very good. When we looked back after turning off the target, a black column of smoke was racing toward our altitude.

That evening we walked up to the barber shop and got GI haircuts. The short hair felt good with the coming of warm weather, but we did look like a bunch of convicts. While in the area, we stopped in at the orderly room and saw the group standings. Though our bombing accuracy score was at an all-time high, we had dropped several positions in the standings. Apparently several other groups had improved more than we did.

The following day our crew took a breather and spent a relaxing day, thinking about the next day's trip to the beautiful Isle of Capri and our mid-tour flak leave. Actually it was past the midpoint for me, since I had completed thirty-five of the fifty missions required for my ticket home. Our brethren in the skies over the Floridsdorf Oil Refinery near Wiener-Neustadt were not so happy, and they weren't relaxing. They were experiencing some very aggressive fighter attacks, which had been on the increase this month, and had lost one plane in the attacks. Two more were lost to flak, one landed at Foggia, two others crash-landed at the base, and seven planes were damaged. Our good friend Rattlesnake Hank Thompson and his crew were among the losses.

On the bright side, we shot down seven enemy aircraft. The report for June was seventeen missions flown and ten losses. The ranks of our original crews were thinning. By the end of June, Ploesti's monthly production was down to 75,000 tons, the result of 584 heavy bombers dropping 1,310 tons of bombs, and the daring low-level raid by the luckless P-38's. There were thirty-four heavies and twenty-four bombing P-38's lost in June at Ploesti.

PART FOUR:
FLAK LEAVE

Chapter 10

ISLE OF CAPRI

About two thousand years ago, Roman Emperor Tiberius visited the Isle of Capri for a few weeks' rest; he liked it so well that he never left. The crew of the *Hangar Queen* went off on a week's leave to Capri, but we knew *we* would have to leave when our stay was over. After a short flight to Naples, we boarded a steamer and headed south across the Bay of Naples to the enchanted island.

When I was in high school there was a lad who ran around all over the school, playing the then popular song, "The Isle of Capri," on some sort of a piccolo instrument called a "potato." I thought about the words to the song, " 'Twas on the Isle of Capri that I found her . . . ," and wondered if it really was all that great.

The Isle of Capri is just seventeen miles due south of the city of Naples, and about three miles off the coast of the peninsula of Sorrento. Capri was just a speck on the horizon for quite awhile, but soon it began to grow. About three hours later we saw the biggest chunk of rock we ever hoped to see. Capri is one solid piece of limestone, about four miles long and nearly two miles at the widest point. What makes Capri unique is that it is the only island or mountain in the area that is not of volcanic origin. Its sheer sides shot straight up from the water for hundreds of feet all around the perimeter, except for a section on the north edge called the Marina Grande, Capri's only port, for all practical purposes. There is a secondary port on the south side, used only when the regular port is weatherbound.

We arrived at Marina Grande and walked quite some distance along the pier to the mainland. At the dock area there were a few buildings, including a restaurant extending out over the water. The first thing that caught my attention was the incline. Back in Pittsburgh there are several inclines located across the Monongahela River from the downtown area. Each has dual tracks that run up the side of Mt. Washington at about a sixty-degree angle. A passenger car on the up tracks is counterbalanced by cable with the one on the down tracks. For years these inclines were a vital link in the commuter transportation system to downtown Pittsburgh. One of the Pittsburgh inclines claimed to be the *only* curved incline in the world. It was so curved that when you looked up the dual tracks they disappeared out of sight around a section of the hillside. They even had postcards depicting this one-of-a-kind phenomenon. I had been impressed with it all my life, and had told many an acquaintance in the army that we had more than just a Major League baseball team and some great college teams in Pittsburgh. (I didn't brag much

Enlisted Men's pier at Capri

The bell

Second curved incline in the world

Smitty and Tyrone

Homer Luke, at ease on Capri

Dusty Rhodes and Ted Newby, July 1944

those days about the Pittsburgh Steelers.) We had the world's *only* curved incline!

"Hey, Newb, look. Tell us about the world's only curved incline," laughed Sherm. All my buddies stood laughing and pointed up to the world's *second* "only curved incline." There it went, up the hill and out of sight around a bend. But there was a difference. It only had one set of tracks, and it was called a funicular. The funicular didn't bother me, but the single set of tracks did.

"You can't win 'em all," I answered lamely, determined to see how they did it with only one set of tracks.

The Isle of Capri has a fascinating history. It is believed to have been occupied since the Stone Age. When Tiberius took up residence here, he built twelve villas as well as some dungeons and other edifices, where he tortured and killed people at his whim. When the city of Capri was established nearly five hundred feet above sea level and its sister city Anacapri nearly nine hundred feet above sea level, they were not accessible to one another, even though they were just two and one-half miles apart.

The only entrance to Anacapri was by way of 800 steps from the water's edge up and through the side of a cliff. At that time they were called the Phoenician stairs. Capri was accessible by a zigzag road that was also hacked into the side of the cliffs. The original road was still there and was the main road to the city. It wasn't until the nineteenth century that a road was built from Capri to Anacapri. The Isle of Capri, while well known in Roman times and during the next few centuries, lay unused and unappreciated until it was rediscovered in relatively modern times—about 1826. We knew nothing about the history of Capri, just that it was a great place to go for a week and not be shot at every day. The area near the port didn't look like much, just a lot of houses between the bay and the beginning of the cliffs. The waterfront restaurant looked like something to be checked out later on.

Our ascent up the old zigzag road was by buggy, and looking over those sheer cliffs with no guard rails was rather exciting for what was supposed to be a nerve-calming vacation. We must have traveled several miles to navigate the 488-foot change in altitude.

The Quisisana was to be our home for this week; it was one of three resort hotels in Capri taken over by the Air Forces for R&R facilities. There was another fine Air Force resort hotel in Anacapri, but we were glad to be in Capri where all the action was.

For a small-town boy, staying in one of the premier resort hotels in Europe was quite a thrill. I had never seen a bedside console with five or six buttons, all symbol-coded for desired services such as valet, room service, wake-up calls, etc. My private balcony faced out over the ocean. This was living!

An important factor in our week's stay was the lack of a dress code: no rules. That meant no uniforms, except at the nightly dances which were rotated among the four hotels. Dusty and I went out and bought a couple of loud casual shirts and some colored slacks. We even bought some seashell neck-laces and flimsy straw hats. Put them all together, along with our G.I. sunglasses, and you had a couple of guys who blended in with the other tourists.

Our first visit to Piazza Umberto resulted in a vain

search for some Scotch or bourbon. It was cognac, champagne, or wine in all the several sidewalk cafes that dotted the square. While "Piazza Umberto" was the official name, the natives called it the "Piazzetta." We called it the square, because that is what it looked like. We tried several cafes and all their cognac was alike, so we decided to get used to it for the week.

In most every shop on the square you could buy the little "Bell of Capri," which we had first seen back in Spinazzola. It was a small silver bell on a small chain. Along with the bell there was a little printed message in English, telling the story of the famous bell. Years ago, when a pirate ship hove into view on the horizon, watchers in the big tower at the edge of the Piazzetta would ring the large bell located at the top of the tower. This warning would give the maidens time to run for the hills and hide in caves, or whatever they could find. The pirates apparently had ulterior motives, which included taking the young girls back out to sea on a one-way trip. They said the bell hadn't been rung since the pirate days several centuries ago.

In the daytime, we spent most of our time at the beach, vying for the attention of the few nurses and Red Cross girls, very unsuccessfully for most of us. At the eastern end of our long beach and out in the water quite a way was a massive rock formation about a hundred feet from a jutting section of shore rocks. It was located in such a manner that the waves coming in would funnel through the pass at an accelerated velocity. A person would have to be crazy to try swimming through the pass, but a lot of half-crazy guys were paddling kayaks through it at a very high speed.

I had never been on, or literally *in*, a kayak in my life. In fact, these were the first ones I had ever seen. Being obviously half crazy, I volunteered to try my hand at this new sport. I fed my legs into the hole in the top, strapped myself in, and tightened the leather cockpit section around my waist. I was well tucked in. They handed me a strange-looking paddle and gave me a push out to sea. There was an outrigger off to one side to give the boat stability, so I managed to stay upright in my new sea adventure.

I swung out to sea past the rock and maneuvered myself around so that I could thread the needle back through the pass. Then it occurred to me, after I was committed to the pass and approaching it at break-neck speed, that if I capsized this thing, I would be upside down in the water and tucked in so snugly, it would take me ten minutes to extricate myself. I would be a goner, no doubt about it. I wasn't half crazy to do this; I was fully crazy. But I *was* doing it, and through the slot I sped at what seemed like sixty miles an hour. It was fun, but once was enough for a guy who was a very poor swimmer. The one latent fear I had in this whole war was that of bailing out over water, and we were usually over an ocean twice during a mission.

The next day we decided to have lunch at the dockside restaurant. We went to the top of the incline, bought two tickets, and boarded the cable car. I was about to ride on the second "world's only curved incline." *One* set of tracks, disappearing down around the bend, still intrigued me, but I was going to learn the secret of how two counterbalanced cable cars could pass each other on the one track. There could be only one explanation.

I wasn't prepared for the sight I saw as we rounded the bend. The set of tracks went into a tunnel in the hillside! Once inside the tunnel the secret was revealed. The tracks split into two sets of tracks for about fifty feet. We passed the "up" car, and went out the other end of the tunnel. This was fancier than Pittsburgh's "world's only curved incline."

The shrimp served at the dockside restaurant was different, but excellent. They placed a big plate in front of us that was filled with very tiny shrimp not any thicker than a pencil and about an inch long. I had never seen shrimp this small before. You ate shells and all. Again, wine was the liquid staple at the meal. I was getting used to wine instead of water when I ate off base. Drinking the local water could lead to diverting valuable vacation time away from fun activities.

One night, after one of the dances, several of us wandered down to the Piazzetta to see what was going on. After closing Luigi's American bar we walked to the end of the square to where the tower of Capri was located, with its famous bell nestled in the alcove at the top. There stood the tower, almost defying challenge. Someone finally said, "I wonder if the old bell still rings?" After some speculation we walked around it a bit and did some calculations. There was an oversized downspout at one corner that ran all the way to the roof. About fifteen feet off the ground there was a port opening about sixteen inches in diameter, but it was some three feet from the downspout.

"I believe it can be done," the ringleader mused. Shinnying up the downspout, he made it to the level of the port opening and swung across so that both hands were gripping the hole in the wall. He chinned himself and squirmed through the opening.

If he can do it, so can I. I followed him into the stairwell, and waited for the third member of our raiding party. Soon we three were stealthily climbing the many stone steps to the top of the tower. I thought we would never get there as we wound around and around inside the tower. Finally we reached the top and found ourselves in a small room with portholes in each wall. The bright moon lit the room reasonably well, so no one stepped through the hole in the middle of the floor where the ropes used to go.

The ceiling had an opening about two feet by two feet, with several iron bars across it. Beyond the bars was our prize, the Bell of Capri, a magnificent sculptured piece of metal hanging there in passive anticipation and almost shouting, "RING ME!" Hanging inside was an equally impressive clapper, the ball at the bottom as big as a very large grapefruit.

"OK, lift me up," I announced, feeling brave at the moment. I had climbed the Matterhorn, but here I wasn't sure just what to do next. They boosted me up so I could hold onto an iron bar.

"Ring it, we can't hold you up there all night."

"OK, OK, I will," I said as I contemplated the fact that the old bell hadn't been rung for centuries. I was sweating, but there was no turning back. My culture kick was taking a new bent. *Oh well, here goes.* I grasped the big ball, drew it back, and threw it as hard as I could at the other side of the bell. Even I couldn't miss at this range, and I didn't. The resulting clang, or whatever it was, just about broke my eardrums and the reverberations made me lose my hold on the iron bar I was gripping. As I came tumbling down, someone yelled, "I'm next."

After each of the others took his turn we scampered down the stairs to our escape window. How we all got out the opening and over to the downspout without falling was a small miracle. By now windows were opening above the shops where people lived. The alarmed citizens were shouting something in a foreign language. We no doubt had kicked one of their sacred cows.

As people began gathering in the square, we disappeared into the night and made our way to our respective hotels. When I wandered into my hotel lobby, I heard comments about hearing a loud bell ringing. I sort of felt famous, except no one knew about my fame.

Our last night on Capri started off like an ordinary night, but at some point I ran into a fellow I had met during the week and he suggested we go visit some friends of his. Having nothing better to do, I agreed to go along. His friends turned out to be two young ladies who were staying at a picturesque villa overlooking the Marina Grande. They seemed quite gracious about our visit. Between the beautiful moonlit night and the soft music from the record player competing for every nook and cranny of the secluded veranda, we could not escape the mood enveloping us.

From an ordinary nothing evening to this in just a few moments was mind-boggling. I kept waiting for someone to jump out from behind a potted tree and hit me over the head. Was this some sort of a setup? Or was it for real? Between the cocktails and the strains of a strumming guitar wafting over the railing, things got pretty friendly. I didn't know what I was doing there and I didn't really care how it happened. From some of the conversation, I gathered they were expecting dates from the mainland who somehow were delayed, and possibly might not show up. We were sort of fill-ins for the time being. The warm-up, perhaps.

It was like a scene from a movie. I couldn't believe my luck. The only catch would be if the phone would ring, or worse, if two huskies showed up on the veranda. It was rather difficult, trying to have a relaxing time while waiting for the other shoe to fall, but we made the best of it and hoped the phone would not signal our defeat.

" 'Twas on the Isle of Capri that I found her . . ."

Our surrogate romance came to an abrupt halt with the ringing of the telephone.

"Oh, I'm so delighted you called; we're waiting for you!" Pause. "Fine, see you in fifteen minutes."

"Sorry, fellows, they were able to rent a motorboat and made it after all. We enjoyed your company."

As we said good night and went on our way, I recalled the old line about the guy living the life of Riley—and then one day Riley came home.

PART FIVE:
PLOESTI KAPUT

Chapter 11

VIENNA FLAK MAGNET

It was sobering to learn that the war had gone right along without us while we were loafing around on Capri. We returned to our base on the Fourth of July to see hundreds of men and officers shooting their .45's in the air in celebration of that great day in American history. Our top people, however, quickly put a stop to that activity just about the time we decided to join in.

While we were on Capri, the England-based Eighth Air Force was in the midst of a daring operation called "FRANTIC," in which they sent 130 B-17's on a three-leg shuttle run to Russia and Italy, and then back to England. En route to Russia they bombed a synthetic oil plant near Berlin, and on the Italy leg they bombed an oil plant in Poland. While in Italy, the cross-continent raiders joined the Fifteenth for its only near-1,000 plane assault on Bucharest and other Balkan oil transportation targets.

While we were on leave, Dick Fowler of Minneapolis returned to the base after more than two months in the mountains of northern Yugoslavia. Dick had been shot down on 23 April soon after leaving the target at Wiener-Neustadt. Six ME-109's and ME-210's flying abreast attacked his plane, causing an explosion in the fuel tanks. The pilot and copilot were killed instantly, and the entire nose section was engulfed in flames. The nose gunner, in trying to climb out of his turret, got hung up by his parachute harness and screamed for help.

Dick fought his way through the flames to get the gunner, but the man succumbed to flame inhalation as Dick reached for him. By now Dick's clothing was on fire. He was in the middle of a furnace, and faced a serious dilemma. He was just a foot or so away from the open nose wheel door, the escape hatch for the nose compartment, and instant relief from the inferno. His chest pack was about two feet beyond the opening, up on the crawl space.

As Dick related it, his dilemma was that the heat was so intense, all he wanted to do was escape the searing fire. He wanted relief so badly that his emotional desire to dive out the opening into the cool air, *without his chute*, was at first stronger than his rational need to move beyond the short-term solution toward the life saving chest pack. It took all of his willpower to move past the beckoning open hatch, through still more flames, to his chute.

At that moment time didn't exist. Reason and the will to live finally won out over emotion. He lunged for his chute, which was also on fire, grabbed it, and leaped through the hole without even attaching it to his parachute harness. When the minus-sixty-degree air jolted him back to reality, he snapped the two chute hooks into the harness rings, and after about ten seconds pulled the rip cord that put him into the last stage of escape from the flaming furnace. It was so cold, he was not aware of how badly his face had been burned. As he floated down to about the 12,000-foot level, an ME-210 fired on him and the bullets ripped through his canopy. Dick quickly slumped in his harness, pretending to be dead, and the enemy plane flew away, the pilot no doubt proud of his victory.

A large group of people were on hand to greet him when he landed. He learned at once that the Germans occupied a town about three miles away, so he asked if there was any Partisans around. A small boy came up and said, "Hello, Johnny." The boy then took a bicycle from a total stranger and gave it to Dick, pointing the way to the village occupied by the Partisans. When Dick had arisen that morning the last thing he expected to be doing that day was riding a bicycle in Yugoslavia.

The local people hid him in a farmhouse and tended to his burned face and hands. They plastered his face with wet tea leaves for three days, and that seemed to help the burns considerably. While he was in hiding, searching parties consisting of over one hundred soldiers continued to look for him. The people began transferring him from farmhouse to farmhouse, mainly by horse carriage. The search parties persisted, and he was hidden in remote rooms and told not even to cough.

The Germans took one of his Yugoslavian benefactors to prison and beat him in order to learn where

Dick was, but the man took the beating and never talked.

Three Partisan soldiers finally arrived and took him under their wing. After a skirmish with some German soldiers who fired on them, they all escaped into the woods.

It was nine days after his escape from the airplane before Dick could open his lips wide enough to eat small pieces of food. Up until then he had been existing on milk, wine, and water which he sucked through a cigarette holder. He recuperated in that general battle area for nearly a month as the Partisans fought the Germans, the Ustasa, and the Chetniks.

He finally met an allied underground agent, and walked with him for eighteen hours a day for eight days through rugged mountain trails to a friendly mission, where he was evacuated by air to Italy.

It was a long nine weeks for Dick.

He told us, "Never again will I let my chute out of my hands while flying in the target area."

"How are you going to get your flak suit around the chute?" I asked. "You'll look like the only pregnant navigator in the Air Forces."

"Simple," he said. "I'll secure it with a short piece of rope or cable to my harness." It made sense.

Dick's face was still red, as if he had a bad sunburn, except for the perimeter which had been protected by his flying helmet. Luckily, his sunglasses had shielded his eyes from the flames.

In his nine weeks of roaming the mountains of Yugoslavia, Dick learned firsthand about the war-within-a-war that was going on below us as we flew back and forth to our Balkan targets. In 1941 the Nazis recognized a right-wing anti-Serbian group called the Ustasa, and established a puppet government in northern Yugoslavia under the leadership of Gen. Milan Nedic. King Peter's Yugoslavian government-in-exile appointed Draza Mihailovich as the commanding general of a resistance group called the Chetniks. The Chetniks fought both the Germans and the Ustasa. A second resistance group was formed, called the Partisans, led by a communist leader, Josip Broz, who went by the name of "Tito."

The Partisans fought the Germans and the Ustasa, as well as the Chetniks. They told us it didn't matter which resistance group we met if we were shot down. Either one would befriend us. We just shouldn't say nice things about the other group. We were also cautioned that when picked up by one of the patrols of either side, we would have to live with them for awhile until they could get us back to an underground contact for eventual movement back to Italy. A very real problem might be that we would find ourselves in the middle of a pitched battle with one or another group and learn that some of our downed comrades were among those firing at us.

The next day I went over to the parachute riggers' tent, and had an umbilical cord fashioned out of a thirty-inch section of control line cable that was about one-eighth-inch thick. My lifeline had snaps on each end, and with one end hooked to my harness and the other to the chute, my chest pack would never be more than two feet away. But it took more than that to assure a successful escape.

When a falling plane starts into a flat spin, the centrifugal force is so great a person cannot move, even though he is conscious and has all his faculties. He weighs a ton, or so it seems, and is simply flattened against the side of the plane. Immobilized, he will soon die without a chance to save himself, even though his chute may be hooked onto his harness. His only chance is for the plane to blow up and shoot him out into the free air. It happened just that way on several occasions according to reports we had heard.

In talking to the riggers, we kiddingly asked if these chutes they were packing were guaranteed to work.

"They better be," one replied. "We each have to pick a chute at random once a month and make a jump with it!"

My parachute confidence level went up a few notches.

While in the riggers' tent I added another touch. I wanted to do everything possible to increase my chances of survival if I should ever get shot down and make it to the ground all in one working piece. I had them sew a sack onto the back of my parachute harness. It was a bright blue sack about a foot square and several inches thick. In it I had some dry socks, a couple of boxes of K rations, a razor and some Kant Rust blades that a friend's dad had given to me while I was home on graduation leave the previous fall. They were stainless steel, and were supposed to last for about fifteen or twenty shaves. Also included in my survival kit was a small compact chess set and a deck of cards. If Dusty or Sherm and I should end up hiding in some Austrian barn, we could while away the time playing chess or gin.

The consensus among all the others was that my blue sack would not survive a parachute opening. I was sure it would, but hoped I would never have to prove it. The next day I thought for a moment that I would have the opportunity to test it. A lot of people have had the exasperating experience, while driving, of having a car on the right decide to cross over in front of them to make a left turn. This happened to us—but it wasn't on a regular highway; it was on the high road to northern Italy. Charlie Hammett had just been made a flight leader, and we were flying in the No. 1 spot in the high box of the second attack unit, on our first mission since our vacation.

The battle plan called for several groups to fly up the eastern coast of Italy, where certain groups would peel off at various points and head inland to assigned targets. Nothing wrong with that, except a group that was assigned a target to the south of ours was positioned ahead and to our right, a few hundred feet above us, as we paraded up the coast. Suddenly the group made a left turn across our bow, and we passed under them. That alone was of some concern, but of more concern was the fact that all of their bomb bay doors were open. *They were on their bomb run!* It was eerie to look up and see all those 500-pounders staring down at us. Bombs do occasionally fall out of planes unexplainably.

After filling the intercom with choice comments about the planners of this mission, we managed to survive the scare and went on to hit the oil refinery at Porto Marghera. We had moderate flak, no fighter opposition, and the bombing was good, with a heavy concentration within the 1,000-foot radius of the aiming point.

After we had landed and were enjoying some coffee and doughnuts, we heard the emergency siren and saw the meat wagon and fire trucks heading down the runway. A crash landing was imminent. Such landings were handled in several ways. When there was a landing gear problem and it required a wheels-up landing, the pilot would be instructed to land on the parallel dirt strip, which would cut down on sparks and avoid ripping up the metal grid runway. This plane seemed all right. All four engines were functioning and the gear was down. It was approaching the metal runway, not the dirt strip. We couldn't figure why the fire truck was there. What we didn't know was that the hydraulic system had been shot out and, since the landing gear brakes work off the hydraulic system, the aircraft had no brakes. The landing gear had been cranked down by hand.

The plane made a fairly normal landing, except that the noise seemed unusually high. Soon after it touched down and was rolling along the runway, a startling thing happened. A parachute erupted from each waist window and billowed out behind the speeding brakeless bomber. The sudden braking action of the chutes caused the nose to come down sharply, where it collapsed because the nose wheel was not strong enough for the shock. Now the sparks did fly while the nose of the plane skidded along the metal runway. Despite this added excitement, the plane came to a fairly quick stop and no one was hurt. Fortunately, the plane did not catch fire.

This improvisation was one of the first uses of a parachute for braking action in the Mediterranean

Theater of Operations. Shortly thereafter, a bulletin came out from Air Force Headquarters, outlining the procedure for this unorthodox but highly effective emergency braking method. Even though the runway was badly ripped up and the nose of the bomber was mashed in, both would be operable again and ready for action, the runway in a matter of hours, the airplane in a few days.

We had witnessed some surprisingly good aircraft rebuilding after some bad crash landings, so we saw a very different result a month earlier, when a fully loaded bomber taxied onto a soft shoulder at perhaps one or two miles an hour. One wheel sank about eight inches into the mud, and the heavy load caused a torque action which warped the frame of the fuselage. The brand new bomber was totaled and dismantled for parts. A new hangar queen was born.

Parts were always in demand by the repair crews, who had been doing a yeomanlike job of keeping the old crates flying. Most of the original planes still around were covered with patched-up holes. Some of the most critical components, and perhaps greatest in demand by the repairmen, were governors for the engines. A very good supply just could not be kept on hand. These were items that seemed to be vulnerable to flak damage and overtaxed engines. It got so bad that when planes crash-landed, the ground crew would sometimes beat the rescue squad to the scene, and could be seen climbing up over an engine to retrieve the governor while the men were still in the burning plane.

On the 8th of July mission to Vienna when our air

force had its visitors from England, our group had a visitor of its own. No one knew his name. He was known as the "carpet man." His job was to operate a new device called "CARPET," a sophisticated electronic version of "window" which was supposed to deflect the radar signals used by the flak gunners. Crew 71 inherited the carpet man, and on the way to the target he pointed to the little black box installed on the flight deck, and told us of its many advantages over "window." "One such device," he said, "could protect an entire group." It sounded great and we bought his sales pitch, mainly because we wanted to buy it since we were going to Vienna, where flak would be well represented in the sky.

Our guests from England soon learned how dearly Germany was prepared to pay to preserve their Luftwaffe *in the nest* and *on the wing*. Where aircraft and oil were in jeopardy, they were fighting like cornered rats. The main targets on that mission were airfields that were chockful of newly built fighter planes, oil refineries, and oil storage depots. But no matter what the target, all the groups shared one thing in common: the GAF fighters were up in full force that day. Before reaching the IP we witnessed some excellent P-51 vs. FS-190 dogfights. It was always exciting and dramatic to watch those adversaries square off for battle. The P-47's however, had flown straight to the target area for the express purpose of engaging this maximum GAF effort. Once there, they symbolically shed their coats as they dropped their wing tanks and pitched in for the scrap. That shedding of the wing tanks always gave me chills. They were *our boys*, and they came to fight for *us.*

A ringside seat to an aerial dogfight is an unforgettable experience. It was reported there were well over a hundred German fighters in the vicinity that day, but the battle was so widespread we saw a relatively small portion of it. However, what we did see was enough for us to appreciate what was happening. We were the lead plane in the high box of the first attack unit. As we turned at the IP and I lined up an oil refinery in my sight, the flak seemed unusually heavy for an IP.

"When are you going to turn on that CARPET machine?" came a plaintive voice.

"It *is* on," the carpet man replied tersely.

"Then turn it off," said another voice. The carpet man was too busy twisting dials and adjusting his machine to answer. The flak was getting worse as we approached the dropping point. As we dropped our bombs and peeled off to head home, the flak got downright nasty. Bad as it was, I still took the time and risk to lean over the bombsight to view our results. We scored high again.

"Turn off that FLAK MAGNET!" someone shouted. It was true that this was the most accurate flak we had seen for some time, so it was easy to blame the new electrical device, because it certainly did not keep it away. Who knows, it might even have backfired on us. The carpet man was furious at the snide remarks that kept coming his way.

You've never heard a sales pitch such as we heard on the way home. The carpet man explained all the reasons why it should have worked and how it functioned, but it was tough selling to this crowd. The device probably worked all right, but if Jerry had a

251

spotter plane sitting just off our wing giving Fritz the word on our altitude, it didn't matter how good the thing was, the flak would be right with us.

We never had the carpetbagger (as he soon became known) with us again. We did hear later that some plane in the group inadvertently had left its IFF switch on during the bomb run. If so, this was a serious breach of the rules. The flak gunners can home in on a radio signal, and when they do this, they don't need radar. The CARPET would have been ineffective if this were true.

IFF means "Identification, Friend or Foe?" Each day the wave length of this radio device was changed, and was given to every Allied bomber and fighter pilot before he went up in the air. If two Allied airplanes approached each other, be they fighters or bombers, and each flipped on its IFF switch, they would automatically be identified as genuine Allied aircraft, with American or British crews aboard. No Trojan horse could infiltrate a flight of U.S. planes when IFF was used.

The IFF had another use. In the likelihood of an emergency bailout or ditching in the ocean, the green IFF switch was to be flipped to "emergency," and it would send out a continuous "Mayday" signal until the airplane crashed. All Allied ships were constantly tuned to this emergency channel; so the longer it stayed on, the better the fix that could be made on the stricken aircraft's position.

Whatever the cause of the accurate flak that day, *Hangar Queen* suffered considerable battle damage, and we were glad to be heading home in one piece. We did make it, and our group improved its proficiency rating with a good bomb pattern. Two of our aircraft were lost, and our group was credited with two fighter "kills" and two "probables."

One of the group's pilots pulled a foolish stunt that had us all sweating for awhile. On the way home from Vienna, his plane's left starboard engine was badly damaged, and he had become that dreaded of all entities, a straggler. In an effort to forestall any hungry German fighters, they went down to the deck, to be more difficult to be spotted from high altitude. As they wended their way through a valley, they were surprised to burst out on a landing strip at a German fighter base.

The pilot reacted to this unexpected development by lowering his landing gear and pretending to prepare for a landing. He apparently was buying time to avoid ground fire. His one feathered propeller added authenticity to the maneuver, and the Germans withheld fire. Just as he got to the touchdown point about midway down the runway, the pilot retracted the landing gear, poured the coals to his remaining three Pratt-Whitneys, and sped away without encountering any opposition. To their credit, none of his crew fired on the men standing around near the control tower.

When the plane arrived home and the pilot reported the incident, he was not a very popular person for awhile. What the rest of us could visualize was another "Cotton Tail" situation. We all kept tuned to Berlin Sally for the next day or two for any signs of a declaration of war on the 460th. Nothing ever came of it.

Two of the replacement crews were sent home on a

thirty-day leave. No one could understand it, especially the ones going home. They didn't complain, but the rest of us did. How come these short timers got to go home early? They had hardly gotten their feet wet. The best we could figure was that it was some kind of an experiment.

After a few days, the Eighth Air Force fliers loaded up with some Fifteenth Air Force bombs and gas and set out for home, with plans to bomb some German targets en route. In the meantime, on 9 July the Fifteenth itself had resumed pressure on Ploesti with the limited use of H2X against the smoke defense. This was the same "Mickey" equipment I had tried out several weeks earlier. Six bomb groups tested Gerstenberg's smokepot defense with the new radar bombsight equipment, and the results were somewhat disappointing; Gerstenberg chalked up six more heavies that day.

The Ploesti flak defenses were augmented by giant Wurzburg and Freya electronic early warning equipment that gave them about forty minutes' time in which to close down the refineries and send everyone into bomb shelters. "Gun laying" (tracking) was done with small Wurzburgs, one or two to a flak battery. It was the small Wurzburgs we were after, with our "window" and CARPET jamming equipment.

The smoke pots had taken their toll too. The rings of flak batteries eventually were expanded to put them outside of the smoke coverage. Apparently enough seasick gunners had complained to management. In the great offense-defense struggle for Ploesti oil, the offense countered the smoke defense in another manner. When there were winds above a certain velocity, they dispersed part of the smoke and rendered its cover relatively ineffective. Taking advantage of this, our strategists later would send P-38's in ahead of the bombers to spot the chinks in their armor. This information would be radioed back to the oncoming bomber forces, who had the option to change targets to suit the occasion. In today's football we call it the "quarterback audible." It was cat-and-mouse all the way.

On 12 July, the Fifteenth went in full force to southern France to hit marshalling yards and bridges. It was at Nimes that day that I learned firsthand what I had been taught in bombing school They had emphasized the difficulty of recovering if you let yourself get too far downwind of the target early in the bomb run. We had practiced this at bombing school and I learned then it *was* difficult—even in a single plane situation. We were warned it would be far more difficult with a formation of bombers on your tail. If the bombardier starts out too far *upwind* of the proper course, it is comparatively easy to make a small correction and let the wind blow you back onto the correct "road" to the target. But when he starts out too far *downwind* of the proper course, he must make his corrections into the wind. When he banks into the wind, the wing tends to blow the plane farther downwind of the intended course. What would normally be a minor correction from an upwind position becomes a major correction from a downwind position.

At Nimes our target was a certain marshalling yard, and we were leading the second attack unit of eighteen planes. The flak at the IP was unusually heavy for a French target, and it was fairly accurate. My turn onto the target, though, wasn't very accurate. I picked up what I thought was the aiming point and instructed the pilot to level out at a certain heading. He did just that and I began my early course corrections. Very routine up to this point. We were well into the bomb run and I was beginning to set up the range hair synchronization, when it dawned on me that the target area didn't look right. All marshalling yards tend to look alike, even though there are distinctive differences. I checked my photos. I *was* wrong. My assigned target was about three miles upwind of my current course—and my stomach about three inches lower than where it should have been. I felt sick.

I first tried to make a small upwind correction, as I did not want to put the plane into the steep bank necessary for a full correction for fear of causing a midair collision, or total chaos in the formation. That move did nothing to correct the problem. I tried another larger correction, and I knew then that I could not make it to the assigned target. The flak exploding around us was the least of my worries. The wild thought then struck me that if a piece of flak would go through my head I wouldn't have to explain this debacle to anyone. I quickly decided I really didn't want that kind of solution. If only I had been upwind of my course, I probably could have made it back to my aiming point.

I gave up and went back to my first target; at least it was a marshalling yard full of freight cars. By now I was upwind of it and had to make a small correction to home in on a new aiming point. Nearly two minutes of my bomb run had been wasted on these aerial gymnastics so I had little time remaining to establish both course and range, but I managed to do so and we had excellent results on this "target of opportunity," as I liked to call it. Others called it a wrong target. I finally learned what they had tried to teach me nearly a year earlier.

I learned something else, too. We had a little fighter opposition on the way home—not much, but enough that we had to fire our guns. Two of our guns jammed and were worthless the rest of the trip. When we complained about the poor quality of ammunition recently, reminding them of all the gun jammings being experienced by others the past few weeks, we were told they knew the quality level was down.

The main purpose of our missions these days was to draw out the Luftwaffe so that our fighters could destroy it *on the wing*. Even though we acknowledged that the destruction of the GAF was a key element of the Allied effort at this time, it didn't give us a very warm feeling to know we were being used as decoys. We realized we meant more than that and didn't like to have it put that way.

While this mission wasn't exactly a rough one, six planes landed at other airfields, due to mechanical problems or a shortage of gas. One plane had to be abandoned near Rome. All the crewmen parachuted safely and returned to the base.

The next day, instead of being our day off, found us on the way back to Porto Marghera. This time, however, we would be passing over the great city of Venice, another highlight on my tour of the famous spots of the Old World. Romantic Venice, with its many canals and gondoliers. One of my boyhood friends, Frank McKenna, had a huge four-by-six painting depicting a Venetian gondolier in action that I had always admired. As a result I had been in love with Venice for years. When the flak began coming up from romantic old Venice, my feeling of love soon faded. This bothered me because I knew Venice was an open city like Florence, and was off limits to our bombing. I didn't like this unilateral interpretation of the rules. However, they were bad shots and no harm was done.

Flak, actual size

Our target was the oil storage tanks, but with the 9/10th undercast the tanks were safe that day. Everyone dropped bombs on whatever he could see through the occasional openings in the clouds. It wasn't a good day. We did arouse some fighters, though, so if our fighters were on the ball perhaps it wasn't a totally lost cause.

It was back again to Porto Marghera the following day, and this time it was 10/10th undercast. Bombs in the ocean again. What a waste! But no one was anxious to land with three tons of RDX bombs aboard. After all, we had plenty more where they came from, or so we thought. That very day a new order was posted. From now on any bombs not dropped on the target were to be brought back to the base. It seems a shortage of bombs was anticipated. Some bomb-carrying Liberty ships had been sunk by the U-boats and the supply was running low.

55th Wing clobbers Friedrichshafen, 20 July 44

Some cynic observed it would take a lot of gall to send us up with reject ammo to sucker the GAF to their doom, with no bombs in our bomb bays; so naturally they didn't want us to run out of bombs. Jettisoning over four hundred bombs in the ocean when the target was unassailable did seem wasteful, but it remained to be seen how many would actually bring home a load of bombs the next time we ran into a 10/10th undercast situation. A proviso in the order did state that a plane with battle damage, or any substandard operating characteristics, would be excused from the requirement, and could salvo in the ocean.

That afternoon we were treated to an excellent USO show. A small stage was set up in the camp area, and we all sat around on the ground or on trucks and heard and saw some very pretty and quite talented girls singing and dancing for us. The juggler seemed to have three arms. But the highlight of the show was the surprise entrance of Joe Louis, who was then World Heavyweight boxing champion, and owner of a long succession of knockout victories. We welcomed Joe Louis's visit as we had a little succession of victories going ourselves. They weren't exactly all knockout victories, but we figured that each time we made it home was a victory of sorts.

Chapter 12

MOONLIGHT ESCAPE

There was to be no rest for crew 71 and its mascot, Smitty's little stuffed horse with the growing list of cities on it. The only one to rest would be *Hangar Queen*. She was in for some repair and patch-up work, and would be out of action for a few days.

The 15th of July marked the fourth straight day Hammett & Co. would go on a mission. It was back to Ploesti again. From this date on, every group would have a Pathfinder plane assigned to it for Ploesti missions. Hopefully the trained operator aboard could read the strange images on the radar scope. This, coupled with the P-38 early-bird target reports, was expected to swing the edge back to the offense.

The prize in this big chess game was Ploesti itself— "kaput" if we won, and a continuing oil source for Hitler if Gerstenberg won.

The new early-bird warning mode of attack was mainly possible because the Luftwaffe was beginning to show signs of attrition and was noticeably weaker. Our three-pronged campaign to destroy the GAF was paying off. Perhaps our "decoy" role was not as bad an idea as it first sounded.

Over six hundred heavies were to hit Ploesti, and some of the B-24 groups were scheduled in at higher altitudes than ever before. We were accustomed to seeing the B-17's up there at 30,000 feet, watching their poor brethren down below. Our group was one of those slated for over 24,000 feet. We knew 20,000 to 22,000 feet was our normal bombing altitude with a full bomb and gas load. We also knew the difficulty of reaching a 24,000-plus altitude. The few thousand feet farther away from the flak guns was of course welcome, but we were concerned about reaching the new heights assigned us. It was all part of the changing offensive and defensive strategies in the battle for Hitler's oil and his Luftwaffe. As the fighter force dwindled, more flak guns were added at Ploesti, hence the higher bombing altitudes.

As our group crossed the Adriatic and began its climb on course at a little steeper angle than usual, we all were nervous. Even the planes seemed nervous as they inched their way up past the 22,000-foot mark. Apparently atmospheric conditions were working against us. The heavily loaded bombers shuddered and shook as superchargers struggled to furnish enough oxygen to feed the thirsty Pratt-Whitney engines. Without the superchargers the engines would be nearly worthless at that high altitude.

Many of the struggling bombers began to show evidence of stalling at around 23,000 feet. As they continued their climb the pilots began making moves to prevent this. Bomb bay doors would open. A 1,000-pound bomb would fall out. The pilot had bought a little time, and could stay with the formation for awhile. No one wanted to reach a stalling situation where the airplane would simply fall over on one wing and start into a dive, or worse, into a spin. The line between stalling and almost stalling is a thin one, and once you cross it, you have your work cut out for you. Bombs began falling out of nearly all the planes in our group. Soon some were discarding their second bomb as the altitude needles crept up toward the 24,000-foot mark. It was this or drop out of formation and go home alone. The decision was simple. Hang in there at all costs! It would be known later that some pilots had dropped all their bombs before they even started the bomb run. *They would rather face the flak with an empty bomb bay than drop out of formation and go home alone.* We had dropped one bomb before we reached the IP and, despite this relief, our engines were suffering.

As we started down the bomb run we experienced a few bursts of flak; not much, but accurate—so accurate that some of it hit our No. 3 engine.

"Smitty, come down here; we're losing oil pressure," barked Dusty. Smitty climbed down from his top turret and joined Dusty and Charlie in the cockpit, after hooking up his oxygen hose to the extra cockpit Auto-Mix, and his intercom to an extra jack.

"There goes the supercharger on No. 1!" shouted Smitty.

"Newby, drop another bomb!"

"Roger," and we were half a ton lighter.

"No. 2 Super is out," cried Smitty as he worked furiously with some valves and controls for the hydraulic and engine oil system.

263

"Newby!"

"OKAY!" And we shed another half ton as another bomb fell away.

Dusty cut in with "The oil pressure is dropping fast on No. 3. I better shut it off and feather the prop. We are starting to lose altitude."

"We can't afford to lose No. 3 with two supers out," suggested Smitty. "There is an oil reserve for feathering, even if all the oil is gone in the engine itself, so let's milk it along for awhile."

"See if you guys can save the engine," chimed in Charlie. "And get rid of the rest of the bombs, Mr. Bombardier!" He didn't want to go home alone.

I salvoed the remaining bombs and closed the bomb bay door to give us some additional lift. Open doors create significant drag. Every little bit would help at this stage. Then I looked at my parachute and made certain it was at the end of my umbilical cord. I had the feeling we were nearing the end of our rope, too.

"Navigator, tell us where we are in case we have to abandon ship," directed Charlie.

"About thirty miles northwest of Bucharest," replied Sherm.

"Keep us posted."

"Anyone remember the address of that hideout in Bucharest?" asked an adventuresome voice.

"You couldn't find it anyhow," answered Tyrone.

"Oil pressure is dropping rapidly," cut in Dusty.

"Shut off No. 3 and feather it," ordered Charlie. With that, Dusty shut off the right inboard engine and reached toward the feathering buttons over his head. He activated the third button, but the propeller did not rotate into feathering position.

"We're too late," said Dusty. "The oil pressure is too low to operate the feathering system." Apparently the feathering oil reserve had been hit by flak, too. Our gamble to save No. 3 had failed, and we also lost the opportunity to feather it. The propeller could windmill from then on, from the force of the air rushing by. We had not been keeping up with the group in their altitude maintenance, due to the power loss from the inoperative superchargers, and now, when we were about one thousand feet below and behind the formation, we lost an engine.

"That's it," said Hammett reluctantly as he shoved the nose down to start a dive that would compensate for the sudden loss of about a quarter of our power. He put a little curve on the dive, so when we leveled out at 13,000 feet we were heading for Italy—alone. We were an instant straggler, 500 miles deep in enemy territory, with a windmilling propeller on a dead engine, two engines without superchargers, and only one complete engine.

The windmilling propeller was a serious problem. A feathered engine, while not pulling its fair share of the load, is at least not a detriment. A windmilling propeller causes a tremendous drag, resulting in an additional twelve miles per hour loss of speed. The inactive superchargers, loss of an engine, and windmilling propeller all combined to cut our air speed to about 135 mph, just a shade over stalling speed. Our problem would be to try and maintain the 13,000-foot altitude at that speed.

We had two orders of business. One was to transfer the reserve gas from the Tokyo tanks into the main tanks and then set up the bypass mode so that all four main tanks would feed the remaining three engines. The windmilling dead engine would be cut off from the main fuel system to prevent it from siphoning off valuable gas and expelling it into the air. The second order of business was to shed excess weight. We were not holding altitude, as the slowly moving altimeter attested. Out went the flak suits, followed by everything that wasn't nailed down. Even some leather flying jackets went out the window. Breaking the ammo belt and throwing out thousands of rounds of .50-caliber machine gun ammunition was like cutting off a leg. We left about a dozen rounds in each machine gun. A big one-second burst for each of the ten guns was our only defense against an ME-109, or perhaps a whole flight of them. The jettisoned ammo was the most significant weight loss, so we had to take the calculated risk of not meeting fighters. Someone asked Sid if we should throw out Bob Kaiser. Sid agreed that he could stay.

Everyone checked his parachute harness and tightened the leg straps just a little. This was no drill. Our odds of making it to the base were not very encouraging. Sherman Wood was experiencing the biggest challenge of his life. On the wall at his navigational training center, several fliers were depicted in a big yellow inflated rubber life raft, pushing away another flier still in the water. The caption read: "There's no room in a life raft for the navigator!" The message came clear now. The fate of the crew—getting to some point of safety—was largely on the navigator's shoulders.

The weight-shedding slowed the rate of drop, but

did not stem it. It would be steady downhill all the way, and Sherm knew the consequences of our relentless descent. We still had the Dinaric Alps to cross. The entire coastal area of Yugoslavia is one series of mountain ranges after another, with peaks of six-, seven-, and eight-thousand feet—a formidable barrier for a disabled B-24 limping along at near stalling speed and not able to maintain altitude.

"Smitty, give Sherm a reading on our gas supply," directed the pilot. "Sherm, when you get this information, let me know how far we can go under present conditions," he added.

After getting the gas figure from Smitty, Sherm advised Charlie, "If we can level out about four thousand feet, and if I can find my way through some mountain passes, we just might make it to Italy."

"There's a whole bunch of fighters behind us, very high." Good old Sid was on the ball, but his report gave nine others a chilling moment.

"Sorry, Navigator, but I'm heading for cover," yelled Charlie as he turned off course and headed for a large bank of clouds. After about ten minutes in the clouds we emerged into daylight; all eyes searched the heavens for black dots.

"Are you relocated yet, Sherm?" asked Charlie.

"Yeah, I know where we are," he replied.

"Yugoslavia, I'll bet," added some comedian. By then we were down to 3,000 feet.

The next report of fighter planes was good news, as three P-38's pulled up alongside of us and the pilots waved. We not only waved back, but must have looked like windmills in our efforts to tell them we were in trouble and would they please stay with us for awhile.

Apparently our four seemingly operative propellers must have looked normal to them, and since we were afraid to break radio silence for fear of attracting the enemy, they were unaware we needed help. They did signal us with a blinker, but we must have tossed ours overboard in our earlier frenzy and could not communicate our plight to them. They waved, dipped their wings, and flew away.

Alone again, and dropping.

Finally Sherm said, "There is a river valley out to the sea about a hundred miles north of our course, and I think we can go through it at about two thousand feet."

"Let's do it!" said Charlie, in answer to a nod from Dusty.

By now Dusty had lowered the Fowler flaps to gain a little more wing area, and thereby lowering the stalling speed of our staggering aircraft. While this was effective in helping us to maintain altitude it did cause us to consume gas at a greater rate. You win some and you lose some.

While Smitty was busy working with the pilots, I had been riding up in the top turret, whirling around looking for German fighters. If I had seen any, I don't know what I would have done, with all of my two dozen bullets in the two guns.

All of us were manning machine guns, which was the procedural thing to do under the circumstances even if all the guns were empty. We had been taught that nothing will attract a fighter to come in on the attack against a lone plane more quickly than limp guns that are obviously inoperative. The rule was to track them with your empty gun; the fighter pilot wouldn't know it was empty. If you had no gun, you should point a stick at them.

We had thrown out the two waist guns and there were no sticks around, so if there had been a fighter visitor, someone would have had to point his arm out the window at it.

"Fire in No. 3 engine!" reported Bob Kaiser. More chills. I mentally started to count to ten; I knew we would be goners if we didn't soon leave.

"It's weird," said Sherm, who had checked it from his side window. "Not a big fire, but just a little flame inside the front of the nacelle, and it appears to be from the friction of the propeller shaft turning without lubrication. The fire is contained in the front cavity of the engine. I don't think it will spread."

"Kaiser, get out of your turret, watch the fire, and keep me posted," requested Charlie. We were starting to lose some raw gas from the area of the dead engine. Apparently a gas line had broken, or a fitting had come loose. With this development, it looked doubtful that we would be able to make it across the Adriatic to Italy.

"Navigator, how far are we from Vis?" asked the pilot.

"We have about thirty more miles to go through this valley, and Vis is about seventy-five miles south of the point where we come out," Sherm answered.

"Italy?"

"Another hundred miles."

"Do we have enough gas for Italy?"

"No!"

"Dusty, call the tower at Vis for landing instructions."

Vis is a mountainous island about fifty miles off the mainland, and for some strange reason it was held by the British, who had hacked a small fighter strip out of the hills. They based a few fighter planes there that would fly over and molest the German troops once in a while, or perhaps just fly "recon" flights over the mainland. They had their own little piece of the war. Vis was an approved emergency landing strip for Fifteenth Air Force bombers that could not make it across the ocean. Any pilot landing there had to file a detailed report to the Fifteenth AF headquarters, explaining why the landing was necessary. They didn't want the place loaded with bombers, since such a condition would invite bombing attacks by the Germans. On one particularly mean day, thirty-seven bombers had landed at Vis.

We wound our way through the mountains and followed a river out to the sea. I immediately felt a sense of relief, and pride in our navigator for pulling us through so far; we could not have gone over the mountains. I also felt a tremendous vibration enveloping the airplane. The plane shuddered so much, my jowls shook; I could actually feel my cheeks shaking like a bowl of jello on a bumpy road. It's funny how your mind works in stress situations like this. I thought of the then popular song, "It must be jelly, 'cause jam don't shake like that."

The airplane felt as if it were coming apart; and it was. The windmilling propeller had been turning all that time without any lubrication, and it finally got to the shaft. The shuddering of the plane was the result of the turning shaft welding itself to the bearing housing. The propeller and shaft finally tore loose from the engine, cut through the fuselage, and spun its way down to the ground. Luckily, no one was crawling through the passageway from the nose compartment to the flight deck, or they would have been sliced up.

When we opened the bomb bay doors and looked down, all we saw was water. Any airplane that shook and shuddered like this one had been doing was obviously about to come apart, and any sensible person should be jumping out about now. But the water down below just didn't look inviting. No one jumped. Of course the bailout alarm had not been sounded, and we were not supposed to jump unless it did sound. (Try explaining that rule to someone when their plane is on fire.)

Charlie looked back at his crew lined up like blackbirds on a fence, as he later described us, and laughed.

"Come on, get back in here," he motioned. "We're going to make it to Vis." It didn't take much convincing to keep us from jumping into the ocean. Actually, the departing propeller was a blessing in disguise. Suddenly, all was serene again, and we picked up twelve miles per hour speed. We would have been better off had the propeller fallen away two hours earlier.

The tower had told our pilots that the runway was just 3,500 feet long, and we were to use parachutes tied to the waist gun positions to help brake the aircraft. The end of the runway was a sheer drop of over two hundred feet into a pile of huge boulders. The gas leak was getting worse; gasoline was now coming out in a steady stream. This added the new concern of a spark possibly igniting it.

As Charlie turned his sick aircraft into the down-wind leg of the very delicate emergency landing, he was of course quite concerned about the short landing area and the consequences of going past the end of the runway—which would be death to all aboard if the plane went over the cliff. He had given instructions to the men at the waist positions to hook parachutes to two harnesses and attach the harnesses to the two waist gun mounts. At a signal from Dusty, after the plane was safely on the ground and rolling, they were to hold the chutes out the windows and pull the rip cords.

When Charlie turned onto the final approach, he was horrified to see a small open cockpit biplane begin to taxi down the runway from his approach end. The pilot, with his scarf flying, no doubt envisioning himself the great Red Baron and blissfully unaware of the fifteen-ton monster descending upon him, was taking his good old time doing whatever he was doing. Both Dusty and the tower were hollering at the pilot, but he either didn't speak any of the languages being used on him, or else had no radio. He kept on his merry way. There was no turning back for us; the red warning light was on, signaling that our fuel was about gone.

What happened next was a study in sheer desperation on the part of our two pilots. Charlie held the plane just far enough off the ground to clear the top of the taxiing biplane, and then dropped it to the ground in front of what had to be the most startled pilot in the world at that moment. The plane touched the ground with less than fifteen hundred feet of runway remaining, and death at the end of the road. A B-24 needs about thirty-five hundred feet of runway for a comfortable landing.

At touchdown Charlie cut the engines, Dusty yelled, "Throw the chutes!" and the men in the waist did their jobs. The shock of the chutes opening was like being hit by a baseball bat, even to us who were braced in crash-landing position. It threw the parachute handlers in the waist up against the bomb bay bulkhead, and they were lucky to escape uninjured.

After the initial slowdown, both pilots stood on the foot brakes while they saw the brink of the cliff approaching at a diminishing rate of speed. I was spared that sight, and was in fact ignorant of the biplane incident. When we were rolling along the ground, I thought our problems were over. Sherm, Bob Kaiser, and I smilingly gave each other the "OK" high sign, blissfully unaware that we were seconds away from death if Dusty and Charlie couldn't summon up a few ounces of reserve strength. They did just that. Somehow, from somewhere, that extra strength came to them, and they braked the stricken bomber to a screeching halt.

As I reached out to congratulate them on a fine landing, I wondered why both pilots were white as sheets. Neither of them said a word. They couldn't. I turned white, too, when I climbed out from under the bomb bay and saw the nose of our plane protruding out over the edge of a cliff that seemed a mile straight down to the rock-strewn ocean shore. *The nose wheel was just inches from the edge.* When we talked to the tower operator, a pilot himself, he told us it was the finest emergency landing he had ever seen, and all he ever saw were emergency landings at his field. He had thought we had no chance of stopping in that short distance; he had seen a number of other disabled bombers go over the cliff.

Because there were two other heavies parked on the field, the operator was a little nervous about having a third one in camp. There was a strong likelihood of a bombing attack that night. We weren't too anxious about being on the receiving end of a stick of bombs, so we agreed with his suggestion of leaving on a boat scheduled to arrive after dark and depart before dawn. He treated us to a dinner of sorts and to strong coffee, and afterward we went on a short tour of the desolate island. It was one big rock, just like Capri, but somehow not as romantic. It was sort of ridiculous to be casually walking around sightseeing while being vulnerable to aerial attack.

We learned later that as we were wending our way to Vis, the largest bomber force ever to hit Ploesti dropped a record 1,526 tons of bombs. Although 607 planes flew into the flak zone, only 587 flew out. It was the heaviest loss to date on a high-level mission to that target.

After dark a boat did arrive. It was not exactly the *Queen Mary*, but it was an ocean-going vessel, a small one with a single smoke stack. We were given a carton of K rations and a hearty handshake, bidden farewell by our host, and left to our own devices on the deck of this Yugoslavian ocean liner. We weren't assigned sleeping quarters; we were just told to find a comfortable spot on deck and go to sleep.

A motley crew we were, but as bad as we looked, we didn't compare to the band of Australian marines already on board. The cleanest-shaven one probably hadn't seen a razor for two weeks. They were the toughest bunch of men I had ever seen at one time, and I was instantly glad they were on our side. They of course had just come from some hard fighting in Yugoslavia, and had no intention of being inspection-ready for a few U.S. fliers who were coming aboard.

Of more interest to them than the new arrivals was some Yugoslavian whiskey in a plain bottle. I supposed it was something like Kentucky moonshine, so when they offered me a swig my first inclination was to refuse it. But with about ten pairs of steely eyes boring in on me, it didn't seem the prudent thing to do. In a sort of hands-across-the-ocean gesture I accepted. That was a mistake. I tipped up the bottle, as all who had preceded me had done, and took a tentative taste. How I managed to keep it down and maintain some degree of politeness I'll never know. It was beyond belief. My throat and stomach burned as if they were on fire. Aside from that, I did enjoy hearing all the Aussies' battle stories and their raw humor.

We roamed around the deck in the semidark, with the only light coming from the bright moon that was shining down upon our escape from Yugoslavia. The boat was showing no lights, except for a few lighted cigarettes here and there. I climbed up on some rope and looked into a window that offered a view I wasn't expecting. There below me was the wardroom of this miniature ocean liner, and seated around the elegantly set table were the captain and his top officers. After the deck scene, it was a shock to see a lace tablecloth, exquisite china, cut glass tumblers, sterling silver, and uniformed waiters attending to the diners' every need.

I was angry at first. I thought, "America is financing the war and these foreigners are living it up, while we who come over here to save them choke on K rations." Then it occurred to me that it was their boat and I *was* getting a free ride to safety. I told myself, "So shut up, Newby, and count your blessings." With that, it struck me as funny and I decided to do something about my situation. Sleeping coiled up on a pile of rope on deck didn't seem a good arrangement to me. Some of the fellows had discovered a room at the ship's stern and had climbed into the tiered bunks. It was hot and stuffy, so I felt there had to be a better way. Although we were told to stay on deck, except for using the cubbyhole at the stern, I decided to see what was behind a certain door. There were some steps. At the bottom of the steps was a long hallway, with a door every eight or ten feet. I had the feeling I was on to something, so I quietly tried the first door. It was locked. So were the next two. Then I found success. The door opened into an empty stateroom; I went in and locked it behind me. I didn't want snoopers like me coming into my private room. I had struck gold! A freshly made bed, covers turned down, with clean white sheets exposed. The room even had a sink with some soap and clean towels. After taking a sponge bath, I put on my pajamas and hit the purloined sack for a good night's sleep.

I was probably the only U.S. Air Force man in history who ever slept in striped flannel pajamas, in a real bed, on a midnight escape boat from Yugoslavia. The reason I was able to wear pajamas was that I came prepared, since pajamas of course were part of my flying gear. In the morning, after washing up and nervously using a straight razor that was provided, I went up on deck to see how the other half was living. I survived my first straight-razor shave reasonably well with just a few little nicks and cuts. As I joined my crew for some K ration cheese and crackers, I casually commented that I usually did not sit around eating breakfast with a bunch of unshaven bums. With that they noticed my shaven face. I naturally gave them a full description of the white-sheeted regulation bed I had enjoyed that night. My popularity probably was at an all-time low about that time. We spent some twenty hours on that boat, finally landing at Monopoli about forty miles south of Bari. There seemed to be no military activity at this little seaport, and we had no way to communicate with the Fifteenth Air Force headquarters in Bari, so we cooled our heels awhile, trying to decide what to do. It occurred to us that we would be considered missing in action, since we doubted that the Vis people would have contacted Bari. Then we began speculating on how many of our belongings would still be there when we got back. We knew of some cases where crews took two or three days to get home, only to discover that the others had helped themselves to their clothes and other items of value. I remember one guy who couldn't even get some of the looters to give him back his clothes.

Our delightful K rations were all gone and we had no money, except the forty-eight dollars in each of our escape kits and my lucky silver dollar I had carried on every mission. My mom had given it to me for a good-luck piece on my last visit home. We debated about whether we could count dinner in an Italian cafe as a proper expenditure for an "evadee." Were we really evadees? The consensus was that we weren't in enemy territory, and therefore weren't eligible to spend it. We decided that if worst came to worst, we could borrow some of the money. What *was* the money for? We had been told it was to be used to buy our way out of trouble or to bribe people for favors if we were shot down over enemy territory. I never had seen how forty-eight dollars was going to make or break a guy four hundred miles behind the line. I had always been intrigued with the idea of writing official-looking IOU's for vast sums and signing for the United States Government. We had been told our government would honor any such document we had to use to help our evasion efforts. We discussed how big a figure we would dare use. I reasoned that any sum a person asked for was good enough for me. I said I thought it would be interesting if, in seeking help, I wrote an IOU for a million dollars, signed President Roosevelt's name, drew a fancy looking seal, and some joker submitted it to our government after the war. We all decided we should not put our own names on such an instrument.

That was good conversation, but it wasn't getting us fed and it wasn't getting us to Bari. While we were still talking, a U.S. Navy LCI pulled up to a dock about a quarter of a mile away. The official greeting party that met them consisted of ten raunchy-looking Army Air Force men in mismatched uniforms, wearing parachute harnesses. Eight were carrying chest packs; one had a stuffed horse under his arm inscribed with names like Ploesti, Munich, and Mostar; and one clean-shaven greeter had rolled-up pajamas under his arm and a strange blue sack on the back of his harness. The ranking officer of the ship was sympathetic to our plight and offered us a ride to Bari, but not until the next morning. We were not in any big hurry, so we accepted. The war would have to wait. That night we all had a decent meal and slept on the Navy ship.

The Navy dumped us off at a pier in Bari harbor, from where we hiked to the mainland, a little band of scraggly refugees. We approached a row of beautiful new tall buildings gracing the harbor that Mussolini had dreamed of making a major showplace. The Fifteenth Air Force headquarters, located in one of the new structures was our target on this mission. We walked down the immaculate halls; Charlie Hammett was finally able to file a report on why we had landed

279

at Vis; he also had them notify our group that we were safe. After a debriefing, we were sent to the hospital for examination, delousing, and a good night's sleep in a real bed. Our truck delivered us back to our base the next afternoon, where we found all our belongings intact. I learned then that I had been promoted to first lieutenant the day I was on the LCI to Bari, but I was saddened to learn also that fellow Pennsylvanian Paul Grinnell and his crew had been lost on the Ploesti mission. Paul had been my pilot on the trip overseas.

Later that afternoon we attended a special meeting for all flying personnel. We had always had it drilled into us that under no circumstances were we to reveal more than our name, rank, and serial number if we were shot down and captured. In the face of all this training and our sincere intentions to abide by all the rules, it was indeed a shock to hear the man on the stage say, "Forget all the name, rank, and serial number business. If you are captured, tell them anything they want to know." We looked at each other in disbelief. The rationale was that the Germans knew just about everything any of us could have told them anyway, so there was no reason to suffer a tough interrogation. We were being told that the war was about over. We had nearly destroyed their oil, the German air force was on its last legs, and it was only a matter of time until they quit. The information we knew, like our base location, names of commanding officers, facts about our airplanes, and so forth, would do them no good. "So talk all you want if captured."

* * *

The day after our return, our group went to Munich and suffered its worst loss ever. Out of thirty-two aircraft that made it to the target area, one had an engine shot out by flak before it reached the IP and limped home alone, seven were shot down by flak, four made emergency landings at friendly fields, and fifteen suffered flak damage. Two crewmen were injured. It was no surprise when we were told that flak defenses had been substantially increased since Munich had become a common major target for both the Fifteenth and the Eighth. Two more of our original squadron crews were among the seven shot down. Little damage was done to the target, due to the 9/10th to 10/10ths undercast. The "Mickey Operator" leading our attack was on his first mission and was of no more value than our regular bombardiers. Our group filed a report to Wing asking that they not send us any more inexperienced H2X operators.

Exactly one week after our three-day trip to Ploesti, we found ourselves on our way back there again. We had company, as over 500 heavies accompanied us while we collectively unloaded 1,334 more tons of bombs on Hitler's oil. Despite our pounding, Ploesti wouldn't quit; but we did have them on their knees. Again it was the old story of a 10/10ths undercast, which was Gerstenberg's best defense. A Pathfinder plane led our group. Because of the undercast, we never did find out how much damage was done to our target, the American-owned Romano Americano Refinery.

Flak was heavy and fairly accurate, but we escaped with no losses and relatively little flak damage to any of our planes. Our tinsel tossers must have been on the ball. Fighters made a few passes at our low box and didn't seem to do any damage. The other groups did not fare as well as we did. Twenty-four bombers were lost that day—the worst loss of the entire high-level campaign against Ploesti.

Oil had a little rest from the Fifteenth, as we headed for France to help pave the way for ANVIL (the invasion of southern France that we all knew was coming). Most of the groups hit airfields. We drew the airfield at Valence, where we unloaded our "frags" with a good bomb pattern. No flak, no fighters. While it wasn't the thrill and satisfaction of weathering a heavily defended target, a milk run like this was certainly welcome once in awhile.

On the way home, a gunner in another plane in our squadron discovered a cluster of six frag bombs hanging up in the bomb rack, and decided to put the safety pin back in before landing. He should have called the bombardier, but he decided to be a good Joe and do it himself. He reached in between the rear grouping of three frags, with the pin in his fingers, intending to place it in position about fourteen inches in from the rear. In order to do this he had to insert his arm up to the elbow with the three bombs encircling his forearm. There was nothing wrong with this; it was the only way to do it. The only thing he did wrong was to grasp the salvo torque bar that ran the length of the bomb bay near the ceiling with his other hand. In grasping the bar he inadvertently turned it and caused the bar to release the entire 120-pound frag cluster. His arm was trapped in among the three rear frags, and the frag cluster took his arm with it. With the arm vent the gunner.

The bomb bay doors were closed at the time, but bomb bay doors were not intended to support the weight of a man, or a falling bomb—certainly not both. The closed doors burst open and slowed down his exit from the plane; he managed to free himself from the bomb and grab the catwalk momentarily. His body was then hanging outside, buffeted by the airstream. Another crewman rushed up and grabbed his arm, but his meticulously oiled leather flying jacket was too slippery for his would-be rescuer to maintain a grip, and he slipped away to his death.

The Hermann Goering Tank Works in Linz, Austria, had just been completed, and a big dedication ceremony was planned for 25 July. It was thought that Goering himself might even show up. The 460th was scheduled to be an uninvited guest for the gathering. We had been told about the big grand opening event, so it added a little extra zest to our efforts that day. We arrived on the scene as planned and were welcomed by a surprisingly heavy flak barrage that was only moderately accurate.

The day was beautiful, not a cloud in the sky; but a good smoke screen was set up that made sighting difficult. Bomb aiming was done by offset sighting; the bomb pattern started where it should have and progressed into the smoke obscured area, and from all indications the main body of bombs hit the tank works. It looked like a very successful mission, especially considering the fact that we lost no planes and had only one minor personal injury. The three other groups in our wing seemed to be impacting their bombs right on top of ours.

As smoke rose from the tank works and we peeled off the target, Sid, from his front row seat, came through with a great exit line.

"Welcome to the club, Hermann!"

The next day the following telegram was posted on the bulletin board, from General Acheson, Commanding General of the 55th Wing:

TO ALL GROUP COMMANDING OFFICERS
CONGRATULATIONS ON A FINE JOB AT LINZ PERIOD
I DON'T THINK WE WILL HAVE TO GO THERE ANY MORE END ACHESON

Chapter 13

MASSACRE OVER THE ALPS

RESTRICTED

HEADQUARTERS C-UPD-bmr
FIFTEENTH AIR FORCE
APO   520

GENERAL ORDERS)   24 September 1944
NUMBER R604) E X T R A C T
Citation of Units..........................I

SECTION I   CITATION OF UNITS

Under the provisions of Circular 333, War Department, 1943, and Circular 89, North African Theatre of Operations, 10 July 1944, the following units are cited for outstanding performance of duty in armed conflict with the enemy:

460TH BOMBARDMENT GROUP. For outstanding performance of duty in armed conflict with the enemy. On 25 July 1944, this Group was assigned the task of attacking and destroying the Zwolfaxing Airdrome Installations which were being used for the assembly of ME109's as well as for repair of enemy fighters and for enemy fighter operations. A successful completion of this mission would inflict a crippling blow to the already dwindling strength of the enemy air force. Throughout the day and night prior to the attack, the ground crews worked untiringly and enthusiastically to have their aircraft at the peak of mechanical perfection to insure the success of this vital operation. On 26 July 1944, twenty-four (24) B-24 type aircraft, heavily loaded with thousand pound bombs, took off, and as lead group of a wing formation, set course for the objective. Intercepted by approximately thirty (30) enemy fighters, displaying outstanding professional skill, coordination and courage, the gunners threw such an effective curtain of protective fire from the extremely tight formation, that the enemy fighters were forced to break off their attacks and withdraw. Severe and adverse weather conditions were encountered and with the target completely obscured by dense cloud formations, the Group was forced to drop to a lower altitude. Without hesitation the Group descended into barrages of heavy, extremely intense and very accurate enemy antiaircraft fire. Three (3) aircraft went down in flames, two (2) were so badly crippled that they were forced to drop from the protective formation, and fourteen (14) others sustained severe damages. Unwavering, despite the intense enemy opposition, these gallant crews continued through the enemy defenses for a highly successful bombing run, inflicting grave damage to vital enemy installations. Through this outstanding achievement the enemy was deprived of one of its most important fighter assembly and repair bases, thus effectively and seriously crippling enemy operational efficiency at a time of great importance. By the great determination, outstanding professional skill and gallantry of the combat crews, together with the superior technical skill and devotion to duty of the ground personnel, the 460th Bombardment Group has reflected great credit upon themselves and the Armed Forces of the United States of America.

By command of Major General TWINING:

R. K. Taylor
Colonel, GSC
Chief of Staff

A TRUE EXTRACT COPY:

OFFICIAL:
/s/J. M. Ivins   /s/William S. Donaldson, Jr.
Colonel, AGD   Adj. 460th Bomb Gp (H)
Adjutant General

-1-

RESTRICTED

The Zwolfaxing raid at Vienna had taken a heavy

toll of our group and, when the weather turned bad for three straight days of stand-downs, no one complained. Again, if you asked someone what the weather was like outside, they would look up at the overcast sky and say, "Beautiful!" Our group was fortunate to miss the 28 July trip to Ploesti. Only 349 planes made it to the target, and suffered one of the highest losses of the campaign when twenty were lost to Gerstenberg that day.

For centuries the city of Buda and Pest sat across the Danube from each other, joined by several bridges. Then in 1872 they became joined in name. Budapest became the capital and the largest city in Hungary. On 30 July 1944 the 55th Bomber Wing set out to separate the city again, at least physically, by removing the one remaining bridge joining the two parts of the famed metropolis. Our group, however, was not assigned the bridge, but was scheduled to destroy the Budapest/Duna aircraft factory.

Our planes were loaded with a full complement of bombs, ammo, and the maximum load of gasoline. That was bad enough, but our real problem was that there was no wind for takeoff. A full load and no wind spelled trouble, as our relatively short runway was not long enough for the fully loaded bombers to be assured sufficient airspeed for lift-off. Every mph of headwind added that much more valuable lift, so badly needed at the critical takeoff point.

Hangar Queen was the second plane in line for takeoff that morning. As we waited, the first plane started down the becalmed runway. When it ran out of runway, it had not yet reached takeoff air speed, and we watched in horror as it plowed into the field beyond the runway, nosed over, and went up in a huge explosion. The towering column of black smoke was a gruesome reminder of an abortive attempt to defy a simple law of physics.

When the starter, standing in a jeep, bravely waved his flag to signal us to take off, our pilot shook his head "no." The starter shook his head "yes." The head-signaling contest went on for a few seconds until someone in authority used his head for what it was intended. Ground crewmen put wooden chocks in front of each wheel. Each chock had a long rope attached to it. The tower instructed both our pilots to apply the brakes and rev all four engines to full throttle. At a signal, the chocks were jerked away and the brakes were released. Our plane shot forward with this new technique as if it had been on an aircraft carrier catapult. We took off without incident, but not without considerable apprehension.

The pilots had also been given instructions to salvo their bombs on the runway if takeoff air speed had not been attained by the time they neared its end; there was no assurance that the new technique would work for all planes. Several of the planes following us did not attain takeoff speed, and had to salvo their bombs. They then circled the area until all of the other planes were airborne so that they could land and call it a day. Salvoing under these conditions sounds dangerous, and there probably was some danger involved; but it *was* an assured remedy for the very serious situation of running out of runway at sub-takeoff speed. The jettisoned bombs did not explode because they were not of the RDX type and an armed fuse was required to detonate them. All they did was

289

break up into hundreds of pieces of TNT that looked somewhat like chunks of brown sugar. Some of the fellows brought small chunks back to their tents for souvenirs.

At the target, flak was moderately accurate, but that was not unusual. What was unusual was the new technique the Jerries were using. Twelve ME-109's dropped bombs on us from about thirty-five hundred feet above our formation. Outside of scaring us somewhat, the new effort was unsuccessful. The bombs exploded harmlessly below our formation. Our target was obscured by smoke from the bombs of the preceding group, so we were not sure how accurate our bombing was. The bridge was also obscured by smoke from exploding bombs, but we thought it was hit. Buda and Pest again. Others hit the nearby oil refineries, so the age-old town knew we were there.

Sherm Wood flew his fiftieth mission that day. When he climbed down out of the bomb bay a few hours later he was grinning from ear to ear. We jealously congratulated him, hoping we could hang on a few more times so he could return the sentiment.

The next day our group stood down, but 154 planes from other groups hit Ploesti again with 435 tons of bombs, and the lightest loss so far. Only two planes were shot down. The July stats on Ploesti seemed to contradict each other. That month the Fifteenth made its heaviest assault on this beleaguered target, with 1,827 bombers crossing its skies and dropping 4,813 tons of bombs on several of its refineries; yet its production for the month rose to 190,000 tons. Ploesti was dying hard. They not only kept the previously bombed units operating, but their defenses shot down

290

seventy-two bombers in July.

After two days of stand-downs due to bad weather, we were ready to resume the destruction of the Luftwaffe. We had them on the ropes and would get them *in the womb* this time. On 3 August it was Friedrichshafen, Germany, nestled on the north shore of Lake Constance, and the site of the Manzell aircraft factory. Across the lake was Switzerland, a little neutral country caught in the middle of a big war.

Throughout our tour of duty, it was an inside joke among all of us that if we ever got anywhere near Switzerland, we would feather an engine and wing it for the promised land. We had heard tales of downed fliers living in swanky resort hotels, drinking fine wines, eating good food, and dating bad girls. They would ski every day in their spare time. That all seemed better than what we were doing. The word also was that if you landed in Switzerland, you had better have some provable malfunction on your aircraft that prevented you from returning to home base. The answer was of course quite simple. Bail out the crew and let the quarter-million-dollar evidence crash to earth. If you are going to do it, do it right! While we all talked a good game about reaching paradise and escaping the rest of the war, most of us chose to try for fifty, and go home holding our heads up.

Our bombing at Friedrichshafen was excellent; the flak was moderate and very inaccurate. There had been no fighter opposition on the way to the target, so we chalked up another milk run as we headed for our base.

Sweet dreams of going home. Just one more mission. German fighter activity had been on the wane for several weeks; Ploesti, the taproot of German might, was on its last legs; Hitler's aircraft factories were a shambles; thousands of German aircraft had been destroyed on the ground, and our own great fighter squadrons were challenging and defeating the GAF at every turn. The United States had complete superiority in the air. The Normandy invasion had been highly successful and our troops were marching south from the northern shores. Our Italian-based troops were moving north at a fast pace, and we had been softening up the French underbelly for ANVIL. Russian troops were moving in from the east and would soon be capturing Ploesti, or what would be left of it.

The outlook seemed so beautiful and rosy, and our euphoria was heightened even more by the breathtaking portrait Mother Nature had painted below us. A cloudscape, if you will, with a half-dozen snow-crested peaks protruding like haystacks on a snow-covered farm. Not a cloud in the sky above us.

Off to our left was another perfect bomber formation, not a single hole in any of its six boxes, white contrails streaming from every wing tip, 360 men thinking our same thoughts. It was a scene worthy of a picture postcard, or even a Christmas card, except for the implication of the bomber formation. A storybook fairyland.

Then it happened. Tail-end Charlie's right wing burst into flames as we looked on. Impossible! Several black specks came tumbling out of the stricken plane, and soon the billowing white parachute canopies could be seen floating down into the clouds near one of the peaks. Then another plane rolled over on its back and more blossoming chutes joined the others on the seeming assault on the mountain peak. Then another . . . and another, and finally a fifth bomber from our neighboring group started down. All of this activity happened in the space of perhaps twenty seconds or so. The twenty or thirty parachutes disappearing into the clouds could have been a parachute invasion, only we knew better.

It was a massacre at 20,000 feet over the Alps, but we did not know how it was happening. There were no flak bursts around. There were no fighters swarming in. What was happening? Our pilots knew. They had tuned in the Bomber-to-Fighter channel on the VHF and heard the plaintive cries for help from the ambushed bombers. A large flight of ME-109's was lurking behind the ill-fated group, lobbing rockets into their midst, while staying just out of .50-caliber machine gun range. They were picking the bombers off one at a time like a duck hunter shooting ducks in the classic manner, last one first and on up to the lead one. The bomber pilots' pleas were heard by our P-38's, and they came streaking to the rescue in time to break up the one-sided match. The GAF was dying hard.

What stroke of fate chose that particular group for the assault? It could have been us. As spectators, we were hypnotized by the unbelievable event happening in front of us. Our trancelike state turned to deep empathy at the realization of what was happening to some two score of men as they landed on the side, or top, of a two- or three-mile-high snow-covered mountain near Innsbruck. We knew their chances of survival were nil.

Our own survival became a matter of some concern, as our old gas hog was up to its tricks again. *Hangar Queen* was burning gas at a rate greater than we could afford and still expect to have lunch in Spinazzola. We landed at Pescara, Italy, about 125 miles short of our base. Pescara was a British air base. During our little interlude there we heard how our British friends had been hitting many of our targets at night. I was surprised to hear they had been to Ploesti several times. Instead of bombing in groups as we did, they went over the target one at a time. They had to dodge searchlights as well as flak and fighters. The thought of *seeing* all that flak bursting at night made me glad we went in during the day. All we usually saw was the smoke from the flak, the red of the actual explosion being barely discernible.

In discussing night versus daylight bombing, the RAF boys didn't think too much of being up there in formation in broad daylight, and we didn't think too much of their methods, so we agreed they could keep their jobs and we would keep ours. Besides, I only had one more to go, and it should be an easy one. We gassed up and continued to Spinazzola.

Two nights later Sherm said good-bye to me. He was leaving for Naples the next day, and I was scheduled up for my fiftieth mission as a replacement on another crew.

Chapter 14

MISSION FIFTY

Our bomb group did have a heart. When someone had completed forty-nine missions, he was usually given something of a choice on his last one. (Somehow Sherm missed out on this deal.) I guess they wanted to send a few home once in awhile to let everyone know it could be done. I was one of the first to be on the verge of completing a tour of duty, so they told me early in the evening where the next day's mission was heading. I passed up two in a row because they sounded like bad ones. I wasn't going back to Ploesti or Vienna if I could avoid it. Let someone else have the honors.

Finally, on 5 August I heard the group was going to southern France the next day. Generally French targets weren't as bad as most Balkan or Austrian targets, so I decided to take this milk run and get my shipping orders cut. I thought it was pretty slick that I was beating the odds like this. I would also be finishing up four days earlier than the ETA date that I had predicted back on D day. In picking this cream-puff target I had to accept a new crew about to go on its first mission, as my crew was not scheduled that day. I didn't consider that too objectionable.

The preflight check and engine warm-up revealed some irregularities in the No. 3 engine, which required the maintenance crew to pull the engine cowling and do some tinkering. I didn't like that, whatever it was, and began wondering how smart I had been to pass up two missions that suffered no losses or injuries for *this*.

In addition to the engine repair, it developed that the pilot's intercom wasn't working. He could not talk to anyone nor could anyone talk to him. I had always been taught that one should not fly an aircraft into combat when the communications system was not functioning properly. This intercom was about as improper as any intercom could be. It did not work at all for the pilot, and there was more interference than normal for the others. When the maintenance chief gave the OK sign on the engine, I immediately told the official in the jeep that we should abort because of the intercom situation. I wanted out of this one. He said it wasn't a valid reason for an abort and ordered us to proceed, even though the group had already gone about forty-five minutes earlier.

Our target was the marshalling yards at Arles, France, and it did offer this world traveler one last fling at some culture, even if I would not be any closer than four miles to where the tormented artist, van Gogh, had cut off his ear.

We were about fifty minutes late taking off and had to fly an intercept course to meet our group out over the Tyrrhenian Sea. They had spent considerable time in formation assembly and the formation itself moved at less than maximum speed, so by flying faster than the formation, we were able to catch up to them about sixty miles out to sea, between Corsica and the mainland.

We were assigned to the number 7 position in the low box of the second attack unit. This was unusual, as we rarely had seven planes in a box. We were in purple heart corner. My first time as Tail-End Charlie—and on my *last* mission! It was a place for rookies, not someone on his fiftieth mission, I reasoned. I was still kicking myself for being where I was because I had no one else to blame. As we approached the formation, I heard a report over the intercom.

"Somebody is shooting at us!"

"Where is it coming from?"

"The bullets are coming *in* from the high right side and *out* the lower left," said one of the eyewitnesses in the waist section.

"It has to be coming from one of the planes in our box," commented the copilot. "They must be testing their guns and have a runaway gun."

"I'm sure it's from number 5," he added, referring to the plane located at two o'clock.

A certain worn part in a machine gun can cause it to continue firing after the trigger is released. All gunners are taught how to handle a runaway machine gun. The procedure is: *first* point the gun away from friendly aircraft, *then* use one of several effective methods of stopping the firing. One method is to twist the ammo belt so it jams the gun. Another is to hook your hat, or cap, onto a bullet in the belt and and let it jam the gun.

* * *

We knew the name of the pilot of the plane from which the stray bullets were coming, and we all vowed to tell him a thing or two about observing that *first* rule—when we got back.

"Every station check for damage, and report," ordered the copilot over his static-choked intercom. All stations reported no apparent damage, and we breathed more easily. Then came the frightening report that made my heart skip a beat.

"I smell smoke!"

"Where is it?"

"I don't know, I just smell it," cried the tail gunner, who was getting a lesson in physics, as had old Sid. Only this time it was smoke from the No. 3 engine and not the Yellow Peril. By now one of the gunners had looked out the right window; he saw the heavy smoke pouring from the No. 3 engine and wheel recess under the right wing. One of the bullets had hit something and we were on fire.

A B-24 on fire! *We had ten seconds or less!*

"Dump the bombs, bombardier," ordered the copilot. I complied as fast as I could, and closed the bomb bay doors out of force of habit. The pilot, who was getting all his information secondhand from a shouting copilot, made a diving turn and headed our plane due east for the closest land. He would soon learn how deadly serious faulty communications could be.

The next move was to cut the right inboard engine and feather the propeller. That action did not stop the fire, as the fire apparently was not in the engine itself. It seemed to be *between* the two starboard engines, so the No. 4 engine was also shut off, and its

298

propeller feathered. Still the fire raged. Then the landing gear was lowered in a vain hope that the inrushing air might subdue the flames in the wheel recess. That not only did not help, but the extended gear added considerable drag, which increased our problem of maintaining air speed. We were down to two engines, which was bad enough, but when they were both on the same side it made control of the aircraft very difficult. The pilots had done all the right things so far. They were performing like veterans, despite this being their maiden trip, and were managing to keep the aircraft on an even keel with full starboard trim.

Target Ploesti, 16 July 44

The engineer was thinking hard, too. He had shut off the gas lines to the two dead engines and was trying to close all gas lines on the right wing of the plane, in another vain effort—this time to stop the flow of gas to the line that apparently had been severed by a bullet.

Nothing was working, and we were way past the customary ten-second blowup time. I felt we should all bail out, and went up to the cockpit and told the pilot to sound the bailout alarm. He shook his head no and said he was going to head south to friendly territory. Our due east course would have put us over enemy lines. I explained, based on my experience in seeing B-24's on fire, that we were way overdue for blowing up and we should not be concerned about where we got out. I was serious. My hooked-up chute pack attested to that. I tried pulling my rank on him, but he reminded me he was the ship's commander. And he was. In a combat bomber no one, regardless of rank, can overrule the man sitting in the left seat. At least so they said.

The radio man had flipped the green IFF switch to emergency, so he, too, was doing the right thing. I told him to stop sending any more hand messages and get his chute on, but he bravely continued to stay with his radio. I wasn't too anxious to jump out into the middle of the ocean either, so I was standing in the bomb bay, debating with myself about whether I should get out on my own right then, or wait until we were near land. If I could have seen what the men in the waist saw, I would have been out before then.

Although the fire had been contained within the wheel well, the intense heat had caused a large bubble to rise on the top section of the wing between the engines. The audiences in the waist had been watching it grow and knew the end was near. They began

300

yelling over the intercom, that the wing was about to blow up, but *the pilot could not hear them*. The yelling only increased the interference in the copilot's earphones, and in the excitement he either did not comprehend the severity of the message, or failed to communicate it to the very busy pilot fighting to maintain control over his disabled aircraft. The bail-out alarm did not sound.

I was off the intercom as I stood in the bomb bay by the door lever. The radio man was sending a "Mayday" message, which was not necessary with the emergency IFF on. The IFF was sending all the information needed by the Air/Sea Rescue people to find us. Even at that moment, while we were fighting our losing battle to stay in the air, the ASR was already en route on an intercept course to meet us. They would fly their planes and steer their speed launches on this course as long as our signal continued. If it stopped, they would know the plane was down and they would head for the spot so indicated.

I hollered once more to the radio man to leave his post and join me, but he dutifully shook his head and continued sending his Mayday messages. *I had chosen all this—to avoid the death skies of Ploesti!* The irony of the situation was lost on the young man in the bomb bay. He had never heard of Maugham's Baghdad servant.

By now all the men in the rear section had bailed out. They had given their last warning to the cockpit, and when they saw the bubble on the wing mushrooming right in front of their eyes, they didn't need a bailout alarm to tell them what to do. I was made aware of what they already knew by a loud thud

301

and a violent lurch of the plane. I was flung up against the bulkhead, and I felt as if I weighed a ton, but I managed to reach across to the bomb bay door lever and yank on it. The bomb bay doors slid open and all I saw was blue sky. *Blue sky through the bottom of an airplane?*

Suddenly I felt light, and with very little effort I leaped, or seemed to float, out through the open bomb bay into the blue. I didn't understand just what had happened at that moment, but later I figured out that when the right wing had finally burned through and begun to fold, it lost all its lift. Because the left wing was still being powered by two good engines, the plane went into a self-induced clockwise snap roll. The initial torque had created a centrifugal force that added several "G's" to my weight for a split second. Then somehow, as a result of the stricken plane's gyrations, I was popped out the bomb bay door by a reversal of that same force, and actually was above the plane for a moment—hence the blue sky I saw through the open bomb bay doors.

Just as I left the plane I heard the explosion as the fire finally reached the wing gas tanks, and then I found myself above a huge ball of fire. The heat was so intense I thought I was going to be burned alive. I also thought I was falling into the fireball, so I took the only action possible to prevent that from happening. I pulled my rip cord so the chute would brake my descent and the fireball would fall away from me. The fear then entered my mind that all the heat and fire might melt the nylon canopy of my chute. I had only two choices, and no decision could well have been *the* decision. Apparently I chose correctly, as my chute did not melt when it opened.

In my complacency, having chosen a milk run, I, a seasoned veteran of forty-nine combat missions, had committed two inexcusable basic errors in the pre-flight period. I had not opened my two Mae West CO_2 containers to see if I had a fresh CO_2 cartridge in each one. I also had not tightened my leg harnesses to the proper tightness. On every previous mission I had pulled the harness so tight I could hardly walk. On this soft milk run I decided to be more comfortable, so I had not tightened them. Even when things began to get grim, I didn't think about tight leg harnesses. About three seconds out of the airplane, I learned firsthand just why leg harnesses should be so tight they are uncomfortable. The relatively minor discomfort before use would have been a small price to pay, to avoid what happened when the chute opened and the loose leg harnesses went together and under the front of my crotch and up its back.

My joy at not falling into the fireball was so great, I didn't realize what was happening to me until seconds later. Then I *knew.*

The beginning of my parachute descent had some-how taken my mind off the burning airplane spiraling its way to oblivion. Once the shock did wear off, I looked down to see the sickening sight of my airplane in a tight spin, its two good engines still droning their death music, and one burning wing flopping around several hundred yards away. The slow throbbing and surging of the engine sounds seemed unreal. It was more of a wail. *That isn't my plane doing that. There aren't really four men still in there, one at his radio, two at the controls which no longer responded to their frantic efforts, and the navigator still up on the flight deck.* The trapped men were victims of the G's of the centrifugal force induced by the spin. They were pinned to their seats and unable to snap on their chutes and escape through the beckoning open bomb bay doors. *Yes, it was all true.*

Go ahead and fly the plane, the starter had said. *One faulty old intercom isn't enough reason to abort a mission.*

I counted six parachutes in the air below. That surprised me, because I knew four men were still up on the flight deck when I left. One must have somehow made it out through the bomb bay after I did. I surmised that it must have been the navigator, as he was the only one with any kind of a shot at following me out. I don't know how the nose gunner got out. Probably through the nose wheel door.

I thought about the navigator's plight. He had flown his first mission the day before as a replacement on another crew, and his plane suffered a near direct hit as the flak exploded under one wing and flipped the bomber over on its back. The pilot skillfully completed the flip and in fact executed a snap roll; a routine maneuver for a fighter plane, but unheard of in a four-engine bomber. B-24's were not supposed to do snap rolls. Now, here he is in a parachute on his second mission. Only forty-eight more to go!

I suddenly remembered then that I had not checked my Mae West CO_2 cartridges before boarding the plane. Surely, they would be OK. But when I removed the first cap I learned to my dismay why the rule clearly stated, "Check your CO_2 containers on the ground." It was a spent cartridge! Someone had cooled his beer with the cartridge and put it back in the Mae West. The other one was OK.

I pulled the emergency mouth-inflating tube from its hiding place and frantically puffed into it. Half of my Mae West became inflated. I realized that half an inflated Mae West would probably add to my discomfort when I hit the water, as the strap went between my legs; but at least that half was inflated. I could inflate the other half after I entered the water by merely pulling on the cord by the good CO_2 container. So much for that.

The world traveler was finally getting to see the great city of Rome. There it was over to the northeast. I had been scheduled to visit Rome in about a week, but the thought of all that culture and fun was the farthest thing from my busy little mind at that moment. My main attention was directed to my personal discomfort. I was hurting. I wasn't even aware that my eyebrows were singed and my face was mildly burned. The shock of my escape and the breakup of the plane was behind me, and I now had time to think of what would happen next. I weighed a ton with my heavy flying gear and heavy boots and, while I could chin myself with both hands to relieve the pressure in my crotch area, I could not seem to hold myself up with one arm to readjust the leg straps with the other one. All I could do was chin myself and hold it as long as I could, then lower myself and suffer for awhile. The trip down wasn't much fun.

The navigator in me somehow compelled me to record the time of this unusual event. I noted that it was 0805 hours. More improbable thoughts crossed my mind. "Now I can join the Caterpillar Club." My experience as a world traveler was being capped by a remarkable ending to my combat career. "Wait till I tell Bill Crippen when we all get home." Bill was another high school buddy who was in India at the time. When I returned to the States I did write to the Switlik Parachute Company, who sent me a membership card in the Caterpillar Club, as one "whose life was spared the 6th Day of August, 1944 because of an emergency parachute jump from an aircraft."

All this was happening right over the bay where the Tiber River enters the Tyrrhenian Sea about fifteen miles southwest of Rome. Our determined pilot had brought his crew to friendly territory and near land, but what a price he paid. The explosion had occurred at about seven thousand feet, and as I floated down, I watched with horror as the plane crashed near the middle of the bay. An instant round oil and gasoline slick marked its grave. As I descended toward the same bay, I saw the oil slick grow larger and larger. I seemed to be in a kind of trance. Suddenly I realized I was heading for the breakwater, which consisted of scattered objects that looked like large dominoes, but were actually slabs of granite or some kind of rock. I knew I would become hamburger if I landed among those jagged rocks.

Somewhere I had heard how to control the direction of a parachute. I grabbed a handful of shroud lines and pulled on them. When I did that it seemed half of the canopy collapsed. All I could visualize was a glob of a parachute material looking like a rolled-up handkerchief in a pocket, so I threw the shroud lines back to where I found them and let nature take its course. That was about the only smart thing I did on the entire mission, as it soon became evident I would miss the rocks and land in the bay.

Landing in the bay presented a new problem: my poor swimming ability. I might be able to swim well enough to make it back to a diving board in a small pool, but I was not ready for swimming a half mile or so from the middle of this bay. My Mae West should take care of me in that regard, but then I began to worry about coming up under my chute. I had heard stories about how one can drown if he comes up directly under a chute that is floating on surface with no air bubble under it. *Perhaps I should try and prepare myself for this possibility.* I unhooked my left leg harness, figuring I could unhook the other one just as I hit water. But after looking the whole thing over, I concluded that if I unhooked the second harness too soon, there would be nothing left to keep me with the chute, so I abandoned that clever idea.

The oil slick was growing larger. Although I was swinging back and forth quite a bit and could not stop it, I managed to hook my two hands around the mating fasteners on my remaining leg harness so I could at least disengage myself from my chute as soon as I entered the water. It seemed like a good idea at the time, even though I was all doubled up.

Suddenly the oil slick was everywhere. And with that, I hit the water flat on my back, which knocked the wind out of me. The impact also knocked out all thoughts of unhooking my leg harness and swimming horizontally for awhile, to avoid the shroud lines and canopy. Suddenly, too, I was under water and fairly deep in it, facing a strange dilemma. I didn't think about it as such; I just sensed it. I knew, from my

307

football days, that when you have the wind knocked out of you the instinctive reaction is to fight to get your breathing muscles back in their natural rhythm. I had to temper that involuntary, almost automatic, reaction with the realization that there would be nothing but water to inhale once the breathing started. A sensed concern was that the breathing system might start up while I was still under water, and *could I stop it? Did I want to stop it once it decided to start? It might not start again.*

Aside from the physical considerations, there was still the matter of shroud lines to enmesh my arms and legs, and the canopy to smother me when I reached the surface. There was only one solution to all this: panic! That was the answer. Panic. I pulled the remaining CO_2 cord, and began climbing up the water dog-paddle fashion. Straight up was what I wanted, and straight up I went, probably more from the fully inflated Mae West than from any effective swimming on my part.

I must have done something right, because my head popped out of the water free of the parachute. In a few seconds I was breathing again. Not fresh air as I had expected, but fume-laden air. The surface was covered with 100-octane gasoline and oil, and I was choking and sputtering in my quest to get some air into my starved lungs. Once my breathing started again, I disengaged my harness and let it fall free. I never did look to see if my blue knapsack survived the chute opening.

The small single-engine Piper Cub circling over-head meant the Air/Sea Rescue people had picked up our IFF signal and had done a good job of locating us. As much as I was thrilled to see the plane, I was more pleased to see the rowboat heading my way, even though it was a long way off. At that moment a fact of life was dramatically revealed to me: money has no intrinsic value. Its only value is a promise of some other thing of value later. My escape kit containing forty-eight dollars was floating about three feet away from me to the northwest. To the east and toward shore was a small yellow oxygen tank that had broken loose from the nearby sunken plane. Still in the clutches of panic, although in no real danger since the Mae West was effectively keeping my head above the water with no effort on my part, I struck out for the oxygen tank, completely disdaining the forty-eight dollars that was just one stroke out of my way. The tank gave me just a little more flotation insurance, something all the money in the world could not do for me at that moment.

The fumes from the high-octane gasoline, which were choking me and irritating my eyes, also added to my panic, because I was convinced someone was going to light a match and set me on fire. I even feared the hot sun might ignite the gasoline. With that, I struck out for shore, the oxygen tank tucked under one arm. Four layers of clothing, heavy G.I. shoes and flying boots at the end of my kicking legs and a generally exhausted condition were all more than one flailing arm could cope with. I ended up swimming in a small circle, yelling for help to the two rowboats converging on me. All I got out of my frantic efforts was tired. Finally I stopped and, while waiting for everything to blow up, I was horrified to see a radio antenna sticking out of the water. I had landed about thirty feet from where the plane had crashed into the bay. None of the rest of the aircraft was showing above the surface, just the antenna. All I could envision was the sight of me impaled on the antenna.

I was one of only two people swimming in the bay at the time, and the two boats were there for the express purpose of picking the two of us up, so I must have presented a ludicrous sight shouting, "Over here, over here!" Nothing like a calm American flier shot down on his last combat mission.

As the two boats approached, one of the young men dove into the water and swam over by my side. With a big smile he said something in Italian to reassure me. It did, too. I was never so glad to see anyone as I was to see the strong young swimmer treading water beside me. For the first time I felt safe, even though I must have looked pretty wild at that point.

The two boats converged on their target and nearly crushed me in the process. Two men in one of the boats hauled me out of the water and dumped me headfirst into the bottom of the boat, my feet still sticking out over the side. I was so exhausted I could not move, and felt like a freshly caught big fish. I did not have the strength to climb to a sitting position for a minute or two. Finally I did manage to sit up and discover I had been rescued, and that the sea had not gone up in flames with me right in the middle. The navigator then greeted me from the other boat.

I thanked the young man in bad Italian, saying things like "Bono" and "Grazzi." In the emotion of the occasion, I removed my official U.S. Air Force watch and gave it to him. Another lesson in the value of the moment. It was probably full of salt water and worthless by then, but it was the only thing of value I had and I sincerely meant it to be an expression of thanks and goodwill.

I asked through sign language how many others had been picked up, and they indicated six of us had been fished out of the water. The four men from the waist landed in the sea a short distance from shore, and the navigator, who departed after me but passed me up in midair, had been picked up a few moments earlier by the other rowboat. The four men who landed in the ocean were picked up by the PT boat that had been summoned by our emergency IFF signal. I somehow conveyed to my rescuers there should have been one more man in the water, so we signaled the PT boat which had entered the bay with the other men aboard. When the boat came alongside, I boarded it and asked the commander to start looking for the seventh man.

We went back out to sea, and while in radio contact with the small airplane circling above, spent about an hour searching for another chute and its occupant. How do you know when to stop looking for someone under such circumstances? I didn't even know the man's name. I hardly knew the names of any of the crew members, as I hadn't cared that much about their names at the beginning of the mission. All I wanted was to get the last one over with and go home.

I kept saying, "Let's make one more trip around the area." The ship's commander let me use his binoculars so I could stand on the bridge and survey the ocean for several miles around. He was very sympathetic with my concern and we probably made a few more circles than the situation called for. Finally he told me that with the combined efforts of the airplane and his boat we could not have missed him if he were still afloat. I reluctantly agreed to abort the search and he took me back to the rowboat near shore, which in turn took me up on the beach where a large crowd of townspeople were assembled. One of the plane's main wheels, its tire still inflated, had washed up on the beach and was the center of attraction until I showed up.

I was dying from the nearly one-hundred-degree heat and my heavy flying clothes, so the first thing I did when I landed on the beach was to begin stripping. After removing my boots I peeled off my canvas flying suit. Following that came the kapok-filled lining. Now I was dressed in army garb except that my pants and shirt were winter issue, which were out of style for this kind of weather. My audience wasn't prepared for my next performance. When I removed my pants and shirt and stood there in my striped flannel pj's, the women giggled. Then when I removed my pj's and stood there in my khaki shorts and undershirt, I brought the house down. I guess I was a rather funny sight at that, but I wasn't embarrassed. Somehow the barriers between us—language, civilian vs. military, rescue vs. bystander—all combined to set us apart in different worlds. I was on a lighted stage and they were seated in a darkened theater. I hardly knew they were there.

My parachute had been picked up by one of the boatmen and was lying on the beach. I thought I would snip off the small pilot chute and take it home as a souvenir. The pilot chute is a small canopy several eet square, with umbrellalike struts, and is the first hing to pop out of the chute pack when the rip cord is oulled. As soon as the pilot chute leaves the pack, the struts spring open and this minichute, caught by the onrushing air, pulls the main canopy after it. By the ime I had completed my strip act and put my pants and shirt back on, the parachute had disappeared. There would be a lot of new nylon shirts and undergarments around that town in a few days. No doubt someone in the neighborhood also would be forty-eight dollars richer the next day, when my escape kit washed ashore.

After awhile, a truck came along from Ciampino Air Base near Rome and picked up us six survivors. As we boarded the truck, we looked sadly at the circle of oil in the middle of the bay and thought of the three men under it. I closed my eyes and thanked the Lord for sparing me this day. I guessed someone would come along and lift the plane out of its shallow grave, and take the three bodies somewhere and bury them. I had no idea how they did those things. It occurred to me we had never had a funeral at our air base; yet quite a few dead men were brought home from missions.

I couldn't get the missing man out of my sight, and felt guilty leaving without him as the truck pulled away from the beach and headed for a little pontoon bridge across a canal. It was the first such bridge I had ever seen. We were in an area that had been an active war zone just a few weeks earlier, and the pontoon bridge was a stark reminder that a ground war was still going on under our war.

Our war was over for me. All of a sudden, my lucky

silver dollar was in my hand. Superstitious? Not *me*!
Somehow, though, I was glad I had carried Mom's
good luck piece. I guess I even silently thanked her as
I looked around at the ravages of war and counted my
blessings.

They gave us coffee and rolls at the air base and
telegraphed word to Fifteenth AF headquarters about
what had happened. They reported there were six
survivors, but gave no names, just the aircraft identification. Back at the base, Sherman Wood was over at
headquarters getting his final papers before leaving
for Naples when he heard about the disturbing report
from Air Force Headquarters that a plane had gone
down near Rome—the plane his bombardier had been
on. All he knew was that six had been saved, so he left
for Naples not knowing if I had survived the crash.

At the air base we were outfitted with clean, dry
clothes. I was given torn, faded fatigues with corporal's stripes on the sleeve, and had all my wet clothing
rolled up and stuffed inside my shirt. All I needed to
do was put the ball of clothes on the end of a stick,
and I would have looked like the classic hobo. The
navigator explained how he got out, but I still didn't
understand it. He said he dove from the upper flight
deck, then went *around* the bomb rack while in
midair and out the bomb bay door without touching
anything. He must have been helped, as I was, by the
centrifugal force when the stricken plane did its
untimely semisnap roll.

They offered to fly us home in a C-47 Paratrooper
plane. I was all for it, as were three of the others. The
navigator declared he wasn't ever going up in another
airplane, and he meant it. He and one other of the

urvivors took off, hitchhiking back to Spinazzola. It
vould take them three days to get back to base.

The trip home was a mixture of relief and anxiety.
Ve all sat in our bucket seats, looking across at the
pen door, which seemed like half the side of the
irplane. I didn't even want to go near it. As we were
lying along at above five hundred feet up one valley
nd down another, the pilot looked back at us and
oared with laughter at the sight we presented. Four
cared-looking, formerly brave American fliers sitting
ke a row of pigeons along one side of the interior,
ach with a parachute strapped to his back. I guess we
new the things worked and wanted to be ready for
nything. The joke was that at 500 feet, under emer-
ency conditions, they were of little value. I finally got
rave enough to walk up and visit with the pilots. I
xplained it wasn't easy getting back into the airplane
his soon after our recent experience. The pilot sug-
ested it was the best thing we could have done to
void a prolonged period of fear of flying.

As we touched down at our airstrip, it occurred to
e that we probably were the only bomber crew
nembers in the war to be shot down and then arrive
ack at the base before the rest of their group re-
urned. We beat them home by at least four hours.
My crew had not yet heard of the accident, as
herman had left for Naples directly from headquar-
rs.

The waiting truck took us immediately to head-
uarters for a special briefing on what had happened.
s we were relating our experiences to an intelligence
fficer, Colonel Campbell came rushing in and asked
Lieutenant Newby was OK. I was surprised at his

concern for me. Although I had flown with him on one mission as well as on the special "Mickey" checkout, I didn't think he really knew me, or cared about me personally. It seems he was very upset at someone scheduling a veteran on his fiftieth mission with a crew on its first mission—a charter member of the group, assigned with a rookie crew on its first combat venture.

When I spoke up and said, "I'm Lieutenant Newby," he did a double take at my corporal's stripes and said, "I'm sorry, Lieutenant, I didn't recognize you in that outfit." He was disturbed at our strong feelings that the shots came from one of our own aircraft. We told him the plane from which the shots obviously came, and expressed our opinion they were the result of a runaway gun. (The alleged offending plane's pilot and crew members later denied having any runaway guns, or of firing any guns at or about the time of the accident.)

In my written report of the incident, I spoke highly of the brave actions of pilot Parker Brown and his copilot in holding the aircraft under control in an effort to fly us into friendly territory before ordering a bailout. I also reported the radio man's bravery in staying with his post to his death. I recommended they be cited for their efforts, but never learned if indeed they did receive any posthumous awards.

During the course of filling out reports and answering questions, an orderly came up and asked me where my escape kit was.

"In the bay," I said.

"Oh, it went down with the plane."

"No, it came down with me."

316

"Why is it in the bay?"

"Because there's where I last saw it floating."

"If you saw it, why didn't you retrieve it?"

"It was floating west and I was traveling east," I answered, using the word traveling loosely. He didn't pursue the questioning any further. He just shook his head and left. I decided that if he were going to ask silly questions like that, I wasn't going to honor them with civil answers. As I was leaving to return home to surprise my roommates and remaining crew members, I saw Colonel Campbell and spoke to him.

"Colonel Campbell, I was gone only two hours," thinking back to my official recording of the time my mission ended. "Will the mission count?"

His hand shot out, and with a big smile on his face he said, "Congratulations, Lieutenant Newby, on flying fifty combat missions."

"Thank you, Colonel."

Epilogue: 12 August 1944

FINAL SCORE

I had been looking forward to my scheduled R&R trip to Rome and all its promised cultural and pleasurable enrichments, so my early departure orders were met with mixed emotions.

Going home won out.

Two days before my departure, my crew was sent on a long mission to France, where the entire Air Force pounded gun positions preparatory to the coming invasion—just two days away. Now it was my turn to sweat out my crew as they sought their fiftieth mission. As the formation came into sight over the hill, there were no missing planes. *All had made it back safely! Hangar Queen* had brought our crew through again, and now we could all go home together.

I was over at headquarters, filling out some papers related to my going home, just as Sherm had been a few days earlier, when someone ran into the house yelling, "Hammett just crash-landed in the field near Poggiorsini. Ran out of gas!"

I ran and joined two others in a jeep that was

heading over to the crash area, and that was easier said than done. There was no direct road to where we presumed the plane had come down. It was like chasing a runaway kite in an automobile: none of the streets seemed to go directly to where you wanted to go. We finally went to Poggiorsini and doubled back on a farm road to the crash site.

From quite a distance we could see the twin-ruddered tail section of *Hangar Queen* pointing up to the sky. *Hangar Queen* had apparently made a good wheels-down landing in the farm field but ran afoul of a low mound across its path. The mound had sheared off its landing gear and the onrushing plane had plowed a furrow several hundred yards through the field, strewing in its path one badly bent propeller, part of an engine nacelle, and the landing gear.

As we pulled up to the crash site, the remainder of crew 71 was standing around silently looking at the crushed hulk of our once proud battlewagon. Smitty had his little stuffed mascot tucked safely under his arm. None of them looked happy about successfully completing their tour of duty. I sensed something was wrong, and then I realized Bob Kaiser was not standing there. *He was still inside the plane!*

Two ground crewmen were standing atop the fuselage, frustratedly peering down through the top hatch at our fallen comrade, pinned in his fume-filled prison. The man we called Tyrone, who had brought us cheer with his songs and relief from our tensions when we needed it, by now was beyond any mortal help.

As we stood by the remains of *Hangar Queen*, a

jeep pulled up and Clyde Gilbert jumped out, his rolled up parachute canopy under one arm and a strange expression on his face. He and the substitute bombardier had leaped out through the bomb bay when the engines quit. He had gone into the valley and his chute had opened in time and saved him. The bombardier was not so fortunate. He missed the valley and his chute had not had time to open fully.

Clyde's face was a picture of mixed emotions. He had just witnessed a crew member plunge to his death, and did not yet know the extent of death or injury aboard his crumpled bomber. He now had to tell the crew of Lieutenant Zimmerman's death, and here were all the others expressing pleasure at seeing him alive.

We quietly boarded the truck for the short trip back to the base. Crew 71 rode together for the last time. Few words were spoken as Smitty's little mascot was passed around for each to take a final look at where we had been, and at the names of all who had shared our odyssey.

Reports were coming in of U.S. fighter planes meeting a new type of German fighter plane, the ME-262, which was said to be about 100 mph faster than any Allied planes. The unique thing was that it was propellerless. The dawn of the age of jet aircraft had arrived just as POINTBLANK was wiping out the Luftwaffe. This one last dying gasp had electrified everyone. How could the bombers combat jet aircraft that could run away from protective fighters? How many did they have? The only consolation was the fact that this new type of aircraft was still in the ram-jet stage, and reportedly could only stay aloft about twenty minutes or so. There had not been any reports so far of any Allied planes being shot down by jets, however, so perhaps speed wasn't the main factor in air fighter competition. In fact, two ME-262's were shot down. Most of us were glad to be leaving before anyone figured out how to keep them up longer.

Unknown to the combatants at the time, the U.S. Air Force was testing a dazzling new jet-propelled aircraft of its own, the P-80 "Shooting Star." This was the realization of Gen. Hap Arnold's years of active leadership in the development of jet propulsion. The results in simulated battle experience far surpassed the wildest expectations of its ability to climb and fly faster than anything else in the air. It made the German ram-jets look like Model T's, and would one day make its mark in aerial combat.

A last look at the group bulletin board showed the 460th to be the top group for the month of July. Its July performance surpassed all previous accuracy records, setting standards never before attained by any other group. Its 53.7 percent of bombs within 1,000 feet of the aiming point was a new high. Ironically, the 460th was destined to surpass that mark for August, but would fall to second place. At that, Colonel Crowder would have been proud of his Black Panthers, as his group had claimed third place for May, first for July, and second for August. It was the only group during the entire war to reach three such high monthly rankings for bombing accuracy. It led the

55th wing for each the first six months in combat.

In the first 100 missions flown by the group, it scored 82.6 percent in effective sorties, the best record in the Fifteenth Air Force. This meant that 82.6 percent of all bombers dispatched for a mission reached the target and dropped their bombs there. To a great degree, this score reflects the quality of ground maintenance, as well as perseverance by pilots and crews.

The group posted a fine record in aerial combat with the GAF during that same period. The 460th was credited with 17 victories per 100 encounters, compared with 15.3 for the entire Air Force, and it had 2.1 losses per 100 encounters, compared with 4.2 for the Air Force. This resulted in 8.1 victories per loss, compared with 3.7 for the Air Force. These statistics seem to justify Colonel Harrison's emphasis on ultra-tight formation flying.

The 460th, however, had paid a high price for its share in the accomplishments. It had left Chatham Field with sixty-two fly-away bombers, and through mid-August it had lost sixty airplanes—most of which were combat-related. The *Hangar Queen* crew's 763rd Squadron had left with seventeen crews. Only four survived.

The 460th received twenty-one commendations from Secretary of War Stimson, Air Force Generals Marshall, Spaatz, Eaker, Doolittle, Twining, and Acheson. Individual awards were as follows:

Distinguished Service Cross	1
Legion of Merit	3
Silver Star	21
Distinguished Flying Cross	551
DFC Oak Leaf Clusters	26
Soldiers Medal	29
SM Oak Leaf Cluster	1
Bronze Star	8
Air Medal	2,279
AM Oak Leaf Clusters	3,388
Purple Heart*	279
PH Oak Leaf Clusters*	8
TOTAL*	6,591

*Does not include Purple Heart awarded
on General Hospital Orders.

Colonel Harrison moved into the 55th Bomb Wing
headquarters in the fall, and later in his career rose to
the rank of lieutenant general in SAC, under the
command of Gen. Curtis E. LeMay. Combat crewmen of the 460th, in the summer of 1944, were
credited with participation in four designated battles
and campaigns: Rhineland, Rome-Arno, Air Offensive Europe and Air Combat Balkans.

Ploesti, that target of targets, was only nine days
away from a near shutdown on 10 August when over
four hundred heavies hit it with 962 tons of bombs.
Fifteen of the Fifteenth Air Force crews ended their
quest for their "fifty" that morning. The 763rd lost
another fine crew when Frank Gydia's plane blew up

over the target. It was the Fifteenth Air Force's sixteenth high-level Ploesti mission, The constant pounding was finally paying off as the second, third, and fourth largest refineries in Rumania ceased production for the remainder of the war.

Steaua Romana, the second largest, had been the heaviest hit in the low-level raid and never did get back to anywhere near its 125,000-ton-per-month capacity.

Concorda Vega, the third largest, was hit hard in the low-level raid but recovered rapidly and was a big producer until the high-level raids began taking their toll. The fourth largest, Romano Americano, while escaping the low-level raid, was a prime target for the high-level campaign and dropped from a high of 109,000 tons in August 1943 to only 12,000 tons in August 1944, before totally succumbing on 10 August. On 17 August, 248 heavies dropped 534 tons of destruction on that battered Rumanian target, with another very heavy loss of fifteen, to be followed the next day by 377 dropping 825 tons and a lighter loss of seven.

When sixty-five B-17's marched across Ploesti skies in the Fifteenth's swan song on 19 August to perform the coup de grace, there wasn't a German fighter plane in the sky, and not one plane was lost to the flak gunners.

The Luftwaffe was virtually kaput.

The flak gunners would be seasick no more because the Fifteenth had written off Ploesti as a bombing target!

On 30 August, when Russian troops marched

across the ground into Ploesti, they found five refineries limping along at about 20 percent of normal production—still linked by Gerstenberg's pipeline web. The Russians were astounded to find the ruins of Romano Americano. They couldn't grasp the idea that America could deal so harshly with its own.

Adding up the toll:

		Sorties	Planes Lost	% Loss
FIFTEENTH AIR FORCE (Daylight)				
1 Aug. 1943	Low-Level Heavies	178	54	30.3
5 Apr. to 19 Aug. 1944	High-Level Heavies*	5,479	223	4.1
10 June 1944	Low-Level P-38's	46	24	52.2
		5,703	301	5.3
*Nineteen bombing raids				
RAF (Night)				
Summer 1944	High-Level Heavies	924	38	4.1
		6,627	339	5.1

Ploesti was known as the "graveyard of the bombers," as more bombers were shot down over that city, by flak, than over any other target in the world.

During the summer of 1944, 188 GAF fighters were shot down by Fifteenth AF fighters and bombers in Ploesti-related action, while the Fifteenth lost 28 of its fighters. During the spring and summer of that year, all U.S. heavy bomber losses in the ETO were 62 percent to flak and 38 percent to fighters. The results were disastrous for Hitler's war machine, and certainly saved many Allied lives in the ground battles. The Fifteenth and the RAF destroyed 1,169,000 tons of oil production at Ploesti, 84½ tons of oil lost for each ton of bombs dropped.

The flak-infested skies of Ploesti produced seven U.S. Medal of Honor recipients (see Appendix). The Fifteenth Air Force fighters and bombers, along with the Eighth Air Force, had destroyed the GAF *in the womb, in the nest,* and *on the wing,* as directed to do several months earlier.

Communication facilities had been severely damaged in Italy and France in preparation for the invasion of France from the south. Oil transportation and oil production in Italy and Austria had been neutralized.

In late August, while the Russian troops were storming across Rumania in their ten-day blitz to reach Ploesti, a most daring rescue operation took place that resembled a familiar scene from a Wild West movie; but it was done with airplanes, not horses.

Lt. Col. James A. Gunn III of the 454th Bomb Group was shot down on one of the final Ploesti raids, and was taken directly to a POW camp. By then the Rumanian guards were aware of the oncoming Russians, so they switched sides overnight, thereby setting the stage for "OPERATION REUNION." Gunn talked a Rumanian pilot into flying him to Italy in an ME-109 on the promise he could have a P-51 Mustang in exchange. It was a rough but welcome ride for Gunn, lying in the belly of a fighter plane without

327

oxygen or parachute. They were farsighted enough to paint some U.S. identification on the side of the German fighter, so the plane landed without incident at Gunn's base. The Fifteenth kept Gunn's part of the deal; they traded a P-51 for the ME-109 and sent the happy flier back home with his prize.

Working around the clock, the ground crews at B-17 bases around Foggia outfitted fifty-six Fortresses as transports. These rescue planes flew a steady airlift operation to the airfield at Popesti, near Bucharest. With the roar of Russian guns in their ears, 1,162 American POW's boarded the rescue planes over a three-day period. Some had fallen out of Ploesti skies just a few days earlier. Others had been there for a year, ever since THE raid. The *Italians* and the *Africans* were going home together.

On 14 August, many 460th fliers were awarded the DFC in recognition of their tour of combat duty, and boarded planes for the long-awaited final trip to Naples. The war was over for them.

For thousands of American men storming the beaches of southern France that same day, the war was just beginning. It was the culmination of weeks of the Fifteenth Air Force's pre-invasion aerial pounding of harbor and transportation facilities, as well as mass preparation on the invaders' part. The joint effort had enabled many to earn their tickets home.

Five hundred of the most seriously wounded survivors of the landings were placed in the best staterooms of an awaiting Navy transport ship. Many would not walk or see again. The fliers had originally been billeted in those staterooms, but in order to make room for the wounded they were bumped to a barracks area five levels below deck. It was hot, stuffy, and cramped in the four-tiered hammocks where they would sleep for nine nights. Despite everything though, it was a satisfactory arrangement, considering the alternatives. The USS *General Meigs* was taking them home.

BIBLIOGRAPHY

Air Force Combat Units of World War II. U.S. Government Printing Office, 1961

Birdsall, Steve. *Log of the Liberators*. New York: Doubleday, 1973

Combat Squadrons of the Air Force in World War II. U.S. Government Printing Office, 1969

Craven, Wesley Frank and Cate, James Lea. *The Army Air Forces in World War II*. Chicago: University of Chicago Press, 1951, Vol. III

Devney, Edward J. *460th Bomb Group*. Cleveland, 1946

Dugan, James and Stewart Carroll. *Ploesti*. New York: Random House, 1962

460th Bomb Group . . . , Historical Research Center, Maxwell Air Force Base, Alabama

Impact, Vol. 2, No. 9, September 1944; No. 12, December 1944; Vol. 3, No. 1, January 1945. Office of the Assistant Chief of Air Staff, Intelligence, Washington, D.C.

Rust, Kenn C. "Fifteenth Air Force Story," in *Historical Aviation Album*. Temple City, CA, 1976

Second Report of the Commanding General of the Army Air Forces of the Secretary of War, 27 February 1945

Sweetman, John. *Ploesti Oil Strike*. New York: Ballantine, 1974

Appendix A

BOMBSIGHT OF OPERATION: NORDEN AND SPERRY

The fore and aft hair is called the *course* (directional) hair, and is comparable to deflection in terms of artillery fire. The bombsight has two concentric course knobs on one shaft. The inner knob corrects for drift. If the wind direction is from the right and the course hair is drifting across the ground to the left, the plane is not "crabbed" enough into the wind. A clockwise turn of both knobs will correct for the drift and place the course hair back onto the aiming point. This action feeds information to the ailerons and rudders, so the bombsight directly controls the direction of the airplane. Once the course hair is "killed," or stopped, *course* is said to be synchronized.

The turning of the outer knob alone will displace the errant course hair back onto the aiming point without changing the course of the airplane. By adroit use of both course knobs, a bombardier can put the airplane on the correct course over the ground so that the bombs, when released, will land somewhere along a line running through the aiming point. The airplane will not pass directly over the target (unless there is a direct head or tail wind). It will fly a parallel course upwind of the target. (See Figure 1).

The bombardier doesn't want his bombs landing just anywhere along the course line, so after he gets the course problem solved he immediately sets out to solve the range problem. Where along the course line should the bombs be released in order to hit the aiming point?

The lateral hair is called the *rate* hair, *rate* being short for "rate of closure." Actually, *rate* is nothing but the ground speed of the airplane—how fast the bomb is moving across the ground before it is released.

There are two concentric knobs on another shaft that enable the bombardier to solve the range problem. The inner knob determines how *fast* the telescope mirror pivots. The outer knob merely adjusts the angle of the mirror and displaces the rate hair without affecting the speed of the pivoting mirror.

The trick here is to "kill" the rate hair so that it stays right on the aiming point, along with the course hair. When both are synchronized, the cross hairs will be glued to the aiming point, even though the plane is moving along the course line at over 200 mph—a beautiful sight for a bombardier.

Although a constant speed motor drives the mirror in its constantly changing angle, the mirror must be pivoting at an *increasing* pivot rate to keep the rate hair on the aiming point. How this is done is the amazing secret of the bombsight. An illustration of this process might be found in the situation where you are driving along a road, and you pick out some object several hundred feet ahead and off to one side. Note how fast you turn your head as you keep your eyes on the object. You will do it slowly at first, but increasingly faster as you come up to the object.

In the process of synchronizing the rate hair, so that the changing mirror angle reflects the ground speed along the established course, the bombsight also determines the exact *dropping angle* based on all the information that has been fed into it. (See Figure 2.) This is that infinitesimal point along the course line mentioned earlier.

This dropping angle is indicated on a calibrated scale with a dropping angle index pointer. Each time the bombardier changes the speed of the mirror, and thereby indicates a new ground speed, the dropping angle index pointer moves to a new reading. When the *rate* hair is "killed," the bombsight has done its job. It has calculated the dropping angle for the established course.

Wherever the rate hair is located in relation to the ground, a sighting angle index pointer indicates the *sighting angle* for the line of sight to that point on the ground. This pointer is always moving along its scale toward the dropping angle indicator. The sighting angle scale is located parallel to the dropping angle scale.

Late in the bomb run, when the rate hair is synchronized on the aiming point, the sighting angle index pointer is almost up to the dropping angle index pointer, and when the two finally meet, an electrical contact is made and the bombs are released. If the course and rate hairs are truly synchronized so that they stay glued to the aiming point when the indices

335

meet, and all other information fed into the sight is correct, the bombs will hit on or very near the aiming point.

The above generally describes the sighting techniques of both the Norden and the Sperry. The Sperry, however, has an electric erection system that maintains the telescope's perpendicular relation to the earth, despite the influence of the curvature of the earth on the attached gyroscope.

A gyroscope maintains its position in relation to the *universe*. When an airplane flies a so-called level flight, it really is flying an arc as it follows the earth's curvature, and the bombsight gyroscope will seem to tip over toward the bombardier. This is apparent precession. The Sperry corrects this precession as it starts to happen.

Norden sights have fore and aft, and lateral bubbles, similar to a carpenter's level, which indicate the amount and direction of any gyroscope precession. The bombardier, late in the bomb run and after he has the cross hairs synchronized, must call the pilot for a "level." The pilot then makes sure the plane is not in a skid, or either accelerating or decelerating, which would give false bubble readings. During this "level" assurance the bombardier then brings the gyro up to its correct position in relation to the earth, as indicated by the bubbles, and displaces his cross hairs back onto the aiming point. He may then need some minor hair adjustments before "bombs away." "Bubble trouble" is the bane of all Norden bombardiers.

Again, with either bombsight the bombardier must remember to arm it eight or ten seconds before the release point. The Sperry helps a little on this. About eight seconds before the indices are to meet, a little flag pops out into the line of vision as a final warning.

Synchronization was just one part of the formula for good bombing. Any errors in the input data, or erratic flying by the pilot, would contribute to a miss of the aiming point, even though the synchronization was perfect. Very small errors in any phase of the bombing procedure could become large errors on the ground.

SIGHTING
ANGLE
POINTER

INDEX
POINTER

RELEASE
ANGLE
POINTERS

INDEX
POINTER
KNOB

Sperry S-1 Bombsight with M-2 Modifications

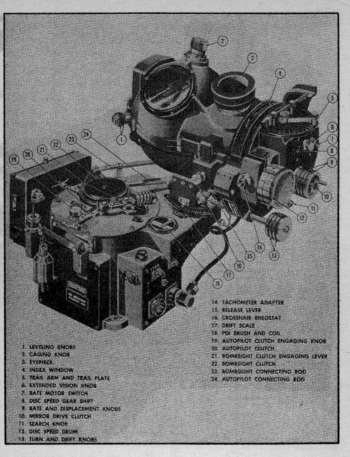

14. TACHOMETER ADAPTER
15. RELEASE LEVER
16. CROSSHAIR RHEOSTAT
17. DRIFT SCALE
18. PDI BRUSH AND COIL
19. AUTOPILOT CLUTCH ENGAGING KNOB
20. AUTOPILOT CLUTCH
21. BOMBSIGHT CLUTCH ENGAGING LEVER
22. BOMBSIGHT CLUTCH
23. BOMBSIGHT CONNECTING ROD
24. AUTOPILOT CONNECTING ROD

1. LEVELING KNOBS
2. CAGING KNOB
3. EYEPIECE
4. INDEX WINDOW
5. TRAIL ARM AND TRAIL PLATE
6. EXTENDED VISION KNOB
7. RATE MOTOR SWITCH
8. DISC SPEED GEAR SHIFT
9. RATE AND DISPLACEMENT KNOBS
10. MIRROR DRIVE CLUTCH
11. SEARCH KNOB
12. DISC SPEED DRUM
13. TURN AND DRIFT KNOBS

The Norden Bombsight

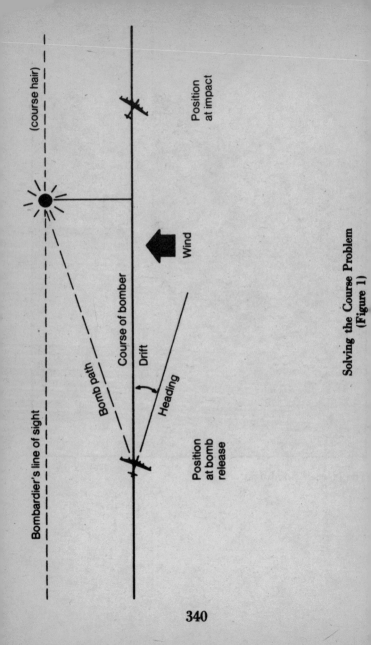

Solving the Course Problem
(Figure 1)

340

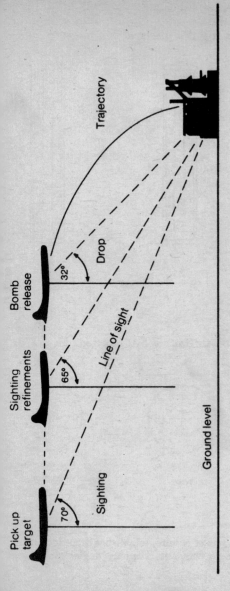

Solving the Range Problem
(Figure 2)

341

Bombardier sees indices on bombsight:
Sighting Angle Index (left).
Dropping Angle Index (right) is displayed as a tangent.

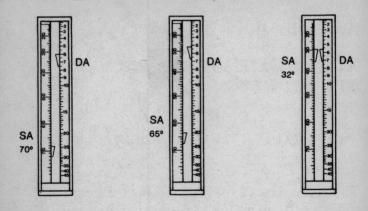

View in Eyepiece: Course Hair is Synchronized; Rate Hair
Movement is:

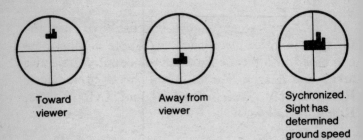

Toward
viewer

Away from
viewer

Sychronized.
Sight has
determined
ground speed

Bombsight determines rate of closure, establishes dropping angle,
and when sighting angle subtends dropping angle bombs are
released automatically.

Appendix B

AIR OBJECTIVE FOLDER NO. 69.1 RUMANIA

EXPLANATION OF FOLDER—

This folder covers the targets within the Ploesti Objective Area, Rumania (69.1). It is primarily for the use of group and squadron commanders and intelligence officers in the planning of operations and the briefing of crews. **NEITHER THE FOLDER NOR ANY PART OF IT MAY BE TAKEN INTO THE AIR ON OFFENSIVE MISSIONS.**

Targets and objective areas are numbered from one to infinity within each country. These numbers are combined into a code showing the country, objective area, and target. For example, 69.1.-38 indicates Rumania (69), Ploesti Area (1) and **TARGET 38,** Rumanian series.

Supplementing the objective folder, target charts are provided separately for the use of air crews. Each

chart is centered on a target; it spots other targets
lying within a four-mile radius; and it identifies
landmarks within a twelve-mile radius. Each chart
bears the number of its central target.

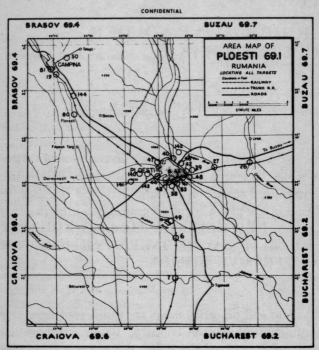

CONFIDENTIAL

SUMMARY AND EVALUATION OF AREA

NOTE: The information contained in this folder is the best obtainable in the U.S.A. Every effort should be made in the field to verify it by photo reconnaissance.

DESCRIPTION: The city of Ploesti and its suburbs constitute an area of approximately 19 square miles with an estimated population of 100,000. The city is situated in the Wallachian Plain 30 miles north of Bucharest; to the north of the city rise the foothills of the Transylvanian Alps and 5 miles to the east of the town the Teleajen River flows in a southeasterly direction. The northern region of the area contains numerous oil fields, particularly in the sector around Campina. Ploesti is almost the geographical center of the area as a whole and is the hub of rail and highway routes converging from all directions. Approaching the area from the south,

attacking bombers would fly near the large city of Bucharest and its environs.

IMPORTANCE: The Ploesti Objective Area (69.1) is by far the most important area in Rumania, as it is the center of the Rumanian oil refining industry, which supplies Germany with approximately 35% of her petroleum products.

There are twelve large oil refineries in this objective area which produce approximately 86% of the refined petroleum products of Rumania and represent 96% of the total cracking capacity. These refineries have a capacity of 189,000 barrels per day and are now producing an average of 170,000 barrels daily. Ten of these refineries are located in the city of Ploesti. One of the remaining two is situated to the south of Ploesti, in the small town of Brazii and the other one 20 miles to the northwest in Campina.

345

The remaining 14% of refined petroleum products is produced in some 39 refineries throughout Rumania. Most of these plants are small and obsolete, and their production would have to be used for local consumption in the event that the major refineries were destroyed.

The Rumanian petroleum production (crude or refined) is of assistance to the Axis only if the oil can be effectively transported from the Ploesti area. Although the pipelines move a considerable amount of oil from Ploesti to Giurgiu, yet 80% of the oil leaving this area moves by rail. Continuous and effective operations against refineries and transportation objectives in Rumania would result in a serious blow to the German war effort.

DEFENSES AND VULNERABILITY: The defenses of the Ploesti area are quite strong and active. Local defenses exist for the various groups of refineries and possibly for certain of the vital transportation points. The Germans have carefully protected the vital parts of the refineries by the construction of protective walls around them. The storage tanks have been camouflaged with paint or by wooden sheds built over them.

A nightly barrage of forty to one hundred balloons is maintained over the city. It has been reported they are lowered at day and that at night they are raised from 6 to 10,000 feet. Included in the various protective defenses has been the construction of "dummy towns" to deceive attacking bombers. A dummy Ploesti was erected on the site of an encampment at Albesti about 7 miles east of Ploesti in June, 1941 and during the Russian attack this "dummy town" was purposely set on fire. It is also reported that a "dummy town" has been constructed about 8 miles northwest of Ploesti. The blackout of the town is said to be very good and the only light likely to be seen is a glow from some of the refinery plants that have not been stopped.

The fighter aircraft defenses of Ploesti were taken over by the German Air Force during the Balkan invasion in the spring of 1941 and since that time they have been shared equally with the Rumanians. There are three principal airdromes in the area supplemented by two alternate bases. Attacking bombers may also receive opposition from the en-my airbases in the Bucharest area to the south of Ploesti.

The outer anti-aircraft defenses of Ploesti form the perimeter of an oval extending to the north, with the north-south axis about 30 miles in length and the east-west axis about 20 miles long. The inner defenses of the city are very strong and in October, 1941, extended for five miles in a belt around the town, with the guns increasing in calibre towards the edge of the belt. In most cases the guns have been camouflaged by nets or "roofs" over them.

CONFIDENTIAL

TABULATION OF TARGET INFORMATION

TARGET NO.	TARGET NAME	APPROXIMATE COORDINATES	DESCRIPTION AND SIGNIFICANCE	TARGET CHART NO.
			OIL	
83	Astra Romana Refinery (Ploesti)	44° 55′ N .... 26° 02′ E	Cap 2,000,000 tons Yr or 18% of Rumanian total: cracking Cap 650,000 tons yr or 32% of Rumanian total. Largest refinery in Europe. Possesses imp modern cracking units. Most southern located refinery in Ploesti: identified by 4 large tanks as approached	83

from south. Giurgiu pumping Sta is within target. (See photos A on page P-1; map on page M-3.)

39	Romano-Americana Refinery (Ploesti)	44° 57′ N .... 26° 05′ E

Cap 1,250,000 tons yr or 11% of Rumanian total: cracking Cap 400,000 tons yr or 17% of total. Third most imp Rumanian refinery with second largest cracking installations in Rumania. 3 mi E of Ploesti near Telajen Station and 600 yds N of Buzau Ry. Prime targets in E part of plant. Includes 2 boiler pumps, power plant for Constantsa pumping Sta, cracking, distilla-

TABULATION OF TARGET INFORMATION

TARGET NO.	TARGET NAME	APPROXIMATE COORDINATES	DESCRIPTION AND SIGNIFICANCE	TARGET CHART NO.
		OIL—continued		
			tion plants. (See photos B & C on page P-2: map on page M-3).	
40	Concordia Vega Refinery (Ploesti)	44° 59′ N 26° 02′ E	Cap 1,500,000 tons yr or 13% or Rumanian total; cracking Cap 210,000 or 9% of total. Imp cracking equipment. Refinery installation, 3 boiler houses, distillation plant. Covers area approx 400 x 550 yds. N Ploesti, E	83

		of Rd and Ry to Vale-nii de Munte, slightly N of Ploesti N Sta. (See photo A on page P-1; photos D & E on page P-3; map on page M-3.)
41	Phoenix Unirea Refinery (Ploesti)	44° 56′ N .... 26° 03′ E	Cap 700,000 tons yr or 6% of Rumanian total; cracking Cap 85,000 tons yr or 4% of total. Cracking plant prime objective and adjoins objectives in Target 45. E of main freight Yds (Target 4), adjoining Standard Petrol Block (Target 45), S of Ry to Buzau, first refinery reached from SE. (See map on page M-3.)

TABULATION OF TARGET INFORMATION

TARGET NO.	TARGET NAME	APPROXIMATE COORDINATES	DESCRIPTION AND SIGNIFICANCE	TARGET CHART NO.
		OIL—continued		
42	Dacia (Dacia-Romano) Refinery (Ploesti)	44° 57′ N 26° 04′ E	Cap 375,000 tons yr or 3% of Rumanian total. Small, Non-cracking, older equipment. 1½ mi W of Romano-Americana (Target 39). Compact with refining units located between two tank farms on NW and SW limits of plant. (See map on page M-3.)	83

| 43 | Phoenix-Orion Refinery (Ploesti) | 44° 55' N 26° 02' E | Cap 460,000 tons yr or 4% of Rumanian total: cracking Cap 85,000 or 4% total. Small but contains modern cracking units. Equipment concentrated. Includes a lubricating oil plant, one of few in Rumania. In S Ploesti within group of several others. (See photo A on page P-1; map on page M-3.) |
| 44 | Colombia (Colombia-Aquila) Refinery (Ploesti) | 44° 56' N 26° 01' E | Cap 300,000 tons yr or 3% of Rumanian total: cracking Cap 150,000 tons yr or 5% of total. Prod high proportion of benzine. Cracking equipment prime objective. Other units, in- |

CONFIDENTIAL

TABULATION OF TARGET INFORMATION

TARGET NO.	TARGET NAME	APPROXIMATE COORDINATES	DESCRIPTION AND SIGNIFICANCE	TARGET CHART NO.
		OIL—continued		
			cluding refinery installations, distillation plant, and boiler house are compact. SW Ploesti, N of Ry sidings NW of "Y" Ry Jc of Ry lines to Bucharest and Campina. (See photos F & G on page P-4; map on page M-3.)	
45	Standard Petrol Block Refinery (Ploesti)	44° 56′ N 26° 03′ E	Cap 600,000 tons yr or 5% of Rumanian total:	83

354

Cracking Cap 150,000 or 5% total. Modern cracking installations and lubricating oil plant. Vulnerable points include distillation plants, boiler house. Located in center of Ploesti refinery concentration. In SE Ploesti, adjacent to Phoenix-Unirea Refinery (Target. 41), S of Buzau Ry. (See map on page M-3.)

| 46 | Redeventza Refinery (Ploesti) | 44° 57' N .... 26° 02'3 E | Cap 260,000 tons yr or 2% of Rumanian total. No cracking, old equipment. N Ploesti, N of Dambul R, S and adjoining Rd to Buzau, N of belt Ry around |

TABULATION OF TARGET INFORMATION

TARGET NO.	TARGET NAME	APPROXIMATE COORDINATES	DESCRIPTION AND SIGNIFICANCE	TARGET CHART NO.
		OIL—continued		
			Ploesti. (See photo A on page P-1: map on page M-3.)	
47	Xenia (Xenia-Redeventza) Refinery (Ploesti)	44° 57' N .... 26° 00' E	Cap 300,000 tons yr or 3% of Rumanian total. No cracking, older, less imp than others. Prin objective within refinery is distillation unit, just W of RR where it crosses Rd to Campina. In NW Ploesti, in	83

triangle formed by intersection of belt Ry and Rd to Campina. (See photo A on page P-1; map on page M-3.)

48	Constantsa Pumping Sta (Ploesti)	44° 56′ N 26° 05′ E	Pumping Sta for oil to Constantsa. Sta terminal for numerous pipelines from Ploesti refineries. Pumps are old but large, vulnerable only to direct hits. E of Ploesti, near Teleajen Sta. S of Buzau Ry. From air appears as mass of storage tanks and one brick bldg which is the target. (See text on page T-9; map on page M-3.)

TABULATION OF TARGET INFORMATION

TARGET NO.	TARGET NAME	APPROXIMATE COORDINATES	DESCRIPTION AND SIGNIFICANCE	TARGET CHART NO.
		OIL—continued		
49	Creditul Minier Refinery (Brazii)	44° 52' N 26° 01' E	Cap 600,000 tons yr or 5% of Rumanian total: cracking Cap 175,000 or 7% of total. Equipped with large cracking units. Modern refinery, including only high octane gasoline plant in Rumania. Other vital points are boiler, power house, distillation plant. 6 mi S of Ploesti, 30 Mi N	49

50	Steaua Romana Refinery (Campina)	45° 08' N 25° 44' E	Cap 1,750,000 tons yr or 13% of Rumanian total; cracking Cap 400,000 tons yr or 17% of total. Third largest European refinery. Large cracking installations, modern distillation uints, and only important paraffin plant in Rumania. NE portion of Campina 20 mi NW of Ploesti. (See photos H & I on page	50

of Bucharest, on W side of Bucharest-Ploesti Ry, 1 mi E of Brazii. Refinery area in shape of triangle bounded by Ry and Rd to Brazii. (See map on page M-4.)

TABULATION OF TARGET INFORMATION

TARGET NO.	TARGET NAME	APPROXIMATE COORDINATES	DESCRIPTION AND SIGNIFICANCE	TARGET CHART NO.
		OIL—continued		
			P-5: map on page M-5.)	
		TRANSPORTATION		
4	Ploesti Ry Yds	44° 56′ N 26° 02′ E	Prin Rumanian Ry center for marshalling of tank cars. Ry repair shops, roundhouse. Extend 1½ mi in ENE direction, S of city, width: 300 to 600 ft. (See photo A on page	83

P-1: map on page M-3.)

6 Prahova R Br	44° 49' N 26° 02' E	Bucharest-Ploesti double-tracked Ry, carrying heaviest traffic in Rumania. Lattice girder construction. Length: 390 ft. (See map on page M-4.)	6
7 Jalomitsa R Br	44° 45' N 26° 02' E	Ploesti-Bucharest Ry. Double-tracked, carrying heaviest traffic in Rumania. Length: 300 ft. Height: 3 ft 4 in above high water. Iron superstructure. (See map on page M-4.)	7
27 Telesjen R Br	44° 57' N 26° 08' E	Ploesti-Buzau double-tracked RR E of Ploesti. Length: 726 ft. Height: 24 to 30 ft	27

TABULATION OF TARGET INFORMATION

TARGET NO.	TARGET NAME	APPROXIMATE COORDINATES	DESCRIPTION AND SIGNIFICANCE	TARGET CHART NO.
			TRANSPORTATION—continued	
			above normal water level. Iron super structure. (See map on page M-4.)	
26	Cricovul R Br	44° 57' N 26° 13' E	Ploesti-Buzau RR at Albesti. (See map on page M-4.)	26
19	Prahova R Br	45° 05' N 25° 45' E	Ploesti-Campina-Brasov double-tracked RR, S of Campina. (See map on page M-5.)	19
			POWER	
80	Floresi Electric Power Sta	45° 02' N 25° 48' E	Supplier for oil industry. Cap 6300 KW, 2/3	None

...mi W of Baicoiu Ry Sta on Ploesti-Campina-Brasov Ry. (See photo K on page P-7.)

None

81 Campina Electric Power Sta — 45° 07' N 25° 45' E .... Supplies oil industry. Cap 22,950 KW, SW of Campina on Prahova R. (See photo J on page P-6; map on page M-5.)

MUNITIONS

83 Concordia Munitions Fcty (Ploesti) — 45° 56' N 26° 03' E .... AA guns Schneider-Creusot type, artillery shells. Area approx 700 x 500 Yds. Bldgs brick, concrete roofs. NW Ploesti S Sta. (See map on page M-3.)

83

TABULATION OF TARGET INFORMATION

TARGET NO.	TARGET NAME	APPROXIMATE COORDINATES	DESCRIPTION AND SIGNIFICANCE	TARGET CHART NO.
		MILITARY AIRBASES		
140	Strejnicul Adrm	44° 56′ N 25° 57′ E	2½ mi WSW Ploesti, 1½ mi SW Ploesti-Campina Ry and Ploesti-Darmanesti Rd Jc. Area 3000 x 3300 ft. Hangars, shops. GAF fighter base. (See map on page M-4.)	None
141	Targsorul Nou Adrm	44° 55′ N 25° 56′ E	SW Targsorul, 5½ mi WSW Ploesti. Area 3300 x 3900 ft. Hangars, fuel, all facilities. GAF fighter aircraft base.	None

142 Ploesti N Adrm	44° 58′ N 26° 03′ E	2 mi NE Ploesti, adjacent Buzau Rd. (No details available)	None
143 Ploesti Air Base	44° 56′ N 25° 58′ E	SW Ploesti-Campina and Ploesti-Darmanesti Rd Jc. Area 4950 x 3300 ft. Fueling facilities. Alternate of Strejinicul, Target 140.	None
144 Floresti Air Base	45° 04′ N 25° 47′ E	N of Floresti, NW Baicoiu, between Rd and Ry to Campina. Area 2100 x 900 ft. Fighter aircraft base.	None

TARGETS 4, 6, 7, 19, 26, 27
The transportation targets in the Ploesti Objective Area consist of 5 railway bridges and the main Ploesti railway yards. The bridges are situated on the lines which carry the Ploesti petroleum production to Central Europe, and the Russian Fronts. 80% of the oil leaving this area moves by rail.

The structures over the Prahova River **TARGET 6** and the Jalomitsa River **TARGET 7**, south of Ploesti, are the largest of the group of bridges. The Prahova River Bridge **TARGET 6**, south of Ploesti, carries the pipeline to Giurgiu. The size and simple construction of all the bridges would indicate that their repair or reconstruction could be made in a short time.

TARGETS 38, 39, 40, 41, 45, 50 Priority should be given to these refineries as they are the largest in Rumania and contain important cracking units. All of the refineries include a considerable amount of tank storage, but, in general, this is not an economical target; the vulnerable units of the refineries being the stills, cracking installations, polymer, lube oil and hydrogenation equipment.

TARGET 48 The Constantsa Pumping Station should be considered in conjunction with **TARGET 38**. The former station could perform the pumping functions for the latter in the event of emergency.

TARGETS 140, 141, 142, 143, 144. The principal air fields in this area are grouped very near Ploesti with the exception of Floresti **TARGET 144**, which is situated between Ploesti and Campina. In addition to these bases there are numerous landing grounds throughout the area.

LIST OF TARGET CHARTS AVAILABLE FOR PLOESTI AREA

Charts are numbered according to the target on which they are centered.

Chart Number	Targets Appearing on Chart	Chart Number	Targets Appearing on Chart	Chart Number	Targets Appearing on Chart	Chart Number	Targets Appearing on Chart
6	6	26	26	49	49	83	4, 38, 39, 40, 41, 42, 43, 44, 45, 46, 47, 48, 83
7	7	27	27	50	50		
19	19						

Appendix C

OPERATIONS ORDER NO. 137: 26 JULY 1944

<u>SECRET</u>

HEADQUARTERS 55TH BOMB WING (H) E-8
APO 520   US ARMY

OPERATIONS ORDER)   25 July 1944
                   :
NUMBER   137)

1.
a.
See intelligence Annex.
b.
6 Groups of 5th Wing destroy Wiener Neudorf Engine
Factory at 1100B Key point time: 0904B. First Alternate Target: PFF on primary Targets. Second Alternate Target: PFF on VIENNA SOUTH M/Y.

4 groups of 47th Wing destroy MARKERSDORF A/

D INSTALLATIONS AND DISPERSED A/C at 1122B. Key point Time: 0931B. Alternate Target: 2 groups Frag A/C on GRAZ/THALERHOF A/D. 2 groups destroy GRAZ-STEYR DAIMLER A/C COMPONENTS FACTORY.

Optional Size force of 49th Wing destroy BERZT KUCOVE NEW OIL DISTALLATIONS AND BARRACKS AREA. Alternate Target: NONE.

304th Wing STAND DOWN.

Fighters of 306th Wing provide penetration, target and withdrawal cover for individual Bomb Wings, paying Special Attention to 5th and 55th Wings.

2.
4 Groups, 55th Wing, destroy ZWOLFAXING A/D INSTALLATIONS AND DISPERSED A/C at 1112B, 26 July 1944. This is plan ABLE.

FIRST ALTERNATE TARGET: SZOMBATHELY A/D AND INSTALLATIONS

BOMBER RENDEZVOUS: Group Rendezvous, 460th and 485th line rendezvous from ALTAMURA TO GRAVINA at 5,000 and 6,000 feet. 460th approaching ALTAMURA FROM TORITTO. 485th approaching ALTAMURA from SANTERAMO IN COLLE. 460th over ALTAMURA at 0819B.

465th and 464th line rendezvous from ANDRIA TO CANOSA at 7,000 and 8,000 feet. 464th falling in behind 465th in 465th area prior to rendezvous. 465th over ANDRIA at 0817B.

Wing Rendezvous: 460th lead over SPINAZZOLA on course at 0830B.

FIGHTER BOMBER RENDEZVOUS: To be signalled later.

ORDER OF FLIGHT: Columns of Wings, 5th, 55th (460th, 485th, 465th, 464th), 47th, 49th.

ROUTE OUT: SPINAZZOLA TO KP SCEDRO ISLE (43°05N–16°42E) to LIVNO (4350N–1700E) to KUTINA (4529N–1647E) to FLIDBACH (4657N–1553E) to MURZZUS CLIAG (4736N–1540E) to IP to Target. Last point to start climb to bombing altitude—LIVNO. Key point Time: 0921B at 12,000 feet.

INITIAL POINT: ALTERNATE (4801N–1559E).

AXIS OF ATTACK: 74 degrees.

TARGET TIME: 1112B.

BOMBING ALTITUDE: 460th—24,000 feet, 485th—23,000 feet, 465th—23,800 feet, 464th—22,800 feet.

TARGET ELEVATION: 580 feet.

RALLY: Right to FRAUENKIRCHEN (4750N–1655E).

ROUTE BACK: Rally point to LIVNO to KP to base.

3.

a.

460th load 5—1000# GP's fused .1 nose and .025 tail.

485th load 10—500# GP's fused .1 nose and .025 tail.

x.

465th and 464th load 36 Frag clusters.

Intervalometer Settings: 460th—100 feet, 485th—50 feet, 465th and 464th—175 feet.

460th and 485th destroy ZWOLFAXING A/D INSTALLATIONS, using MPI as shown on attached target charts, 464th and 465th Frag dispersed A/C on ZWOLFAXING A/D, using MPI as shown on attached target charts.

PFF STAND DOWN

Attention of 464th and 465th is directed to 55th Bomb Wing Operations Memorandum No. 5–8, dated 16 May, 1944.

Groups will maintain close column enroute and over the target to assure maximum protection and bombing accuracy.

Lead ship will maintain 155 MPH after rally until Wing is reformed. 155 MPH will be maintained if any stragglers need protection.

First Alternate Target: 460th and 485th Groups destroy SZOMBATHELY A/D Installations. 465th and 464th Frag SZOMBATHELY A/D.

IP—LOVO (4730N–1648E).
Axis of Attack: 205 degrees.
Target Elevation: 721 feet.
Rally: Left to (4700N–1700E).
Route Back: Rally point to LIVNO to KP to Bases
Method of Attack: Column of Groups using MPI as shown on target chart.
Intervalometer Settings: 460th—75 feet, 485th—50 feet, 465th—250 feet, 464th—175 feet.

4.
No change.
5.
a.
Command Radio Assigned Group Frequency for communications within the Group. VHF Wing Channel "B" for Group to Group within the Wing.

b.
VHF Channel "A" for Bomber to Fighters and Wing to Wing.

c.
Bomber Call Sign: 5th Wing—KIDDIES 47th Wing, FIRTREE, 49th Wing—SHORT BREAD, 55th Wing—CANTAB (460th—CANTAB LEADER, 485th CANTAB 2, 465th CANTAB 3 464th CANTAB 4).

d.
Fighter Call Sign For: 5th Wing—PUSSCAT, 47th Wing—BURGLAR, 49th Wing—SENILE, 55th Wing—IMPISH

e.
Recall Signs: 5th—PRISM, 47th Wing—FEATHER, 49th Wing—COMIC, 55th Wing—PLANTER, 306th Wing—SHANTY.

x.
Carpet will be employed by all units so equipped. Load 3 cartons Window in lead attack unit of each Group dispensing 6 units every 20 seconds from 2 minutes before IP until clear of Flak.
All groups will check in at Wing Rendezvous with Wing VHF ground station on Channel "B".

By order of Colonel Acheson:

DEWITT I. JONES
Captain, Air Corps,
Assistant A-3.

DISTRIBUTION:
    1 cy CO, A-2, A-3, PI 55 BW
    2 cys ea GP 55BW
    1 cy CG 306th Fighter Wg.
    1 cy CG XV AF.

Certified true and correct copy.
_____(SIGNED)_____
SAMUEL WILNER, 1st Lt., AC

Appendix D

MISSION NO. 150: BATTLE ORDER FOR *HANGAR QUEEN*'S LAST MISSION, 12 AUGUST 1944

SECRET

MISSION NO. 150 (Plan BAKER)   12 August 1944

BATTLE ORDER

1. Breakfast   0345
   Briefing: 0450
   Transportation: 0525
   Stations: 0540
   Start Engines: 0615–0625
   Taxi Out: 0625–0635
   Take Off: 0630
   Depart Assy Area: 0724
   Depart Altamura: 0732
   Rendezvous: 0741 Spinazzola.
   Target Time: 1110
   Time of Return: 1500

2. LEADER: Major Anderson.

DEPUTY LEADER: Capt. Carroll.
2ND ATTACK LEADER: Major Lincoln.

3. RENDEZVOUS: 460th (9000') lead 485th (10,000') over Altamura. 460th & 485th fall in behind 464th (9000') & 465th (10000') at Spinazzola.

4. ORDER OF FLIGHT: Loose column of wings: 55th (464th, 465th-first wave), (460th & 485th-second wave).

5. ROUTE OUT: Spinazzola to Melfi to KP (41°01'N–13°56'E) to Control Point, Cape Rocco (42°13'N–08°32'E) to IP to Target. KP Time: 0852–1200

6. POINT OF CLIMB: Follow the lead group.

7. FIGHTER RENDEZVOUS: P-51's at 1055.

8. BOMB LOAD: 10-500# G.P.
   GAS LOAD: 2700 gallons.

9. BOMBING: 160 mph at 16,500'. 464th–16000'. 465th–17000'.
   460th–16500'. 485th–17,500'.
   (a) Primary: GUN POSITIONS in the SETE AREA SOUTHERN FRANCE. Interval 25'. N 43°03'N–03°46'E. Axis: ABLE BOX 290°. BAKER BOX 304°. CHARLIE BOX 314°. DOG BOX 317°. Rally—464th & 460th Left to 42°58'N–03°25'E.

10. **BOMBING FORMATION:** By Boxes.

11. **ROUTE BACK:** Rally to 42°53'N–04°37'E then reverse route out.

12. **RADIO PROCEDURE:** 460th & Dolly 4040; Bombers to Fighters VHF "A". Group to Group VHF "B".
    AIR-SEA RESCUE: VHF "D"; Radio Op's on 4535 KC's. ASR Launches VHF "A".
    SQUADRON CALL SIGNS: 760th 761st 762nd 763rd R/T YOUNGIRL CAMPCHAIR BACKSIDE SWEEPER W/T FBP OLJ FDS HTD
    BOMBER CALL SIGNS: 464th Gp—CLEARSOUP Leader.
    465th Gp—CLEARSOUP 2.
    460th Gp—CLEARSOUP 3.
    485th Gp—CLEARSOUP 4.
    FIGHTER CALL SIGNS: PLATOON
    RECALL SIGNS: 55th Wing—PORTRAIT

13. (a) Turn IFF on immediately after take off; Turn off at 08°00'E going out; Turn on again at 08°00'E on return.
    (b) Turn Carpet on when IFF is turned off and turn Carpet off when IFF is turned on.
    (c) Two (2) cartons of chaff will be loaded in each ship of the 1st Atk Unit dispensing according to SOP, four (4) units every twenty (20) seconds from IP until clear of flak.
    (d) Boxes will break off at the IP for individual

runs. Boxes will reform in Group Formation after rally.

(e) At Control Point 460th & 485th will execute a 360° turn and then continue on course maintaining at least ten (10) minute interval between second and third groups.

(f) There are no alternate targets. Only targets specified will be bombed. No bombs will be jettisoned over France.

(g) Any convoy encountered will be avoided.

(h) Group Leader will fire a double green flare to designate IP and as a signal for boxes to break off.

(i) Box Leaders will report results of bombing to Group Leader on 4040. Group Leader will report bombs away as follows: Three (3) boxes MSOK. One (1) Box MFOK.

(j) This flimsy will be turned into the Intelligence Officer at Interrogation.

Mason		Shackleford		Anderson—Bonetti		Crawford		Carroll—Parker		Hertrich		Henninger		George		May—Haller		Milanoski		Fielder		Drybread
W	D	W	S	R	L	W	M	W	R	W	T	R	V	W	J	R	S	Y	V	R	E	W	G

Lincoln—Lowe
W | B

Alexander
Y | J

Boniface
Y | O

Hester
Y | P

Hammett
Y | C

Galarneau
Y | R

Peterson
Y | G

Burt
R | H

Granger
B | C

Hostetler
B | I

Walker
B | J

Hannan
B | H

Beam
B | G

SECRET

379

BEFORE TAKE OFF CHECK LIST

(a) Parachute
(b) Oxygen Masks
(c) Life Vests
(d) Escape Kits
(e) Winter Flying Equip.
(f) Steel Helmets
(g) Flak Suits
(h) Navigation Equip.
(i) Bombardier has proper bombing tables and target maps.
(j) Radio Operator has proper flimsi
(k) Entire crew have proper knowledge as to their destination.

MARKINGS OF THE 55TH WING

460 Gp - O
465th Gp - —
464th Gp - I
485th Gp - X

Appendix E

FACTS ABOUT PLOESTI

Ploesti was the first really important strategic target to fall into Allied hands immediately after a bombing campaign had ended. The production information on the following pages was published in a U.S. Air Force publication in December 1944, just three months after the capture of Ploesti. *Impact*, Vol. 2 No. 12, December, 1944.

Astra Romana, Ploesti's largest refinery, during low-level attack by 8th and 9th Air Force on 1 August 1943.

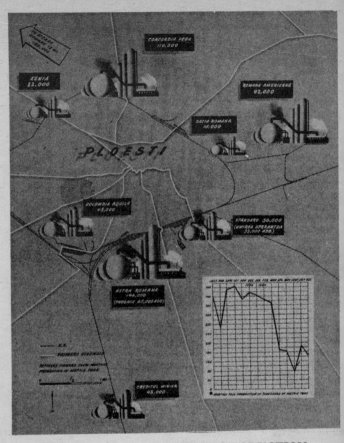

WHAT WE DID TO REFINERY PRODUCTION

Largest and most modern refinery in Rumania surrounds Phoenix, located outside of photo at rear left. Excess standby facilities enabled Astra to rebound quickly after low-level attack of 1 August 1943.

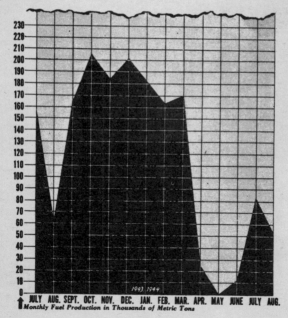

1943 1944

JULY AUG. SEPT. OCT. NOV. DEC. JAN. FEB. MAR. APR. MAY JUNE JULY AUG.

Monthly Fuel Production in Thousands of Metric Tons

The fourth largest refinery in Rumania escaped the low-level raid. However, this American owned facility was not spared in the summer of 1944. It was brought to a standstill on 10 August, along with two others.

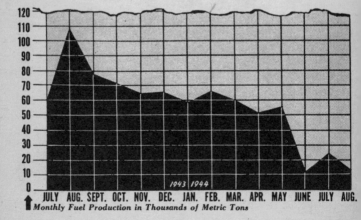

Monthly Fuel Production in Thousands of Metric Tons

The third largest unit was hit hard on the low-level attack, but recovered rapidly and was spared until 5 May 1944 and several times after that. It was finally flattened on 10 August.

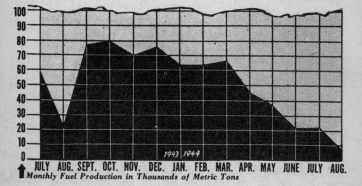

Monthly Fuel Production in Thousands of Metric Tons

Visitors are viewing the remains of a treatment plant after the very
effective low-level attack which shut down this second largest
refinery for several months. On 6 May the 15th put it down again,
after the RAF had blasted it the night before. It too shut down for
good on 10 August 1944.

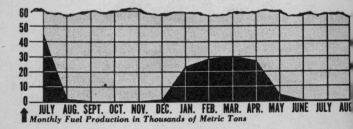

Monthly Fuel Production in Thousands of Metric Tons

While production facilities were virtually wiped out in the low-level attack, the tank farm was generally intact. When the large refineries were severely damaged in the high-level attacks, Colombia was patched up and put back into service.

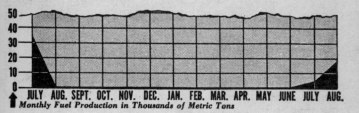

Monthly Fuel Production in Thousands of Metric Tons

This smallest of Ploesti's significant refineries was not bothered by the 15th, and when the larger ones began feeling the effects of regular bombing, it was pushed to capacity in the summer of 1944.

Monthly Fuel Production in Thousands of Metric Tons

Destruction here and at Colombia Aquila and Steaua Romana testify to soundness of 1943 low-level planning whch depended on each plane's hitting the specific building assigned to it. Where formations approached target on proper heading, attacks were astonishingly effective. Where they did not, some refineries were missed all together, some slightly, some seriously damaged.

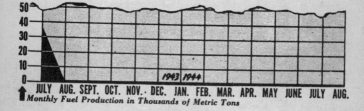

Monthly Fuel Production in Thousands of Metric Tons

Typical distillation tower for gasoline was knocked over, righted again in an effort to keep refinery running. Note guy wires holding it in place. Small tanks are heat exchangers.

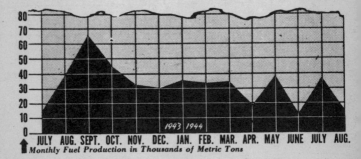

Monthly Fuel Production in Thousands of Metric Tons

Closeup of tank that suffered direct hit. Blast wall is typical of those at all Ploesti refineries.

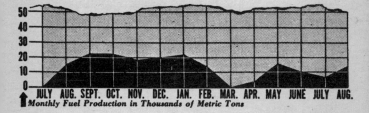

Monthly Fuel Production in Thousands of Metric Tons

Appendix F

PLOESTI MEDAL OF HONOR RECIPIENTS

1 August 1943

Hometown

* Lt. Col. Addison E. Baker   Chicago, Illinois
* 2nd Lt. Lloyd H. Hughes   Alexandria, Louisiana
* Major John L. Jerstad   Racine, Wisconsin
   Col. Leon W. Johnson   Columbia, Missouri
   Col. John R. Kane   McGregor, Texas

23 June 1944

* 2nd Lt. David R. Kingsley   Portland, Oregon
9 July 1944

* 1st Lt. Donald D. Pucket   Longmont, Colorado

* KIA

INDEX

394

399